Great Betrayal

Dedicated to the memory of Cossack
men, women, and children sacrificed
by the educated West

Gen. V. Naumenko

Great
Betrayal

Repatriation of Cossacks at Lienz and Other Places
(1945-1947)

Collected Documents

Volume 1

Copyright by the author

Translation and added notes by William Dritschilo

Cover by Jamie Dritschilo

All Slavic Publishing House
New York
1962.

Table of Contents

Preface

By the spring of 1945 it became very clear that Germany was nearing collapse.

More importantly for us, large groups of Cossacks were present in northern Italy and Croatia.

In Italy, the Cossachi Stan, as it was called, led by Field Ataman General T. I. Domanov, numbered in the tens of thousands of Cossacks and their families. There, also, was the Cossack Host's main command, headed by General P. N. Krasnov.

In Croatia, the 15th Cossack Cavalry Corps was desperately fighting off pressing Red hordes. Commanded by German General Helmuth von Pannwitz, it numbered up to fifteen thousand in its ranks of combatants.

Besides this, many small Cossack combinations were sprinkled in among separate German divisions. Some Cossacks worked in peasant households and factories in Germany and Austria, which then constituted the Third Reich.

The war ended in the beginning of May of 1945. Most Russians found in territories being occupied by the western allies, Cossacks among them, began to gather together into special camps under the direction of occupying forces.

At that time we had no information whatever on the fate of the Cossachi Stan or the Cossack Corps.

Fantastic rumors began to spread that units of the Corps were breaking through companies of Titoists into Greece; that General Shkuro, with a group of Cossacks, was holed up in some unassailable Italian castle, and so forth.

In June, a German woman announced to us that one of her relatives had just come from Italy with a story about some sort of bloody incident had taken place there in which many Cossacks had suffered. It was not until July 16th that someone could give us a credible account of the fate of the Cossachi Stan. It came from a native of the Kuban region who came to Camp Kempten (in Bavaria) from southern Austria. He verified that, indeed, there had been a bloody incident, but it had been in Austria rather than Italy.

He explained to us that in early May, in anticipation of the end of the war, the Cossachi Stan relocated from Italy to southern Austria, which was then being occupied by British forces. By order of the British Command, they were distributed along the Drau River on a portion of land between the cities of Lienz and Oberdrauburg, stretching some 25-30 kilometers. All were placed under English control. Then the Kuban native told us about the remote events that became the subject of this book.

As to what happened to General von Pannwitz's Corps, we were long left in the dark, even in the face of measures we adopted to discover it. Not until the beginning of 1947 did we learn from Soviet newspapers of the executions in Moscow of Generals P. N. Krasnov, Sultan Kilech-Ghirey, S. N. Krasnov, and Helmuth von Pannwitz.

How they fell into Bolshevik hands, we learned much later. On this there is also discussion in this book.

Of the fate of the officers and Cossacks of the corps, we had no knowledge until 1953, when we happened to make contact with an officer who managed to escape the betrayal. He sent us a written account of the tragic end of the 1st Cossack Division, but of the 2nd Division, we learned only later.

General von Pannwitz's Cossack Corps suffered the same fate as the Cossachi Stan. In the same year of 1953, we received a communication from a certain officer, Besskaravayny, who had been turned over with the officers of the Cossack Corps. He then wound up in the concentration camp in Siberia where the remaining officers had been sent, escaped from there, made his way to Baghdad (in Mesopotamia), and sent us a detailed account, excerpts from which can be found in this book.

A German officer who commanded a company in the Cossack Corps, on his release by the Soviets, verified Besskaravayny's account in full.

Finally, beginning with the summer of 1955 and totally unexpectedly, several of those turned over to the Soviets in 1945 began to return, having served their 10-year terms of prison labor. That is, at least those who could prove they were other than Soviet nationals. Those who could not claim such alien nationality for themselves, the Bolsheviks would not let leave the USSR.

From them we obtained a great deal of evidence concerning the tragedy that befell Cossackdom in 1945.

––––––

From the time we first received reports of forced repatriations until the present, I have been collecting all that relates to this terrifying crime by the allies of the Bolsheviks.

Over fifteen years, I have gathered hundreds of exhibits, letters, notes, various observations, diaries, and other materials from survivors of the drama of the betrayal, of its witnesses, and of the inhabitants of places where the betrayals took place. I have also collected many maps, schematics, sketches, photographs and portraits of individuals, and everything that has appeared in Russian periodicals and foreign presses, books and pamphlets, in various languages.

I contacted authors working on the issue of forced repatriations. From them I also obtained many valuable materials.

With the goal of familiarizing the educated public with the Cossack tragedy that took place in 1945 on the banks of the River Drau in Lienz, and in other places having large concentrations of Cossacks—fighters against communism—and in order to preserve the materials collected for posterity and future historians, I offer this book, which came to fruition through the kind assistance of Sergey Vladimirovich Zavalishin, director of the All Slavic Publishing House in New York.

––––––

From the great mass of materials available to us, we included in this book all that seemed to us to be important at present, but in our "Archives of the Tragedies of Forced Repatriations," historians will find many details that appeared non-essential to us, but may be of value to them.

––––––

It is difficult for us to evaluate all that happened, because, due to the brief time that has passed, we still suffer strong emotions over what we have gone through. We empathized with those who lived through this tragedy when we listened to their tales or read their writings. From human weakness arising from our personal relation to them, we might sometimes have believed what perhaps we should not and disbelieved what we should have.

Future historians will be in a different situation. By the passing of years, they will come from afar, as the saying goes, to evaluate all that happened many years in the past. They will come with cool temperaments, with the single goal of properly evaluating all that we lived through.

Keeping the above in mind, I did not attempt to give an overall account of what happened, but only hoped to gather as much information as possible and only in certain instances did I find it necessary to explain issues that arose.

For this reason, materials in the book are grouped neither chronologically nor in any order but that by which they were received.

On publishing them, repetition has been unavoidable, since different authors often write what they remember of one and the same event in the tragedy.

However—the repetition is only apparent. Each observation was made under extremely strained conditions, with its author in danger of being seized, and sent into the hands of Bolsheviks. In addition, the events usually took place over a large spatial extent and in crowded gatherings of people, when each might see only what occurred in his immediate vicinity.

For example, several thousand people were gathered on the large field of Camp Peggetz. Nerves were drawn taught to their breaking points. Each experienced what happened individually. The majority of survivors of June 1st, 1945, on the field of Camp Peggetz attest to the complete inhumanity of English soldiers who butchered all resisters. Such was the general impression; but others viewed instances of humanity by several English soldiers, one example being when a girl carried a note from her father to one of the tank crews.

Or, when fleeing from Italy: a column of people spread over ten kilometers was mired in snow. Those extremely exhausted people could see only what happened immediately around them. Thus, several saw instances of complete inhumanity, when the healthy and strong passed by— with cutter indifference—children perishing in the snowdrifts, or ignored elderly people too exhausted to go on. Others saw different ones: some saw Cossacks climb down from their conveyances in order to put an old man or a child having no strength left on them.

One can not take a general measure or make inferences from a single occurrence.

It remains for future historians to give accounts in their impartial words.

———

I tirelessly requested individuals to send their testimony, and in accord with the amount of material that came my way, I must announce with great gratitude that many answered my call.

But, aside from the act of being forcibly abducted, several episodes in the tragedy and following it remain unexplained to this time.

For example, to this day, it has been impossible to establish where the Bolsheviks sent those taken away from the scene by train, among whom were the members of the Cossachi Stan.

Still unexplained, also, is the important question of the executions at Graz. There exists some knowledge of them, but no conclusive evidence. One of our compatriots had a film, obtained from a foreign officer, that was made at the stone quarry where the Cossacks were shot, as the images clearly showed. This film was sent off to me from Europe, along with the diary of this compatriot. But even though the package was sent off several years ago and after endless reminders to the dispatchers, to this day, nothing of the sort has arrived.

There are other issues, less essential, but still of clear interest. For example, it is well known that General von Pannwitz was on May 29, 1945, together with General Krasnov and others, imprisoned in a factory in Judenberg. The next day, he, along with them, was transferred from Graz farther toward Vienna, but there his trail disappears. All the others were sent by train to Moscow, but where he went is unknown. Then it was learned that he was given over to the Americans, and on June 10th was sent to Austria, to Enns Station, with an echelon being driven for repatriation to the USSR as a gift to that regime. Where he had been in the meantime, we could not establish. There exists unverified testimony that he had been summoned to Trieste.

Collecting information was very difficult, because so many still fear it, regardless of the number of years having passed since the repatriations. Several of our compatriots still do not reveal their true names and try to hide like bears in hibernation, hoping that even their compatriots will forget them.

And it is not only our compatriots, but also several foreigners who at present still suffer pursuit and repression or are involved in armed struggles.

One foreign journalist, who is energetically investigating the issue of forced repatriation, is required, to this day, to hide behind a pseudonym.

And is it not a significant event that, last year, fourteen years after the end of the war, German General Manteufel was sentenced to prison as a "war criminal?"

———

Much of what transpired is still not clear. For example, many are troubled by the question of how a thousand officers could allow themselves to be fooled into being driven from Lienz on the pretext of a "conference" with English generals.

From our vantage point, it seems that the cleverness of the English was "sewn with white threads." But at that time in Lienz, the situation was not comparable to what we see in hindsight. We must focus on the preliminary methods used by the English at that time to blind Cossack vigilance.

On this question much has been written and many opinions given.

In considering in full the setting in which the trip of the officers of the Cossachi Stan took place, one must allow that the main reason that the officers let themselves be fooled was their training as Russian officers. They could not conceive of the idea that an officer, even English, could lie, then disguise that lie as the "word of honor of an officer in the Royal British Army.

The documents studied show that the most trusting were the old regimental officers, such as General P. N. Krasnov, for example, whose last words to his wife before leaving for the so-called conference were:

"I will return around six or eight in the evening."

And here is another typical occurrence with one of the old generals. When seated in the auto waiting to go to the "conference," one of the officers expressed doubts on noticing English machine gunners accompanying the vehicles. General Ye., sitting with him in the same automobile, answered:

"You understand the new situation poorly, *Sotnik* [Cossack rank, the equivalent of lieutenant—*trans.*], and the way things are done now in democratic armies, but as to your observation of the presence of machine gunners, they are simply our guard. Obviously, somewhere along the route we are to follow, there must be groups of partisans."

It must be admitted that such trust shown by old veteran officers greatly calmed the others.

————

As to the cunning of the English, it is not without interest to remember their own history.

At the end of the 16th century, England's Queen Elizabeth I had her relative, the Scottish Queen, Mary Stuart, beheaded.

As a consequence of a revolt against her in Scotland, Mary Stuart hid in England, finding refuge in a private castle by the sea. From there, she sought asylum for herself in England from Queen Elizabeth. The latter very warmly answered that she was ready to accept her with all the deference due a queen, but first of all, a thorough investigation needed to be conducted on the reasons for her fleeing her Scottish borders.

Mary Stuart resolutely informed her that as a queen, she could not submit to any kind of inquiry regarding her person.

Then, with the intent of having her drop her vigilance, she was told that there would be no investigation of any sort, but that a "conference" would be held, instead.

On this bait was Queen Mary Stuart caught. She her sent approval.

This was all that Elizabeth needed. Instead of a "conference," an actual court trial was conducted, at which Mary Stuart was sentenced in her absence to life imprisonment. That ended after eighteen years in Fotheringhay Castle, when she was beheaded on the new charge of plotting against the life of Queen Elizabeth. Mary Stuart was executed in the same castle hall in which she suffered imprisonment for so long. She had carelessly believed in a "conference" in the same way that, three hundred fifty years later, on the River Drau, in Lienz, more than two thousand officers of the Cossachi Stan did, too.

———

Why Cossacks and other anti-Bolsheviks did not want to return to their homelands when the war ended, even preferring death to return, is best understood by those most familiar with the nature of Bolshevism and the purpose of Communism.

Individual foreigners who study the issue of forced repatriations and collect documents about them understand it.

Several members of legislative institutions in America and England, such as US Congressman Albert Bosch and British Members of Parliament G. G. Stokes [This should be Richard Stokes, Member of Parliament after World War Two, not G. G. Stokes, the noted mathematician and physicist, who died in 1903—*trans.*] and Nicholson [English spelling could not be verified—*trans.*] also understand it. They are determined to get an explanation of the circumstances and who was responsible.

It must be put that the nature of Bolshevism was very clear to the participants of the Yalta Conference, and that those who supported the use of deception with prisoners of war created the basis at the end of World War Two for forced return to their homelands of those who were unwilling to return voluntarily. Did they know what they were doing, when they knew what fate awaited those seized on repatriation, but nonetheless carried out this historically unheard of seizure, only to please Stalin?

But it was not known then in Europe and America, as it is still not known, what Soviet power in Russia represents. For that reason, it is possible that doubts may have arisen about those unwilling to return to their homelands after the war and led to the belief that they were criminals who feared legal reprisals.

But they were not the criminals. Soviet power, having kept the Russian people in slavery for more than forty years now, was and is.

And it must be known that it was not only Cossacks and other Russians who did not want to return voluntarily after the war. Neither did Ukrainians, Caucasian Highlanders, Poles, and Baltic peoples, all allies of the Bolsheviks. Not all of them were repatriated. Particular attention was given to Russians, Highlanders, and Cossacks, who, as freedom-loving people, were the mortal enemies of Soviet power.

The public of free countries does not know, or does not want to know, that Soviet power does not arise from the people in Russia, but from a band of criminals, who remain in power through unprecedented use of force and terror.

The Russian people, half-starved and half-naked, toil in compulsory labor, under conditions of slavery. The Russian people hate Soviet power. Soviet power deludes free nations by conducting fictional elections, under which one must vote only for specified candidates, under fear of death or abduction into forced labor camps.

With the goal of achieving its main aim, enslavement of the entire world, the Communist leadership widely uses the strength of its people for free labor by driving them into *konslagers* and *kolhozes* [concentration camps and collective farms—*trans*.].

Konslagers are filled completely by people that Soviet power considers to be dangerous. If there are not enough such, government agents fill the need with people accused of crimes against Soviet power. It is to these camps that those who were forcibly returned to Stalin by the allies of the Bolsheviks arrived in 1945.

Millions of people now suffer in these camps, while millions more have already perished in them.

Bolsheviks do not falter before their massive requirement for people. For example they sent every single inhabitant from several Cossack *stanitsas* (*selos*) [Cossack settlements (villages)—*trans*.]

into a fierce winter blizzard without allowing anyone to take any of their things. They perished in hordes, especially children and the elderly, during their transport and imprisonment, where they were often let out and left in places without a single dwelling, surrounded only by barbed wire.

In order to destroy the more resistant populations, such as Cossacks and Ukrainians, the Soviet government created an artificial famine on their lands, removing all provisions to the last grain. Millions of people perished as a result.

One of the executioners sent by Stalin to destroy the people of the Ukraine, Nikita Krushchev, the current dictator of Russia, is now met with great respect in the countries of the free world.

What is life like in Russia, and in all the other nations enslaved by Bolsheviks? Unbearable. Evidence on the condition of life there is that, when the Germans invaded Russian territory, before the inhabitants knew the true intent of the latter, but considered them to be their liberators from the Soviet power they hated, Russian people surrendered by the millions to the Germans and eagerly bore arms in order to fight against their hated Bolshevik oppressors.

It is well known that, when the Germans retreated from within Russian borders, millions of Russians went with them, seeking nothing but to no longer remain under hated the Soviet power. These people hoped to find shelter in free countries, but were only bitterly fooled in their expectations, being returned to Bolshevism to find only death and imprisonment.

After the end of the war, the Soviet leadership feared leaving masses of prisoners of war and laborers in Europe, because these would be living witnesses capable of opening the eyes of free countries to the intolerable Bolshevik regime in Russia.

Nor could the Bolsheviks leave the returnees from Europe free to mingle with others, because they could tell about what life is like for free a person. This is why Soviet authorities vigorously sought the return of all prisoners of war and laborers to their homelands. But, on getting their hands on them, they killed some quickly and drove others into brutal compulsory labor in konslagers, thus increasing the number of free hands, willing-unwilling, available to work to strengthen the power of their own oppressors.

The allies of the Bolsheviks, having forcibly turned over millions of people to them after the war, strengthened through this action the might of Soviet power and undermined any trust in them by the yoked Russian people.

Russian people hate Soviet power. They hate it because, in the passage of decades, they have tested it out on themselves.

The Russian nation prefers a free life, even if difficult, but not the unjust life they have, under constant threat of loss of freedom loss of families, loss of all that is dear, that squeezes and oppresses all inhabitants of Russia.

A Cossack, as do other Russian men, desires little—only the return of that human existence that has been taken from him by Soviet power. He wants the life lived in the rest of the free world.

This is the reason that the betrayed Cossacks, other prisoners of war, and laborers, did not want to return to their homelands after the war. But the allies of the Bolsheviks, for their own economic interests, gave them over to the justice of the Red beast.

V. Naumenko

Fleeting Dawn of Cossackdom

It sparked in the darkness of the Soviet abyss from the storm of war in '41 ... began to shine hope on subjected people ... flashed a sword at Communism ... once more shone light on it before the world, shone light on all its lies and failures, all its cowardliness and its satanic villainy.

In vain did a million slaves suffer prison hardships to erect endless defenses of antitank ditches, parapets, minefields, barbed wire enclosures, foxholes and trenches, chains of artillery fortifications, *dots* [pillboxes—*trans.*], *dzots* [pillboxes of earth and wood—*trans.*], and so forth. The true condition of the flower of the Red Army became known. Until then it had been gloriously heralded by noisy communist propaganda, just as it is heralded now.

With strong resolve, the German Army cut its way through Communism. It cut into Communism's stronghold with forged steel, overcame the opposition of the Red Army, urged on as it was by rear fire from NKVD forces behind the battle lines, and pushed it farther and farther east. The Red Army was pushed back because, in the end, it had no spirit nor desire to defend the universal imprisonment, the arbitrary rule, and the other "attainments" that are Communism. Red Army units surrendered *en mass*. The Red kahal trembled to its very bottom. It lost its long-standing haughtiness, and it came to see the true cost of being "ever-ready" to subjugate the world. From fear of retribution for all its inhuman crimes, it swallowed its pride. To save itself, it brought back the priesthood it had trampled underfoot into bloody filth. It bellowed, even from the churches that it had abused and destroyed, words tested by the ages: "Our native land, our mother country, is in danger…" It called on the public to take up arms, created medals named after heroes from Russia's history, attached epaulets to shoulders, and even restored officer ranks and many other things for which, before then, it had persecuted us and executed our grandfathers and fathers.

Still, not pinning its hopes on such "slander," Communism in due time began its curtain. On retreat, it took with it equipment from its mills and factories, robbed its own populace, drove off livestock by the millions, and destroyed any weapons held in village households.

To the east moved long columns made up of crucial "co-workers" and their kin and automobile caravans, overloaded with the goods of the populace. Innumerable livestock herds were driven straight into fields.

After the Red Army retreated, the NKVD left. First, however, they blew up and mined the abandoned mills and factory buildings; burned archives; destroyed railroad tracks; cut telegraph lines; burned or poisoned granaries, huge stores of foodstuffs, and other provisions; shot prisoners or set them afire alive, packing basements with their corpses, even of those only held for interrogation; and killed anyone "suspicious" found out on streets or roads.

Fulfilling in this way their responsibility to "care for the public welfare," Communism doomed to hunger and deprivation "its people"—to the last man—and its retreating army, as it lined its path with corpses and lit it with the fires of all that could be burned.

What resulted was something never taught by the "wise leaders." An even greater hatred arose for it in the people. It also fostered trust in them for the German Army that was chasing out the Communists.

Hatred by Cossacks of Communism was unbounded. It sparked up from the first days of Communist rule. In those accursed days, Communism flooded Cossack lands with Cossack blood and death, covered with Cossack bones the most bleak, out-of-the-way places of exile, canals, and konslagers. It exterminated through hunger even those left to toil in kolhoz prisons, filled Cossack hearths and homes with its own trusted selections, and wrapped Cossacks in its final fierce tyranny.For this reason, the soul of the Cossack was lifted by the storm of war. It blessed his suffering soul, and put fire in his dimming eyes. A wave of hope went from the upper reaches of the Don and Khopr, on to the Kuban, into the Caucasus, to Stavropol, along the Kalmyk Steppes, to the north, rolling over the Caspian Sea, the Volga, and Ural, into Central Asia, Siberia, and the Far East.

On Cossack lands in the Northern Caucasus and farther into the mountains, Stavropol, and other places, Cossacks, Kalmyks, and Highlanders brought out their rifles from hiding places, along with blades, *Nagans* [Nagan, the name of the manufacturer, became synonymous with the product in Russia—*trans.*], daggers, and swords, and sharpened their pitchforks and axes.

In Novocherkassk, secret military organizations, in the main under senior officer Pavlov, sprang up for the liberation of the Don, long before the approach of German forces. In Chechnya, in the Shatoysky District, an armed uprising began and spread to other *auls* [settlements of Caucasian Highlanders—*trans.*]. The rebels fortified the city of Grozny. Kubans, Tereks, and all the Caucasian nationalities began to rise up. In many distant, overcrowded konslagers, all the inmates rose up. Prisoners overpowered guards, freed their neighbor comrades-in-misfortune, and successfully escaped into the taiga. In places holding exiled "dekulakized" Ukrainians, Cossacks, Caucasians, Russians, and others, along the River Pechor, beyond the Urals, along the River Ob, in the Narimsky region, and elsewhere, exiles took up arms against Communism.

Males dominated among exiles. All were men who were not welcome in the Red Army. Cossacks of the Ural, Orenburg, Siberian, Amur, and other hosts swelled partisan numbers. Frightened Communists abandoned entire regions, sent in elite punitive units of the NKVD against the uprisings, and spared not even children in refilling their prisons with malcontents and suspicious persons. Terror was fomented through the power of the USSR.

In Cossack lands and in the Ukraine, revolt against its inhumanity heated up in answer to what were by its own measures the monstrous piracy and tyranny of retreating Communism. Partisans lay in watch for their executioners everywhere. They rescued those arrested who were close to them, neighbors, and any prisoners held temporarily. They recovered the livestock that was driven off and the transports that were taking away their goods. They rolled Communist convoys down slopes into ravines, killed activist left in their midst to instigate disorder, and fought in battle those punitive units sent against them, along with those sent with them from the Red Army, replenished from the ranks of recent deserters.

From the first day of the German attack, Cossacks, Highlanders, Ukrainians, Russians, and other prisoner-of-war volunteers began to appear among German forces. They worked as chauffeurs, stretcher-bearers and ambulance drivers, cooks, weapon masters, radio technicians, and anything else they could do.

Everywhere, on their own responsibility, individual commanders in Germany's attacking forces began to create combat sub-units from the volunteers and partisans who had joined up with their units along the way. Reports of their bravery in advanced reconnaissance positions against the Communist Red Army became more common. Many rose in the ranks to command positions. German commanders requested to have more of our volunteers enrolled in German formations—on even terms with Germans. They were never refused.

In this way, the foundation was put down for future Cossack, Highlander, and other cadres of volunteer troops. It was facilitated by the German Army having no small number of Russian speaking officers. Meanwhile our emigrants, who had become naturalized citizens, were serving as officers in Rumanian and other armies.

As one of these, I commanded a Highlander-Cossack reconnaissance team in a unit of the attacking German Army.

Breaking through powerful, deeply entrenched lines of Soviet defense, forces of the southern wing of the German Army quickly moved to the east. On October 16, 1941, in territories it liberated, it came upon the first points of habitation of the Greater Don Host: Novo-Nikolaevskaya Stanitsa, in the city of Taganrog, and its western *khutor* [Cossack farmstead—*trans.*], Sinyavkskiy.

Moving on, the first German units came to the city of Rostov-on-Don. They destroyed its Red defenses and took the city. Toward the end of the same month, they left under strong fire from Red artillery, coming from the direction of Bataysk, which resulted in many casualties among the city dwellers. These units left the main line of their army, crossing the near banks of the Sea of Azov through Sanbek Selo of eastern Taganrog.

News of the liberation of the high command of the Don Host crossed the front lines and spread far and wide through Cossackdom. Dark expectations changed to joyous hope.

With passionate tears, Cossacks praised God, but the severe winter tempered our hopes. It was that winter, not the "wisdom" of leaders frightened out of their minds and having run away to the home front, that stopped further progress by the German Army. That and the strained lines of communication through the vast roadless land of scorched earth left by the communists.

Winter also prevented further retreat by the Red Army from the stalled Germans lines and gave it a chance to reinforce itself. Communism had time to recover from its fright as its western allies stepped up to save it with through various means.

Deep winter cold and the blizzards of 1941-1942 not only kept German forces from attack, but also caused great losses, despite all the efforts of its command and its men.

At that time, Communism made greater efforts at saving its own skin than its army, causing incommensurate losses, especially on the central and northern fronts. Poorly equipped Red Army troops perished *en mass* from exposure and lack of bandages. Those with serious wounds froze before they could be transported to field hospitals. Those lightly wounded or frostbitten were not released from the front. They died there of blood poisoning. Those with "self-inflicted" wounds were executed on the spot, as lessons to the others. Rifle bolts and automatic weapons failed from improper care with inadequate substitutes for gun oil. The metal of weapons also froze to the skin holding them. So many weapons were out of action that Red soldiers could not offer any serious resistance in hand-to-hand combat with Germans and allowed themselves to be taken prisoner. The number of deserters was great. The Soviet defense held, however, mainly through uninterrupted artillery fire, German passivity, and fierce thrusts by defensive units on the Red Army front lines.

But the worst human losses occurred on the orders of the "Generalissimo" and his "Baby Generalissimos," who drove their entrenched defensive forces into throwing themselves at the German position.

Commonly, these attacks were chosen for nights during blizzards blowing from the east that blinded the German forces. The massive Red attacks began only after minefields were laid. A mad artillery barrage held down the Germans while the Reds prepared for engagement. Their attack came wrapped in the haze of the storm and in places where snow was drifting. Red forces themselves got stuck in snow that drifted up over the barbed wire defenses and sunk into wolf holes and anti-tank traps. They blew themselves up in their own minefields, for which maps did not exist.

Surrounded by flashes from especially powerful German rockets within range of them, the Red Army fell under the ruinous fire and turned back. But the storm blew snow back at their frozen eyes, knocked them off course, and cut them up once more in those same obstructions…

The "lucky ones," who moved out of their initial position, were fired on from advanced positions, now strengthened in response to the new sorties, and were once more driven back to perish…

Only those who managed to reach German lines could save themselves.

In the days of calm that followed, cries and groans carried out from the dead zone from those wounded and stuck in obstructions. But rescuing them was difficult. German medics who tried were met with a rain of fire from Red machine guns. Red "medics" finished off those of the wounded who tried to reach us on their own. The cold finished off the rest. The dead zone soon fell silent ... until the next assault.

Many in the Red Army fell in this way that first winter on the orders of Communism. But it was not out of love for it that the majority of the overwhelmed soldiers fought on. They fulfilled their criminal orders out of fear of execution and dread of becoming the executioners of their own loved ones, for everyone knew that not following orders, or even surrendering, counted as "treason against the motherland." Those guilty of this were threatened with death on the spot, and their loved ones with prison and confiscation of all their belongings, according to Section 58 of the Criminal Code. After "release" came loss of all "rights."

Only these satanic means then kept—and still now keeps—Communism in power.

That winter, the front stalled on the shores of the Don and Kuban Hosts. Beyond its lines, Soviet tyranny ruled. Day and night, mass arrests were made of former prisoners, escaping prisoners of war, and deserters from the Red Army, among whom were mainly Cossacks and Caucasians. Justice for them was "swift and fair." Some were shot on the spot, others sent for further "investigation" in unspecified directions. Still others, in the best of cases, were "accompanied" in convoys to the better known penal regions.

Out of fear of possible new German attacks, Communism drove its "own free," half-naked, starving populace, out during typically hard freezes to construct new defensive structures. Its own *oprichniks* [Ivan the Terrible's special guards—*trans*.] built barbed wire enclosures and, as if for animals, hunted out the deviants held there, then filled transports with them and herded them under guard on foot to work.

A deep freeze and prison labor carried off many.

The situation of Cossacks beyond the front lines became unbearable ... despair was everywhere ... In the beginning of March 1943, a sotnik of the Don Host, A. A. Syusyukin, got through defensive lines at the Sanbek position. Reaching the Germans, he informed them that he had been sent by the full Staff for the

Liberation of the Don to convey the critical situation Communism had put Cossacks in and their readiness to revolt against it. He requested that appropriate arrangements be made with the German Command. He asked to be directed to General P. N. Krasnov to present information on the basis of which he would solicit the General to his side. In further communications, Syusyukin repeated his message to the staff of Army General Wittersheim. It is understood that the Germans had already learned much of his information from prisoners and deserters, but the journey of Sotnik Syusyukin had no other goal intended than the salvation of Cossackdom. After seven days, Cossack volunteers accompanied him to Berlin, where he informed General P. N. Krasnov of his mission.

In the spring of 1942, one hundred thousand leaflets were dropped beyond the front lines with General Krasnov's call to all Cossacks. Again, renewed hope brightened the Cossacks. But the leaflets were not the only things from which they could seek comfort.

Back in February of 1942 in Vinnitsa, *Yesauls* [Cossack rank, the equivalent of captain—*trans.*] of the Don Host, Ilyin and N., with assistance from Sonderfuhrer Richter, acting then on his own initiative, set about organizing large groups of Cossack prisoners of war under a single command. By the end of April of the same year, there were already more than 1000 Cossacks in these combined units. On June 3, they were placed under the command of Russian-speaking Captain von Braude, the newly arrived Assistant Commander of prisoners of war in the Ukraine. Even more German officers came with him. On June 6, these battle-ready Cossack sub-units were sent to the front. The rest, enlarged with new volunteers, continued their preparations. On June 18, orders were given to move all Cossacks from Vinnitsa to Slavuta and to establish there a center for Cossack formations. On June 28, there were 5826 Cossacks in Slavuta. After a few days, all were transferred to Shepetovka, where they were organized into the 1st, 2nd, and 3rd Cossack Regiments. But they were not the first and were far from the only formations made up solely of Cossacks. For example, among the first Cossack-volunteer formations, there was already on November 3, 1941, a group of 26 men from Nevelia in a Smolensk prisoner of war camp that grew in a few days into the 1st *Sotnya* [Cossack company, consisting of one hundred men—*trans.*] In April 1942, German Oberlieutenant Count Rittberg, with the permission of General von Schenkendorf, organized four Cossack sotnyas and a battery near Mogilev. I will speak of other formations later. This was the start of the conversion of Cossack forces for the liberation of Cossackdom ... It appeared to be very near ...

And they burst forth ... They burst forth in a big way, never to be forgotten by any of us.

On July 11, 1942, the 40th Tank Corps, comprising part of the German 6th Army of General Paulus as it advanced on Stalingrad, attacked first from the northwest into the territory of the Don Cossack Host. On that day, its advance guard reached Bokovskoy Station in Astakhov. The commander of the Corps was General von Schweppenburg.

On July 14, the 4th Panzer Army of General Hoth arrived on the Don and fought off the Reds between the upper reaches of the River Chir and Millerovo.

On its right, between Millerovo and Kamensk-Shakhtinsky, the 1st Panzer Army of Colonel General von Kleist advanced in the direction of Rostov-on-Don, while farther on the right was the Army Group of Colonel General Ruoff, consisting of the 17th German Army and the 3rd Rumanian Army of Colonel General Dumitrescu.

South of them, near the Sea of Azov, in eastern Taganrog, a group of tank forces under General von Wietershcim, the 14th and 57th Panzer Corps, was in action. Farther south, in Kerch, preparing to attack the Kuban, was the Rumanian Mountain Corps, formerly part of the 11th Army.

On July 21, the 57th Panzer Corps of General Kirchner defeated Reds fortifying Sanbek and moved on to Rostov.

The full attack of the main Army Group on the outnumbered forces of the Don began along the line of Taganrog-Kursk under the command of Field Marshal List. Rumanian units in Kerch did not take part. On orders from the 2nd Army Command in Crimea, they waited for the arrival at the Red rear of the main German forces in the east.

On July 23, the 125th Infantry Division and the 13th and 22nd Panzer Divisions occupied Rostov in force. The Reds began to retreat south, with the German 5th Army following them.

On July 30, the 4th Panzer Division, units of which reached the Manych River, was reinforced by German Army Group "B", acting to the north. It then turned to attack Stalingrad from the south. The rest of the army, Group "A", continued its movement toward the Caucasus and the Caspian Sea.

In mid-September, 1942, the German Army freed the western and southern parts of Don Cossack lands from the Communists, Kuban Cossack lands to the foothills of the Caucasus, the Stavropol area, and a large part of the Kalmyk Steppe. The first detachment from the 1st Panzer Army reached the Caspian Sea in the area of Sosta and Yashkul.

When it entered Cossack territory on July 11, 1941, the German Army set loose a wide wave that washed Red death away with it. Its overthrow of the Communists revived Cossackdom. Everywhere, as in ancient days, Cossack organs of self-government sparked to life. Cossacks who had been scattered in all directions rushed to their native stanitsa and khutors, replenishing their depleted ranks. Their shrines and ancestral hearths were reestablished. Life began anew. In the bright rays of the following days, cap bands and trouser stripes blazed with scarlet. Silver sparkled from Cossack arms, greatcoats, and saddles. These sights brought joy and pride to the once tear-filled eyes of Cossack women. Veteran Cossacks, with feigned strictness, taught the young how to trick ride on horses of the former kolhozes, take care of weapons, and mend and wear their native dress. Cossacks prayed in churches for those who had perished. For those still living, they prayed for a return from their places of Diaspora. They put up crosses over the group graves of unknown dead. They passionately asked God for the return of their lost Cossack freedom. They prayed for him to give them victory over the satanic power that had oppressed them and forever to help them guard against all usurpers. At the end of each working day, they retired with a cup, reminisced over the past, dreamed of the future, and harmonized in song.

The Cossack's love of freedom, his industriousness, keen wit, and courage was particularly appreciated by the German Command. It gave its good offices through directives rendering assistance to the reestablishment of Cossack life, the return of local laws, rearmament, etc. Pillaged and half-destroyed by Communism, Cossackdom began to heal its wounds through hard work. Once more, Cossacks attained the mighty stature of the ancient knights of Russia, the *Bogatyrs*.

In Rostov, Novocherkassk, Yekaterinodar, and other cities, newspapers appeared. The restoration of local industry continued, new undertakings were begun, etc. But the enemy was not sleeping: as it retreated, the NKVD left behind not a few of its secret agents, and continued to slip in new ones, in order to commit murder, sabotage, and similar acts of provocation within the populace that remained.

German forces were overextended along a precarious front, so there was to be no peace for us at home.

Far from it. Cossacks did not distance themselves from German soldiers, who were dying on Cossack land in battle against a rash common foe. They looked to take an advantage from the heat of the foreign arms. Close behind the front lines, Cossacks established a home guard. In stanitsas near the front, Cossacks, armed with trophy weapons, maintained defensive details along with German soldiers, and carried out all the duties of war alongside them.

On the Don, from the first days of liberation of Novocherkassk, the Field Ataman of the Don Host, Colonel Pavlov, working out of his own household, spared no efforts to bring back the glory of Cossackdom. His assistants, Colonel Dukhopelnikov, Colonel of the General Staff Ivanov, Under-Yesaul Domanov, Sotnik Syusyukin, and others of the General Staff gave him important help.

On a square in Novocherkassk, a cast iron Yermak testified to Cossack deeds. Rising above him was a majestic cathedral. Pain that could be solaced only through vengeance boiled up in Cossack souls at the sight of its once-gold cupolas, looted bare by Soviet atheists.

At this time, many Cossacks were still outside of their native *kurens* [Zaporozhian Cossack settlements; dwellings of Don and Kuban Cossacks–*trans.*] They got caught for various reasons in other cities and villages and were found in prisoners-of-war camps.

German camp administrators were instructed to free any Cossacks in their camps. This was difficult for them, however, because they could not tell who was a real Cossack. For this reason, the Field Ataman directed Sotnik Syusyukin to reconnoiter various places in search of the men indicated, to organize proper Cossack centers with them, and legitimize their organization.

Sotnik Syusyukin completed the tasks and created the centers. The main centers were in Mariupol, Taganrog, and Rostov-on-Don. The Field Ataman decided on his own initiative to improve them by naming leaders for each center. Of them, *Starshin* [Cossack elder, approximately a sergeant in rank—*trans.*] Zhelokhovsky [the English spelling of this and many other Russian names that follow could not be verified—*trans.*] was named commander of the Mariupol unit and Starshin Stefanov, Taganrog. War Minister Odnoralov was chosen for the Rostov center. The work of these centers was as follows: they registered and trained all Cossacks found among the wounded, saw to their needs with the help of the local authorities, and kept them on track in Cossack matters, local regulations, etc. Besides this, the centers were required to search the camps and passing parties of war prisoners in order to free any Cossacks in them, organize them into new units, and provision them. The German Army Command directed all of its local officers to cooperate accordingly.

In 1942, Cossacks, for the first time in all the years of their enslavement, could openly and freely celebrate their traditional holiday—"*Pokhrova*" of the Holy Virgin.

The Field Ataman, knowing the hopes of Cossacks for the holiday, decided that the main ceremony should be held in Starocherkassk. To this end, an announcement was made in advance throughout the entire host. The elders in charge of putting on the Cossack holiday received written notification under the signature of the Field Ataman. It had few pages—altogether only four thin, yellow leaves, but its simple Cossack words gave the pronouncement a strength that was irresistible.

And from all directions, men of the Don came to the cradle of their native host. Some came mounted, some on wagons, but most came on foot. The old and the small took routes straight through swampy glades, even directly into the thick marshes still drying from the smoothly flowing waters of the Don. Steel glistening, in an easy trot, the Goldina Sotnya, in the uniforms of escort guards, with swords and carbineers at their shoulders, overtook those on foot. Enraptured glances from those meeting it greeted the company. The arms of elders flew into the accustomed salutes and hid the sweet tears that sparkled unbidden.

The ancient cathedral could hardly fit all the people. They crowded its entrance and stood in its square. A triumphant fate, shining in Cossack eyes, penetrated deep into their very hearts, transforming their emaciated faces...

For that reason, with a cross at the head of the procession, they went to the Urochishche Monastery ... The autumn sun gave the crosses and church standards a golden color. High above, under a white cloud, martins flew overhead, calling to each other. Here and there along the banks of the Don were yellow marshes. Yellow dust rose lazily about feet.

The sotnya formed itself up before the platform to the decaying chapel, under which rested the bones of the hero of Azov. Cossacks stood at attention for the prayer. Kleist's staff officers stood frozen in place beside them. People bowed their heads and fell to their knees.

They could not hold back their pain through the sorrowful words of the requiem mass ... Cossack mothers, orphans, and widows started to cry ... Weeds about the sacred ruins trembled ... Gleaming white wings cried out in answer ... The ancient Don River flowed with dark blue ripples.

The appearance of the holy throne lifted the grief of the Cossacks...

After the priest, Field Ataman Pavlov addressed the Cossacks. Briefly, but resolutely, he spoke of the past glory of Cossackdom, fell to one knee, and read the letter from the hero of Azov to the Tsar. When he rose, his words had once more dried Cossack tears and enlivened their eagle eyes.

When they returned to the ancient stanitsa, they gathered around a cup of plain wine and shared pieces of wheat bread. The conversation was heavy and so was the Cossack song they sang. For dark clouds were already creeping over the Cossacks at the sunset of their day.

It is obvious that from the start of the war, the decisive forces of the West threw themselves into helping the Bolsheviks. From all sides, they sent a crowning flow of massive quantities of aviation, tanks, artillery, munitions, ships, transport trucks, equipment for military production, strategic and other materials, fuel, medicine, etc., to the USSR. Even when denying the quantity and effectiveness of such help, the Bolsheviks themselves write that they received from the USA alone "hardly even" 14,000 airplanes and 7,000 tanks. No matter how they belittle the real scope of the help they received, one is required to assume from their bragging that they somehow built up to 40,000 airplanes, 12,000 pieces of ordinance, over 30,000 armored tanks and self-propelled equipment, all on their own. Of course, the Bolshevik claims ignore that they left in ruins on the lands they abandoned all the industry and sources of raw materials required for such production. Neither do they like to make more precise that they apparently received 11 billion American dollars.

Thanks to this help and the winter respite, its back protected by the Red Army, Communism had time to collect itself from its first fright. Knowing that strength of spirit could raise its millions of people to safety, it put into action all of its resources to cultivate that spirit. Publicly spitting on its own mug, it abolished its institution of commissars, increased the proportion of national minorities in its leadership to its very heights, forbade anti-religious propaganda, freed, for show, its minor political opposition, etc. All this might lead one to think that Communism had started on a path of self-destruction for the sake of instituting freedom for its peoples and protecting it into the future. And, with the exclusion of root units of the populace of Cossack lands, the Kalmyk Steppe, Stavropol, and the Caucasus, the great bulk of the populace began to fall for Communism's new deceptions.

This is the reason that the whining address Stalin made to the army and people on July 31, 1942, when for the first time he hid nothing, reproached and threatened nobody, and revealed the terrible losses and the desperate situation of the country, became one of the turning points of the war. About ten days after this address, mass surrenders came to an end and the number of deserters fell significantly. The Red Army's strength at the front grew sharply.

In November 1942, those in front positions could see a new phase beginning in the war.

At this time, the Red Army, supplied with arms by the West and effectively holding Germany and its allies on all fronts, was reinforced by reserves and gained even more strength.

The opposite took place with the anti-Communists. Reinforcements in German, Italian, Hungarian, and Rumanian armies was almost nonexistent. Their infantry companies often numbered no more than 70 soldiers. Anti-tank weapons and ammunition stores were insufficient. Shortages of fuel were critical and spare parts were cobbled together from worn out tank units, in which, at times, only one-third of the vehicles remained in service. For example, the 48th Tank Corps consisted of the 33rd German and 1st Rumanian Tank Divisions, but only 46 tanks were still whole in the former, while the latter had only about 40 tanks. These mostly appeared to be light German tanks and Czech trophy vehicles. The attack strength of the entire "Corps" could be equated to that of a single tank regiment.

Communications were spread thin, extending some 2500 kilometers from the mouth of the Don. As for the condition of army supplies, there is not much to say.

The West had its own concerns...

The front line began between Novorossisk and Gelenzhik and went southeast. South of Maykop, it followed the ridgelines of the western Caucasus to Elbrus. South of Mozdok, it swung to the north, stretching through the Kalmyk Steppe past eastern Sosta, Yashkul, and Tundutov. It went west of Stalingrad at Rynok [English spelling of this and some of the place names that follow could not be verified —*trans.*] Then, turning northwest, it passed through the Tatar Horn to Kuchalin, and crossed the Don. Continuing with changing prospects up to and along its southern bank to Voronezh, it cut off the top part of the Don Host and left it to be ripped apart by Communists.

This front troubled Cossack hearts. Still, the local populace, as everywhere, did not believe the leaflets dropped on them by the Reds that proclaimed their new "charity." Neither did they believe that the unnatural union of capitalism with communism was never to end, nor did rumors of approaches from Hitler to make peace with the west fade away. They waited for the peace, waited for their united strength to sweep communism away and forever free the world of its menace. All hoped for this result as they continued to toil on their own land ... The German Command had not erected extensive defensive fortifications. Nor did it meddle in the affairs of selos, even near the front lines. So the populace huddled together in its native ruins, preparing their sparse inventories for fall work. More than a few refugees were there from Kremensky, Kletskoy, Yelanskoy, Kazanskoy and other leading stanitsas, khutors, and villages. Some were their waiting for near and dear ones. Others contemplated that future spring in which their hearths and homes would be free from the Reds. They tolerated the losses they suffered from gunfire and lived on a hope poisoned with dark foreboding. In mid-November, their worries, regardless of German success in Stalingrad, were increased even more through suspicions raised by the work of Reds who surreptitiously got beyond their lines under cover of the powdery haze and smoke of damp moonless nights.

November 17, the day after participating in the German capture of the Stalin Tractor Works, my unit was transferred to the northwestern wing of the 6th Army, which acted jointly with the right flank of the 3rd Rumanian Army, to take a defensive position alongside German units, as ordered.

But we were not there for long. The worries that were torturing the populace, to which the command did not pay the attention needed—or value reports from the front lines—were confirmed with frightening accuracy.

By simultaneous twin attacks on the Rumanian forces, the Reds increased their pressure both on the 8th Italian army, that was holding the left flank of the Rumanians from the west, and on the 6th German Army in Stalingrad, to the east on their right flank, against which they had moved storm troops.

On November 19, 1942, at 7:30 on a foggy, dank morning, there, northwest of Stalingrad, the Bolsheviks began an artillery attack against the 3rd Rumanian Army, which was joined with a wing of Paulus's 6th Army on its right flank. Its hellish intensity and extent had never before been seen. The attack began with the requisite blasts from *"Katyushas"* and snatches of all manner of artillery and weapon fire along a line of front on the Don of more than 100 kilometers, from Melo-Melovksy Khutor in eastern Kletskoy Stanitsa, to Rubeshinskoy Khutor, west of the city of Serafimovich. The strength of this fire, which continued for 1 hour and 20 minutes, can be judged in regions of Bolshevik breakthroughs. On every kilometer of the front, they often used more than 150 rounds of ordinance. The ground and the gloomy sky shook with deafening blasts of artillery that blended together into a single roar.

In accordance with their own infernal plan, the Reds did not with this hell just sweep away the Rumanian defense, whose entire artillery consisted only of 37 millimeter cannon pulled by horses, which were out of action from the beginning. They took their destruction, fire, and death deep into the rear, into dense populations of civilians …

The aim of the Reds—to spread horror among the latter, drive from it the legs of possible reinforcements, and create a panic in wavering soldiers, so as to ease its prospects in Stalingrad.

At 8:50, the 21st and 5th Soviet Tank Armies dashed through their bridgeheads, first on the right flank of the Rumanians at Kletskoy, then in western Serafimovich, where they were closer to their strength.

This action prevented the German Armies from rescuing the Rumanians.

The Soviets met the first part of their objectives: iron hail from their heavy artillery covered the population at the rear with its fire and death for almost four hours, creating the affect required. On a line more than 100 kilometers in width, thousands of half-clothed residents ran south from stanitsas and other habitation points destroyed by their enemy. Many were wounded and soon fell from exhaustion … They tried to crawl away from horrible deaths … Cossack children, mothers, and elderly ran … Only the dead were left. A shroud of snow began to cover them on this horrible morning of a black day.

Too far removed from the blow delivered, the German High Command did not realize its magnitude and extent—or its threat to

Stalingrad. Because of this, they delayed moving their single Rumanian reserve, the aforementioned 48th Tank Corps, from its initial position in the area of Perelazovskoy and other khutors, to face the Reds. This delay divided their strength. As a result, the Reds overcame the desperate opposition of the Rumanian forces and managed to succeed in attacking in both directions.

The right flank of the Rumanians was destroyed. Some Rumanian units were surrounded and perished heroically in the one-sided battle. Meanwhile, their main strength was in tatters and ignored.

Both divisions of the 48th Tank Corps, divided and tardy due to orders from on high, then engaged the center of the attacking 5th Red Tank army and were surrounded.

Moving southeast toward the approaches to Stalingrad, Red tank forces whiplashed the weak German reserves, shooting them on the go. Cossack refugees on roads and fields were thrown into panic. Special, red-hot Soviet propaganda about its cavalry corps and sharpshooter divisions, who kept an eye on the second echelon, followed the Cossacks, shattering their hopes. The horrid "business" was finished with Red tanks. There was no safety in the open spaces … Along with the blood of Rumanian and German soldiers, the blood of Cossack refugees spilled on the frozen snow…

This was the way the first evil shadow of Communism moved in, from the north, once more bringing repression and death to the Cossack populace.

On November 19, 1942, the Red Army inflicted mass exterminations on the Cossack populace.

This was repeated on another day, when the 51st Soviet Army broke through south of Stalingrad in the area of Krasnoarmeysk, on the left flank of the 4th Rumanian Army, and joined with the 21st and 5th Tank Armies, which were sweeping around Stalingrad.

In the evening of November 22, 1942, those armies locked Stalingrad in a ring of death and permanently cut off the 6th German Army within it. Not just Rumanians and Germans were left in the west. Along with them was a group of local inhabitants and Cossack forces, pushed there by the encircling Red attack. Most had not survived the horrors of famine, cold, typhus epidemics, and hellish bombardments during the time of the siege or the reprisals of the NKVD after surrender.

The front line of the encircling ring was more than 200 kilometers in circumference. Of the unbearable fate of all those unfortunates, we can guess from the boasts of Soviet Marshal Yeremenko, who said that 330,000 man had been surrounded and further explained that 200,000 of them perished and 90,000 men had been taken prisoner. What they did with the remaining 40,000 men, the Marshal was silent about.

In any case, these "loose ends" sooner or later discovered a new Communist "Katyn" at Stalingrad.

Little could be done to save Cossack refugees, even inside the ring, within the ineffectual front of the 3rd Rumanian Army. Eyewitnesses to the Soviet brutality could not escape on foot over roadless areas without being overtaken by Red tanks, cavalry, and bullets.

The few who were saved managed to reach units of the 15th Rumanian Infantry Division of General Lasker, who broke through the encirclement at Raspopinskoy, and the 48th Tank Corps of General Geyma [spelling could not be verified—*trans.*], who broke through encirclement in the area of Zhirka and Ust-Medveditskoy.

Among the ranks of encircled German forces in Stalingrad, likewise were units of the 20th Rumanian Infantry Division, which was cut off from the left flank of the 4th Army, and the remainder of the 1st Rumanian Cavalry Division of the 4th Corps, which had been destroyed on the right flank of the 3rd Rumanian Army during the aforementioned breakthrough by Soviet forces.

My unit, 46 Cossacks and Caucasians in number, also turned up in this encirclement and found itself on the western edge of Stalingrad's defenses.

Due to the enormous extent of the front and the different situations even of neighboring units, one can speak credibly only of one's own, and even then, only within the limits of its particular circumstances.

Nonetheless, it will be necessary to write of this separately. For now, I cover the following: from the first day of encirclement, it was clearly evident that supplies of all sorts were insufficient. From the beginning, the army's battle reserves barely reached 10% of the standard, while provisions were sufficient for 10-12 days, based on 500 grams of bread. From the first, weapons were provided with approximately 10 rounds per day, but soon even this could not be expected. Even during the beginning of the siege, there was not enough fuel for tactical redeployment of units, while later there was not even enough to reposition individual tanks and mobile artillery when necessary. They had to resort to endless dripping to gather enough fuel even to light firing points. Machine guns and automatic weapons were used only in highly dangerous situations. It became necessary to engage attacking Reds by resorting to hand-to-hand combat, in order to preserve cartridges and grenades for counterattack. And toward the end, it became necessary to engage often. Even the Reds now admit that they tried up to 700 distinct sorties during their encircling siege.

Cold, hunger, terrible support conditions, shortages of medicines and bandages, all these increased death rates among the wounded. A dysentery epidemic started and spotted fever spread throughout. Fatalities became massive. Corpses were barely removed. Invasions of rats brought on horrible rumors that the Reds had inoculated them in advance with typhus then released them to increase the spread of the disease among the beleaguered.

Pressure by the Reds, which was stepped up sharply beginning November 20th, became even greater. Their hellish bombardment continued without interruption. It broke connections between units on the edge of defenses and required some parts of the lines to be abandoned. Typically, this took place under cover of night and bad weather.

On December 13th, a sweeping, high-angle mortar fire covered our section and broke contact between my unit and the nearest command post. By nine o'clock that night, this fire was transferred half a kilometer past the line our section held. The terrible thought arose that neighboring units had retreated, but for some reason or other were unable to warn us. Scouts sent by me returned to inform me that the second line, that had been behind us, was abandoned, while about a kilometer further off, on the north side of their gun emplacements, mechanized Red forces were rapidly accumulating in a shallow ravine parallel to our position. It was clear that we were being over-run and would perish in any attempt to break through to our side, should we remained in place until morning.

Only one thing remained—to risk slipping through the Red lines on the west.

Losing no time, I gathered together my group of thirty-eight remaining men and told them of our situation, the plan I had, and its risks. Abandoning unnecessary gear and camouflaging ourselves for the snow, we first tried to the west, maintaining close order in case we found ourselves to be surrounded. We were prepared to die as free men. Then we chose a different direction. We moved southwest and only on foot. Crossing the tracks of the railroad into Kalach, then the frozen Marinovka River, we learned of a relief attack toward Stalingrad from the south by the Army Group of General Hoth that began December 12th. We turned to meet them. On December 17th, we crossed over the ice of the Mishov River northwest of Nizhnaya-Kamskaya [English spelling of this and names that follow could not be verified—*trans*.] The night of December 18th, we went south another 10-12 kilometers, after which we had to hole up to avoid a large movement of Red tanks and motorized units. The heavy geological relief in the area was very opportune for us. The thunder of artillery and the sounds of rifle fire made us aware of a tank battle underway very near us. Not too long before sunrise on December 19th, we had to step into battle with a motorized Red company that came upon us. We were saved from annihilation by the arrival, just in time, of a company from the 17th German Tank Division. We suffered seven Cossack and two Caucasian dead, specifically: Degtiareva, Nikolai Kriulkov, Aleksei Kotchetkov, Mikhail Perov, Tchikmasov, Ivan Miliutin, Arutiunov, Shiliy. We also had fourteen wounded. In addition, four Germans died in rescuing us. Those who fell in heroic death were buried there in two graves. We used rifles instead of crosses. We could not describe our joy at being saved ... We choked back tears ... Merciful God! May peace be on the souls of the heroes.

Due to our wounded and general exhaustion, the Germans did not permit us to take any further part in the operations on Stalingrad.

We were allocated an ambulance and one light transport vehicle, along with a light tank to cover us, which occasionally lost us due to our greater maneuverability in skirmishes. They delivered us to Potemkinskaya. Our wounded were sent to Rostov from there, the same day. We served to replenish von Pannwitz's group, which was ordered into battle with other German and Rumanian units in the regions of Karachev, Pimeno-Cherni, Derganov, and Sharnutovsky, against the most entrenched Reds.

The Second German Staff had formed Pannwitz's group November 25th. It was linked with and subordinate to the defense of Kotelnikov, towards which Reds streamed after the breakthrough on the left flank of the 4th Rumanian Army at Stalingrad. It was made from non-combat soldiers from the commandant's office, construction units, railroad workers, those cut off from units with which they served, and a small number of Cossacks, found in the rear areas of the 6th Army. The majority of the men were poorly trained and poorly equipped. They barely could fill two battalions, but were nonetheless bestowed the designation of regiment. Pannwitz was expected to perform feats of bravery with them. The day after taking command, he hit the Reds on the northern flank as they were nearing Kotelnikov, tore them to pieces, and destroyed them. The next day, in concert with the similar Battle Group Bischoff, which at most consisted of a motorized division with two mobile artilleries, he pushed north of the city into the Red rear lines, where forces were concentrating for an attack on it, and crushed them.

My future designation by Pannwitz as commander of a half sotnya of Cossacks, Kalmyks, and Caucasians gave me ample opportunity to confirm that he was in all ways gifted and stood out from others. He personally examined tactical situations on the field of battle, the way the enemy was situated, and the location of its greatest vulnerability. His decisions were without fault, his attacks decisive with minimal losses on our side. His concern for his underlings was such that we never saw him just resting, even after the most intense of battles. On his orders, not one wounded German, Cossack, or Red Army soldier was left on the field of battle, and every single one of us got equal attention from him. And how many refugee families he saved, rescuing them often from being surrounded or covering their rear with a quick and decisive maneuver. It is they, the refugees, who first brought to Cossack lands the glory and valor of Pannwitz, his selflessness, and his love for Cossacks.

No one in Pannwitz's group was ever offended or felt downtrodden or ignored. He was with us heart and soul.

For this reason, we never lost hope in the worst of moments. We knew that, with no concern for himself, he would do everything to get us out of the most hopeless situation. The German Command also drew on the cooperative spirit between Cossacks and Pannwitz. In the end, this was the main reason that he was designated as the head of the Cossack unit that was created and turned over to him, the 15th Cossack Cavalry Corps.

And when he once more led us into Yugoslavia against the Reds, everyone knew that Pannwitz had adopted Cossackdom to his dying days. Born a German in Poznan, he happened upon Cossack land even at the beginning of the war. He proved his love for Cossacks by imperiling of his own life during the dreadful days of surrender. In hope of easing the chances for his Cossacks, Pannwitz rejected the chance to save himself as a German. He stayed with his Cossacks until the end. He was the first on the Cossack execution block in Moscow ... Perpetual memory ... perpetual glory to him—a Cossack.

Pannwitz was capable, fearless, a great organizer. He lived many years among the Polish populace, learned their language, and connected with them in such a way that made it easy for him to obtain what was necessary to provision his division. He stimulated interactions between German and Cossack officers, considering it to be absolutely essential for the creation of a unified spirit. The German officers he chose for the division were chiefly those who had lived in Russia or the Baltic countries before the revolution and therefore knew the language.

There was an edict from higher up forbidding Cossack officers from the 1920 emigration, but Pannwitz paid no attention to it. If they appeared suitable to him, he took them.

His own military career began as a sixteen-year-old cadet volunteer, going to the front in the war of 1914-18. Within six months, he was wounded and awarded the Iron Cross. After the Treaty of Versailles, he wrestled against Bolshevism in Germany in the ranks of the German Volunteer Corps, but after they seized power, he left its borders and did not return to his homeland until 1932.

In operations against Poland, France, and the USSR, he commanded a reconnaissance division, the division's flight squadron, and many other military groups.

Soldiers loved him and called him "Old Man."

Colonel General Kleist intended to commission Pannwitz to form a Cossack Brigade in the northern Caucasus in November 1942, but the early withdrawal of German forces interfered.

On March 27, 1943, Pannwitz, then a colonel, was ordered to form the First Cossack Division.

The Division, formed in a camp near Mlawa, was officially given its designation on May 1, 1943.

July 1, Pannwitz was promoted to major general.

Pannwitz earned battle glory when the German Army attacked Pinsk, in counterattack at Piriatin and near Stalingrad.

South of Stalingrad, his battle group coordinated with other German and Rumanian units in the Kalmyk Steppe to fended off many Red forces of superior strength, completely destroying two Bolshevik cavalry divisions.

General Pannwitz was awarded a Knight's Cross on September 1941 and oak leaves for it on December 23, 1942.

From the first day of the Stalingrad breakthrough, besides Pannwitz's group, naturally, there were other German Battle Groups formed at battalion strength or greater. The better known were: Sauber, Pruskowsky, Sauvant, Birkenbiehl, Bischoff, and others. Depleted in numbers, these poorly armed detachments, unfit to be German soldiers, in whose ranks were Cossacks from among the few remaining refugee groups, took on themselves great parts of the blows of breakthroughs by Reds, who by far exceeded them in all things but courage. Red fear of counterblows slowed in significant measure any faster spread of Soviet successes and provided the time to save units that were retreating.

On December 23, 1942, the German breakout from Stalingrad, which started from the south December 12th with Army Group Hoth, was stopped by orders from higher up. The order was given because on that day, the Reds made another breakthrough 300 kilometers to the northwest of Stalingrad. This time it was directed at Rostov and threatened the main strength of the Army Group "Don" of Manstein and Army Group "A" of General Kleist, who had been put in command of the latter on October 22nd.

The main blow by the Reds was made on both sides of Verkhniy Mamon, and also Kazanskaya, western Vershenskaya, Skosirskaya and other stanitsas, and spread fear equal to that in Stalingrad among the inhabitants and in Cossack parts of settlements.

Elements of the destroyed Rumanian and Italian armies retreated from the Reds in disorder, increasing the panic. Only 170 kilometers separated Red-occupied Tatsinskaya from Rostov.

It was a repeat of the night of December 15, when Red mechanized units broke through to the west over the front of the 57th Tank Corps of Army Group Hoth, south of the Aksai River, and reached the bridge at Shestakaya with their tanks. Here the Germans held, but their situation became critical, because the day before, the Reds, in sequence, destroyed the 6th, then the 7th Corps of the 4th Rumanian Army. In effect, they no longer existed.

Thus, the battles, simmering from the first day of encirclement of Stalingrad, flared up on the north and west of the Don Oblast [political region, equivalent to state or province—*trans.*] and the Kalmyk Steppe, then continued toward the Caucasus, the Terek, and the Kuban Oblast.

The answering attack by depleted German units against the Reds, who were armored in steel and armed to the teeth through the help of the Western confederates of Communism, weakened. Engagements took place with changed success, and Cossack lands more and more disappeared into the depths.

Duped anew by Communism, Red Army soldiers, instead of turning against it, as by the example of General Vlasov, forced themselves on our land, tore our people to pieces, and sowed the horrors of Communism within our blood kin.

Terrible were the fortunes of those who failed to flee from Red-occupied regions. Not uncommonly before occupation, there arose nests of those not born on Cossack lands. Some of them, wanting to serve Communism and show their devotion to it, became brutal, finishing off wounded soldiers, lynching and hanging Cossacks. When there was no one left to kill, they dug up the graves of those who fell in the fight against Communism, dragged them out to display, then hung the corpses and set them on fire, mocking the dead in every possible way. Attacking groups of our refugees who remained behind, they robbed them naked and threw them out to perish from the 20-30 degree Christmas time cold. The blizzards that started then ended this "business" of the activists and covered the unfortunates by snowdrifts. They were not idle threats of execution and the gallows in the million leaflets with which they flooded front-line regions through their propaganda brigades and aviation. Their air attacks against the Cossack populace were without mercy. We, as participants in rear-guard battles, stand as witnesses to the satanic cruelty of Communism, as do all those who succeeded in saving themselves from being among those remaining behind. For this reason, the threat of death, Don, Kuban, and Terek Cossacks, along with Caucasian Highlanders and others, had to abandon their native lands and defend themselves to a man and protect their kin from Soviet killers and saboteurs. They went away to the west in order to save themselves from the Communist tyranny that the Red Army brought to them.

The German Command, knowing of Communist reprisals against peaceful inhabitants, from the first days of Soviet breakthroughs, simultaneously ordered elements of its forces and its military commanders to notify the local authorities of their withdrawal from endangered points and to render all necessary assistance to those fleeing. Mechanized German forces who had been within regions now occupied by the Reds, in breaking out of Red encirclement, picked up, when they could, the refugees that were falling behind. They even shared their own scant rations with them.

Commander of Army Group "A", General Kleist, displayed particular concern for refugees. He was already an honorary Cossack of the Kuban Host. Despite the difficult situation on his part of the front, he found time to worry about the material conditions of refugees on the road. Following his orders, local militia units were required to maintain contact with the German Command. In addition, all those serving in various ways in any city establishment or stanitsa authority, from those in charge to those on guard duty, were given two months pay in advance on the day of evacuation.

Several days after the fall of Stalingrad, which took place February 2, 1943, Novocherkassk also faced a direct threat from the Reds. Following a warning he received, Field Ataman Pavlov gathered together transports from those wishing to withdraw and, covering them with the strength of a regiment gathered for the purpose, went off in the direction of Krivogo Rog. At this time, his assistant, Colonel Dukhopelnikov, who, even before the ataman received the warning mentioned, had been sent by him to collect Cossacks in the Azov region, found himself surrounded by Soviets. Breaking out with several Cossacks, he reached Taganrog and, in view of the evacuation by the Field Ataman, he was designated by General Kleist to be in charge of gathering and directing Cossacks near Kherson. All the registration points that were organized earlier in Rostov, Taganrog, Mariupol, Berdyansk, and others up to Kherson were subordinated to him. Their staffs were increased and their powers enlarged correspondingly. Their tasks consisted not only of registering passing Cossack groups and individual commands, they also had to classify them according to capability for combat service, assemble in separate organized entities, provide them with ration cards and *marchbefels*, and then direct them to destinations farther west of Kherson.

At the same time, German military units were ordered to free all Cossack sub-units and individuals found in their organization, including those who were foreign nationals and had served in union with the German Army.

Following this order, we separated with our established commander and moved toward Kherson, not suspecting that von Pannwitz would soon lead all of our combat units.

Beneath Mariupol, my unit caught up with the almost two-hundred-man group of Sotnik Talalaev. He was traveling at its head in the same direction from Rostov, along with Colonel Dukhopelnikov, who was in charge of gathering Cossacks. With him was a part of his staff and his darling spouse, Nadezhda Yevgenievna.

Knowing Sotnik Talalaev as one of the better officers among the Cossacks being gathered, Colonel Dukhopelnikov sent him to collect a new unit. He put the entire Cossack group that remained under my command.

At the very beginning of March, I took this group to a place designated for us—in Muzikova (near Kherson), where we organized ourselves into units at a nearby church square.

While still en route from Kherson, we were pleasantly overwhelmed by the martial appearance, fully outfitted, of the Don Kalmyk regiment of Military Starshin Nazarov. At the time, they were engaged in highway work and were waiting to be armed.

Almost at the same time as us, the large group of Terek Cossacks of Colonel Kulakov arrived, and, after it, the similar group of Kuban Cossacks of Military Starshin Salamakha, who I knew personally from the fall of 1941, when he was a sotnik in rank. After him came the group of Don Cossacks of Yesaul Berezlev, the group of Kuban Cossacks of Military Starshin Malovik, and the Don group of Sotnik Moskvitchev. All Don Cossacks and a major portion of the Kuban Cossacks settled at Muzikovka. The Terek Cossacks and the rest of the Kuban Cossacks occupied a neighboring selo.

The head of the gathered Cossacks, Colonel Dukhopelnikov, consolidated all Don Cossacks under Yesaul Popov (former head of the Novocherkassk police).

Biliy, arriving with the previous group of Kuban Cossacks, stopped at Kherson and carried on there in such a manner that he quickly became the angry talk of the town. He surfaced among the Kuban Cossacks at the beginning of the withdrawal and announced to them that General Kleist had designated him as the military ataman. In fact, this was a lie, because General Kleist did not make such designations, never meddling in internal Cossack affairs. It was a confused time. Taking advantage of it, Biliy fooled Cossacks into believing that he had been designated military ataman and the Germans into believing that the Cossacks had elected him.

The head of the preliminary organization of Cossack regiments turned out to be the German, Captain Lehman, who had been sent for that purpose by General Kleist.

At first, our Cossack groups were called: 1st Terek, 1st and 2nd Kuban, 1st Kalmyk, and 1st Don regiment. Soon after, the Kalmyk regiment left for parts unknown. After this, Captain Lehman, in charge of the Cossack groups formed during the time of our stay near Kherson, renamed them in the following manner:

1st Don Regiment—commander, Yesaul Popov,

2nd Terek Regiment—commander, Colonel Kulakov,

3rd Kuban Regiment—commander, Military Starshin Salamakha,

4th Kuban Regiment—commander, Military Starshin Malovik.

Already at that time, the 1st Don Regiment totaled 1,100 Cossacks and 14 officers. A large number of them were unfit for combat duty and in a so-called reserve based on their age, physical condition, etc. For this reason, Yesaul Popov could not designate the required number of company commanders. All the Don Cossacks were first redistributed in our three infantry sotnyas, but were later separated out as a mounted platoon.

By this: I was left in command of the 1st Sotnya, 2nd Sotnya —Yesaul Berezlev, 3rd Sotnya—Sotnik Moskvitchev, Mounted Platoon—Sotnik Tchikin.

The Terek and Kuban regiments consisted of 700-800 Cossacks each. Their situation with military command staff was no better than ours.

By Holy Easter, no fewer than 6000 Cossacks had been collected. All this time, we lived in hope of a return to the front. We were losing our patience. We forgot about the critical shortage in our officer cadre, about the absence of appropriate weapons, etc. All our thoughts were on our Cossack land, which was being ripped apart by Soviet dogs … Dark, evil news came to us from there … It flew among us, striking deep into our hearts … A burning, deadly hate of Communism simmered…

In the end, on Passionate Thursday, Colonel Dukhopelnikov and Captain Lehman told us that all our regiments had been placed under Colonel Pannwitz and that we had to go the next day for Kherson to be boarded on trains and sent to Mlawa to form the 1st Cossack Cavalry Division.

Our joy was great. Truly, there was not a Cossack among us who, even if only by reputation, did not know of Pannwitz, of his valor, and his love for Cossacks.

On Friday, our regiment arrived at the city of Kherson and bivouacked in a freight yard.

On Sunday, we formed up "on parade" and accepted General Pannwitz. The Cossacks could barely hold in the loud "Hoorah" they shouted on his greeting, which he gave in strict Russian.

After a meal, we began to load onto freight trains. A first-class coach was attached for officers.

On the second day of Holy Easter, April 26, our train set off.

On our arrival at Mlawa, the regiments detrained and marched to a military camp located approximately nine kilometers to the west. There, each regiment took quarters prepared for them in a comfortable barrack.

In the days that followed, on orders from General Pannwitz, several special committees were formed and immediately set to work. Among them was a committee of older Cossacks who knew their own forces, stanitsas, and departments very well. This committee classified Cossacks by their membership in a Host, place of birth, or origin, and verified that they were truly Cossacks, their previous service, etc. Its work went very well, thanks to the presence of thousands of Cossacks who knew one another.

At the conclusion of the committee's work, all our regiments were brought to a large field and arranged in front of the leaders in columns in their full original compositions.

When Pannwitz approached, the command was given, "attention."

Greeting us, he spoke of his good fortune in being with us, of the necessity of reorganization and of preparation for coming battles against communists, of the situation of our senior officer staff, and of his intention to name new commanders here from our own ranks. With this aim, he asked all combat officers to step out of formation to the left flank and stand there in one row.

After his command, "at ease," while we were walking to the place indicated, specially designated members of the reorganization committee s approached the regiments. One group stopped at each regiment, approximately at a distance of forty paces. Each such group had lists of the complete composition of each future regiment, by division, sotnya, and platoon, with which they began calling out individual Cossacks, giving the number of their regiment, division, sotnya, and platoon. Each Cossack who was called out moved behind the reorganizing group and took his proper place in the platoon being made up for his sotnya.

At that time, General Pannwitz came to us with an escort of several German officers and other ranks. He questioned each of us about our military training and our service, the names of our combat units, places of action, etc. Then, depending on the answers, he designated us to battle duty with the indicated regiment. With those designations, General Pannwitz let himself be guided only by the current military insignia of an officer and his battle experience. His decision was completely independent of whether he had until this time fought on the side of the Germans, or the opposite, that he had fought against them in the ranks of the Red Army.

When the reorganization ended, we took our places in the new regiments. Those officers who were left off for various reasons were placed in reserve, with the right to serve in non-combat duties in our division.

Toward evening, the reorganization was completed. All our regiments were renumbered as follows:

1st Don Cavalry Regiment,
2nd Siberian Bicycle Regiment,
3rd Kuban Cavalry Regiment,
4th Kuban Cavalry Regiment.
5th Don Cavalry Regiment,
6th Terek Cavalry Regiment.

I remained in command of my sotnya in the 1st Don Regiment when it became the 7th in the 2nd Division.

After the regiments had been reorganized in this manner, they were taken to the new quarters designated for them. There, each sotnya settled into the barrack to which they were assigned, one-by-one by platoon. Commanders and the staff of the sotnyas were led to separate barracks.

The next day, all of us received new German uniforms, which we put on after good, hot baths. The old Soviet-issue weapons we had up to then were turned in. After that, we began to be outfitted for service.

After a few days, General Pannwitz assembled our entire officer combat staff and said a few words to us. He told us that, due to the lack of suitable senior staff in all our regiments, with the exception of Kononov's, they would have to name the better German cavalry officers to the necessary regimental and divisional positions of command. They were to remain in place until the time that our Cossack officers were ready. He assured us that, toward the end of the preparation of our divisions, he would choose the most capable officers from among us and send them for accelerated courses in the city of Bromberg. Then, having received the required combat knowledge there, he would use them to replace as many commanders in the divisions as necessary.

All this was said in a sincere, fatherly tone and was fully understood by all of us. We knew that during the years of Soviet dominion, Cossackdom suffered much more persecution than other Russian peoples did. Indeed, the ranks of our staff officer had been destroyed almost to a man and those who survived were found either in prison or in hiding, with the result that they fell completely out of touch with any knowledge of modern warfare and were practically incapable of carrying out battle duties. Our Cossack youth had been disenfranchised under Soviet power. Communism did not let them into any sort of military school. Those who were impressed into Red Army units were there under close watch. Therefore, as a result of Soviet persecution, we did not have a properly prepared officer corps.

After Pannwitz had his say, we dispersed with our souls in peace. We knew and believed him. He confirmed our trust in him in future events.

Every Cossack regiment of Pannwitz's 1st Cossack Division consisted of two sub-divisions of four squadrons, along with a separate heavy squadron. Commanding these sub-divisions were German officers, but Cossacks led the squadrons, with the exception of the latter. Each squadron consisted of three battle platoons, an auxiliary platoon, and a mortar unit. Cossack officers commanded the battle platoons, but the auxiliary platoon and the mortar squad were led by higher-ranking noncommissioned officers [Cossack sergeants —trans.] Platoon assistants were likewise noncoms.

Each battle platoon consisted of three squads. Each squad was commanded by noncoms. The squads consisted of three teams of four-to-five Cossacks and one medic. Of them, the first was a machine-gun squad. They were armed with the hand-held Model M. G. 42s, famous by the name of "Stalingrad," thanks to its speed of fire and other distinct advantages. At the same time, the first member of the squad was armed with a pistol; the second, third, and forth, with Model 98/K carbines. The second was a sniper team; third—grenade-rifle.

The mortar section was made up of nine Cossacks. It had one light 5-cm cavalry mortar. Its commander was armed with an automatic weapon.

The fourth—the auxiliary platoon of the sotnya, consisted of a horse-drawn kitchen and the required number of vans for ambulance use, provisions, ammunition, fodder, blacksmith forges, etc. In this team there were also twelve to fourteen Germans, among them, a senior smithy, weapon master, cook, clerk, forage specialist, quartermaster, etc.

The weapons of squad commanders and officers were pistols.

Each regiment's heavy squadron consisted of five teams:

1st had three heavy machine guns,

2nd—three 8-cm packed mortars,

3rd—three 37-mm horse-drawn anti-tank cannons,

4th provided covering fire.

5th was a helper.

Division artillery consisted of three batteries of seven 6 mm horse-drawn cannon [certainly a mistake and should be 60 mm or 6 cm—trans.], which were replaced by ones that were more convenient and effective for use against Soviet tanks, except the T-34 tank. These were 105 mm and similarly horse-drawn.

In a typical formation used by general Pannwitz, there was also one escort sotnya.

Along with that, the division had one team of reconnaissance tanks and one reconnaissance aircraft, one engineering, and one transport division.

On June 18, all ranks of the division were given a duty book in Russian and German languages, called "Kennbuch."

Right after reorganization, all of our regiments began to drill, followed by tactical lessons.

Soon we received horses.

After some time, a group from within our command staff was sent for a week on an excursion to Germany, the populace of which treated us with exceptional warmth and goodwill.

The division continued to fill out, following which a reserve regiment was detached. Soon there were more than 5000 Cossacks in this regiment, the number increasing almost daily.

About the second half of July, due to lack of space for tactical lessons, our 1st Don Regiment and one of the Kuban regiments were transferred from the camp at Mlawa to a military camp near the city of Prausnitz, some thirty-five to forty kilometers from Mlawa.

At this time, the 2nd Siberian Regiment turned in their bicycles and received horses.

General Pannwitz did not forget his promise. In August, by his personal choice, our group of officers was sent to the Cavalry War College in the city of Bromberg, in two squadrons of commanders from each regiment, to prepare there to take on the duties of commander of a division. I was designated as the leader of this group. Unfortunately, our preparation had to be compressed because of the catastrophic situation at the front. For this reason, on General Zeitzler's orders we began the transfer of our Division to Croatia to fight against Tito. We caught up with our regiment while it was already en route there.

We landed in Pančevo and marched across Belgrade to the front. Our reserve regiment was sent to Langres (France).

In the fall of 1944, our division was converted into the 15th Cossack Cavalry Corps, consisting of:

1st Don Division: Regiments:
    1st Don,
    2nd Siberian,
    4th Kuban.
2nd Don Division: Regiments:
    3rd Kuban,
    5th Don,
    6th Terek.

Colonel Wagner was named to command the 1st Division, while 2nd—Colonel von Schultz.

During the period of conversion of our division to a corps, there was a brigade created to be commanded by Colonel Kononov. It consisted of the 7th and 8th Plastoon [Cossack infantry—trans.] Regiments.

In February, this brigade was converted into the 3rd Division and Colonel Rendell [English (or German) spelling could not be verified—trans.] was named as its commander.

A single book is insufficient to fully describe the performance in battle of the 15th Cossack Cavalry Corps. The heroism of the Cossacks, their officers, and their valorous leader in the unequal battle against Communism is written in gold letters in the history of Cossackdom.

But Communism was saved by its accomplices from the West.

It was not our lot to wait until our own clear Cossack day … Our dawn became clouded in bloody fog and anew our native lands were darkened by Soviet death … By the stupidity of the West, it is widening and crawling in every direction. Ever more brazenly, Communism threatens not only there, but its own recent friends and saviors … They fawn cowardly, are hurt, and retreat before it. They betrayed to its horrible sufferings mothers children, widows, and the elderly. I speak not only of those tens of thousands of people living then, who were betrayed at Lienz, Plattling, in Italy, and other places. I speak of the hundreds of thousands of our unfortunate refugees who never managed to reach such places, but were spread along roads west: in Ukraine, in Bessarabia, in Rumania, in the Baltic states, and Poland. They were cut off there by quick, deeply penetrating blows from Soviet tank units and parachute descents on the communications of retreating German, Rumanian, Hungarian, and Italian armies. They were prevented from being saved by the treason of the leadership of Rumania in chorus with Communism. There, on orders by the latter, on the night of August 22, 1944, the Rumanian Army went over to the side of the Bolsheviks, closed its borders, and cut them all off.

Имена их Ты Господи, веси.

N. Nazarenko

•

Germans on the Kuban—Evacuation—1ˢᵗ Cossack Division

Alarming news of the rapid approach of German forces on the Kuban and the evacuation of all livestock deep into the rear brought on great consternation in local party members. In the end, an order followed on August 4ᵗʰ to evacuate our region. The last rear guard units of the Red Army pass by.

On August 5ᵗʰ, in order to avoid the compulsory evacuation, I hid myself that morning in a field brigade, where the members of the kolhoz were committing theft of the barleycorn left to air dry before being delivered to the elevator. Wheat in our fertile Kuban, considered so vital to the inhabitants of Russia, from 1938 to 1942, inclusively, was not grown in most areas: during every year of that period wheat was unrelentingly devoured by the voracious turtle bug. Turtle bug infestation allowed wild growth, every kind of weed possible, to dominate the remaining, untilled fields.

On August 6ᵗʰ, the first units of Germans arrived, to be met by the Cossacks with great enthusiasm.

On the day before their arrival in the stanitsa, part of the populace robbed the property left in place by Soviet authorities.

All day, explosions could be heard in the area of the stanitsa's mill, workshops, etc. In the elevator, the Bolsheviks made a huge mass of grain worthless by pouring kerosene and oil on it. Where petroleum products were stored, benzene, oil, and kerosene were poured on the ground. All this took place on orders from the Kremlin.

Thoughtless destruction of edible and feed grains, stores of provisions for times of terrible need by residents for bread, and the suspension of spring and summer planting campaigns, all became strong factors in intensifying the hatred of Cossacks for their communist oppressors.

An ominous silence fell over the stanitsa on the evening of that day. I too did not await the arrivals of the Germans free of anxiety—and then I suddenly thought, could the news in the lying Soviet newspapers on the monstrous inhumanity of Germans turn out to be true? What a bitter fate awaits me, as one of the few men left in the stanitsa. I was reminded of the attitude of the Germans, based on information in the newspapers, toward those of the populace remaining in villages and stanitsas. Supposedly, they chased all the inhabitants out on a square, after which the more respected elders were subjected to their peculiar method of execution: each old man was tied to two tanks, which were then set off in opposite directions, and the elderly one was ripped apart into two pieces.

In the final issues of the Krasnodar newspapers, it was asserted that, in the stanitsa of Batayskaya (by Rostov-on-Don), on occupation by the Germans, a registration of every female was carried out, and the more attractive of them were sent to German brothels.

Contrary to our expectations, the Germans made an excellent first impression: the smart appearance of their soldiers, the quality of their equipment, exceptional discipline, respect toward foreign customs, and the respectful attitude by their officers toward residents. All this had a winning affect on members of the stanitsa—more accustomed to seeing Soviet units completely the opposite. What impressed us most of all was the modest way officers treated soldiers and the equality of their rations. At that time, there was an impassable gulf between the officer staff and the rank-and-file of Red Army soldiers.

The democratic structure of the army, the abundance of motor parts, the firm belief of the Germans in absolute victory over Bolshevism, awed the populace, weary as it was of the tyranny and violence of Soviet power.

Here, I must tell of one lady, escaping the area of her stanitsa to one in which her mother lived on the day of the arrival of the Germans. The distance between the two stanitsas was fifteen kilometers.

"I was going," she says, "along a graded road and carrying two suitcases. The weather was marvelous. Quiet. Not a soul anywhere. Then suddenly, to my horror, through a cloud of fog raised by passing German units, mainly motorized, I saw Germans in their uniforms, which were easily distinguishable from Red Army uniforms. My whole body began to tremble from fright. My legs became shaky. In my mind, I said farewell to life: without question, what awaited me was execution as a spy. But to my deep amazement, not only was I not arrested, but they paid no attention to me whatsoever. I have yet to get over it."

The lady's amazement did not appear strange to us: we were used to an entirely different regime.

About the nightmarish conditions of life in German prisoner-of-war camps, mass exterminations of Jews, pillage and destruction of Russian cities and villages, we learned only later. In our stanitsa, Ukrainians and Don and Kuban Cossacks who were taken prisoner were released after a brief interrogation to go in peace in all four directions.

The two German *unter*-officers quartered in my apartment were always polite. When they learned that our cow had not yet started giving milk and that we bought milk at the market, they turned down, with characteristic formality, the glasses of milk we offered them.

Moreover, the six-month stay by the occupiers in our stanitsa was not darkened by even a single instance of theft or violence. On the contrary—when a Rumanian unit passed through our stanitsa, they pilfered the kolhoz beehives in the night. The Germans quickly organized a pursuit of the thieves. They were caught, the honey was returned to the kolhoz, and the guilty suitably punished.

On August 7, I went to Krasnodar to see the Commandant of the city with the intention of offering information I had learned about Kuban volunteer units.

On seeing me, the Commandant haughtily repudiated what I had heard. With arrogance, he told me—"The German Army is so strong and capable that it will take care of the Bolsheviks without Cossack help." Then, noting that there was a need by the Germans for educated talent on the economic front, he quickly wrote out an order naming me the director of the kolhoz in which I worked. On having the order typed, the Commandant continued: "Return to your area. Go to the Economic Commandant of your selo. Inform him of this present order and obtain from him the necessary instructions for your future work."

Within an hour, I was before the economic commandant of my selo, who, handing me the required mandate in two languages, ordered me to come to an all-kolhoz gathering the next day to elect an economic manager and an agricultural technician. The haughtiness of the Yekaterinodar Commandant in refusing Cossack help in combat organizations against Bolsheviks, was the first dark factor in a series of bitter disappointments by the unseemly actions of National Socialism that followed.

And so, in some respects, I became the owner of the kolhoz and not an assistant, since the true right of ownership—general meetings—was barely if ever permitted by the Soviets.

I was worried by the required election of two coworkers. Only the elderly and invalids had been left in the kolhoz … But the next morning, I was struck by the arrival on the kolhoz doorstep of a large number of men who had already been mobilized in the Army of the Field.

Later, German conduct in great measure changed the previous favorable view of them by the members of the stanitsa.

The fundamental reason for disillusionment with them was the refusal of the Germans to disband the kolhoz, which naturally was the inner desire not just of Cossackdom, but the entire population of Russia.

The second reason for dissatisfaction was the conciliatory approach the Germans had toward communists, whom they treated better than their enemies: many obvious communists were named to higher administrative-economic posts, such as directing the milk and cheese production facility, heading the regional electric station, etc.

Protests by residents were ignored. The Commandant typically answered: —"We have no interest in their pasts. Back then, these communists fulfilled their duties to the Soviet government. Now there is a different regime. We are watching them carefully. At the slightest attempt at sabotage or damage, they will be quickly terminated."

Frequent requisitions of vital foodstuffs, butter, eggs, domestic fowl, pigs, sheep, etc., from the populace, undermined its living standards and further increased dissatisfaction.

Side-by-side with this, concern by the populace for their own needs was brought on by extremely strict measures: an absence of transports for manufactured goods and seeds for planting practically never being released jeopardizing the future existence of the inhabitants.

The absence of a Russian press left the populace in complete ignorance of what was happening at the front.

Middle and higher educational institutions, under the pretense of lack of space, did not function.

Insignificant numbers of arrests of persons suspected of being sympathetic with the face of Communism, arrests of traitorous people, carried out on the initiative of Cossack police were, systematically, on one ground or another, countered by the directives of the German Command.

By the way, during the time that the Germans were with us, Cossacks repeatedly had reason to have their judgment reinforced that Soviet information was all lies and provocation. Let me relate a characteristic episode. Soon after the occupation of our stanitsa, my friend and I turned to an *unter*-officer living with us, a signal man and radio operator, with a request to allow us to listen to a radio broadcast from Moscow. In transmitting a war communiqué, the radio, in exceptional detail, dwelled on German atrocities in recently occupied places, among which was our own stanitsa:

"In this stanitsa, the occupiers have committed mass executions of inhabitants by hanging them from telegraph poles, hung with garlands of corpses. Children from the ages of two to twelve were driven by the Germans into cellars and to a head suffocated by gas."

On the fourth month of the German presence with us, when it became clear that they were losing in the Caucasus, belated permission was given for the formation of Cossack battle units in Krasnodar and in the ranks of stanitsas, ours among them.

A Cossack from Staroderzhelievskaya Stanitsa, Colonel M., who was commissioned to form a separate battalion of *plastoons* in our (regional) stanitsa, suggested that I take the post of Chief of Staff of the latter, to which I quickly agreed. We took the matter up with great enthusiasm. Quickly forming three sotnyas and thoroughly remodeling the middle school into a barrack, we organized a unit of needed masters (shoemakers, tailors, stewards, and blacksmiths.)

Since our battalion was not yet integrated into the Wehrmacht, we, with the approval of the selo's Military Economic Commandant, and similarly the Regional Ataman, set about taxing kolhoz food stores for rations needed to last for several months.

The formation of the battalion, with unbelievable enthusiasm from the inhabitants, went so well that we were obliged to turn away, based on the their advanced age or major physical infirmity, many Cossacks who wished to join.

But the existence of the battalion soon came to an end when retreating German units took over our barracks.

On our own retreat, the Germans did not force the populace to evacuate, but almost every resident of a stanitsa tore up his roots and left to meet an unknown fate.

In March of 1943, in the settlement of Muzikovka, Kherson Gubernia, two Kuban and one Don regiment were quickly formed. The command staff consisted exclusively of Cossack officers. The role given to the German major who was with the regiments was reduced entirely to observation and coordination.

Battle and tactical lessons were regularly given, by the book, under strict discipline.

Interrelations with local inhabitants were excellent. One instance of rape of a girl by a Cossack was an unpleasant exception and entailed bringing the guilty to trial. The function of a court, following ancient Cossack tradition, was carried out by the full composition of the regiment. The violator was unanimously sentenced to death and quickly executed in the presence of the court, that is, the entire regiment.

In April, these three regiments were transferred to Mlawa (in Poland), in order to bring the 1st Cossack Division to full strength under the German, General Helmuth von Pannwitz.

Seriously wounded on the journey, I got into the division after my recovery and received my orders, first as an observer, then as the first chairman of the Cossack divisional military court. Up to that time, Cossacks were tried in German courts, which were often severe in their procedures. They often gave out sentences that did not correspond with the offense and arrived at judgments that either totally misunderstood Cossack life and traditions or were prejudiced against Cossacks, as if they did not have full rights.

It was in Mlawa, where many Cossacks who were former Red Army prisoners-of-war joined our units, that we first heard of Nazi cruelty to prisoners. But there was nothing we could do: from two ash piles, we needed to choose the better, the opportunity to fight the hated Communists, as if pre-ordained.

The belief of Cossacks in their mission of liberation caused stanitsa members to continue to work alongside Germans.

The policy pursued by the Germans in their panicky terror over the restoration of a powerful, united Russia had consequences for us: instead of the Western Front, we found ourselves in Croatia, where the bands of the communist, Tito, were operating at the time. Knowledge that the battle against Titoists appears as a main link in the chain of fights with International Communism, Moscow at its head, to some extent smoothed over Cossack unhappiness with being sent there.

Actions in battle by the 1ˢᵗ Cossack Division (later the 15ᵗʰ Cossack Cavalry Corps) come under the heading of substantial victories. This splendid fight gave clear expression of the exceptional character of Cossackhood: selfless bravery, native savvy, and knightly majesty.

Soviet propaganda, and after it, to our regret, some Russian and foreign presses, accused Cossacks of various sorts of evils, trying to hang on them banditry, robbery, mass rapes, participation in the murder of Jews, and others.

On my honor before world public opinion, I can, fully responsibly, confirm that the Cossack Corps absolutely did not take part in any persecution of Jews or their extermination. As for rapes, a military court mercilessly punished any occurrence of the sort. Widespread advertisements in Cossack presses and decrees given to all units and subdivisions of the corps constantly cautioned Cossacks to immediately leave areas where rapes or illegal requisitions were taking place.

Not wishing to be without proof, I will allow myself to disclose several instances from my own court practice.

Back during the formation of the 1st Cossack Division in Mlawa, the division's security service exposed a group of conspirators having the goal of blowing apart the Division from within, causing demoralization and dissolution.

The organizers of the conspiracy turned out to be a group of NKVD agents who infiltrated the division in the guise of rank and file Cossacks. The most serious conspiracy took place in the 6th Terek Regiment.

On September 20th, an informant told the division's security service and the division's court that, in the regiment named, a communist nest had been organized. It planned to steal arms that had yet to be distributed to the Cossacks on September 21st from division stores, kill the officer staff, and take the Division to join Polish Communist partisan bands operating in the region of Mlawa, led by a Soviet NKVD officer.

The conspirators, seven in number, were soon arrested and, after a brief period of denial, confessed under the weight of the irrefutable evidence given by witnesses and admitted they were under orders from Moscow to infiltrate the Division, solely to commit acts of sabotage and espionage. All seven conspirators turned out to be officers, starting from colonel and ending in a junior lieutenant. They pretended to be uneducated in the regiment and asked that other, educated Cossacks, sign for them when they received their pay and supplies.

The second instance of the NKVD acting in the guise of Cossacks took place in Croatia. In one sector of the front, two armed "Cossacks" came to a woman, a mother of three small children and wife of a railroad man. She treated them to a fine, substantial breakfast. But, instead of thanking her, the visitors pressed vile suggestions on her. The woman fell to her knees before them and begged them to spare her for the sake of her children. But the rapists were implacable. Struggling with them, however, the woman broke free and took off running. But one of the bandits, with these words:

"None of your tricks! You won't get away from us,"—fired his rifle and killed her. Then both fought over her flesh.

Investigation revealed that both had been sent by the Bolsheviks as provocateurs. The one who killed the woman was a native of Vologodsky Gubernia, an actual member of the Communist Party, by the name of Parfenov.

Concerning the honor of Cossacks, it must be said that of all the criminals during that time, there was not a single Cossack or a non-native resident of Cossack lands among them.

Units of the 15th Cossack Corps continually defeated Titoist partisans. It was toward the end of the war that they met units of the Soviet Red Army. After the first clash, the Soviet Command, fearing demoralization of its own units by the Cossacks, replaced them with Bulgarians.

A. Sukalo

•

Arrival of Germans on the Kuban

The German Army came to the Kuban in 1942. Our stanitsa found itself without any controlling authority over us for two weeks: neither Reds nor Germans.

Our *stanitsa* at the mouth of the Lada had up to 3,000 Red Army soldiers left in it. They put all their rifles in a pile on the square.

A single German arrived, gathered the teachers who could write in German, and began to give passes home to all Red Army soldiers. If there were two or three or more from the same selo, he gave a single pass for them all.

Our stanitsa was part of the Ust-Labinsk Region, from which it received instructions. German control was established in the *stanitsa* through a chief and police who were chosen by them.

They harvested seeds, corn, and sugar beets. All of it was given to members of the kolhoz, but the wheat that was owed the Soviets, they left. They took rest with them.

Plowing began. The Germans brought wheat by truck and made us plant it. Where it came from, I do not know.

Two or three weeks passed. Cossacks began to gather from all directions, and complaints arose that the village elder was incompetent. The non-native population quieted down—as if they no longer existed.

When the Cossacks familiarized themselves with the situation, a group was formed, which I joined, to go to the headquarters of the German Commandant. We explained who we were and why we came. We told him everything. He gave us documents.

We returned to the stanitsa and showed those documents to the village elder in order that he turn control over to us.

We removed him, as ordered by the Commandant, and took control ourselves in the stanitsa. We set about to elect an ataman.

All 117 of the Cossack men who were at least seventeen years of age assembled.

We had to take control away from the hands of the communists ourselves, because the Germans, on their arrival, announced that everyone should stay in the position in which they were serving. All it required was to elect a chairman of the soviet, since the chair had run off.

Partisans appeared in September 1942. The Cossacks asked them to leave, since the Germans had made it clear that a hundred residents of the stanitsa would be shot for every German killed. Fearing this threat from the presence of partisans, the Cossacks required them to leave the stanitsa. The partisans obeyed the request.

Life in the stanitsa passed peacefully and quietly. There were no German abuses. On leaving, they offered to evacuate the entire male population above the age of fourteen along with them, but they did not take anyone away by force.

On January 31, 1943, I abandoned my stanitsa. My path was to be as follows: Yekaterinodar, Slavyanskaya Stanitsa, Temryuk, and Fontalovskaya Stanitsa. Beyond Kerch: the city of Melitopol,

Dzhanskoy. I stayed in the Crimea until the beginning of March 1944. Then I went to Odessa on a German steamship, from which I traveled by train across Rumania, into Poland, to the city of Radom. There I met Colonels Y. V. Kravchenko and Mikhailov. There, two sotnyas had been formed: Kuban and Don. An ataman had been chosen: K Yesaul Bogaevsky. From Radom, we moved to the city of Nemirov, near Rava Russkaya, and from Nemirov—to the area of Novogrudok, in the village of Zapolye. Here, there were new elections, myself, anew, the *izban* [hut (?)—*trans.*] ataman. From Zapolye we came to Dvoretz (Dvorzhetz), from there to Zdunska Wola, where the entire group of Field Ataman Domanov was gathered. This is where separation into hosts was made: Don, Kuban, and Terek with the Astrakhans. Kuban Cossacks were further divided into sections. I was chosen ataman of the Maykop Section.

In Zdunska Wola, we were loaded onto a train and brought to Italy. The Maykop Section was stationed in Osoppo. From there, we went to Covazzo [This location could not be verified; possibly, the city was Cavasso Nuovo—*trans.*]; from Covazzo—to Lienz.

Then, after the betrayal of the Cossacks of the Stan to the Bolsheviks, I was caught by the English and put in a camp surrounded by barbed wire in the stanitsa of Dölsach. I spent four months under the open sky.

I. V.

•

From the Kuban to Italy

The Germans came to Maykop at dusk on August 9, 1942, and stayed there to January 31, 1943.

The city and its environs were not evacuated, apparently because the Reds, on retreating, tore up the railroad tracks. The Germans had not yet repaired them.

As the interpreter for most of the Maykop factories, I left the city earlier, on the morning of January 23, in a large German vehicle loaded with rifles. It took three days to get to Yekaterinodar, because the entire way was blocked by four rows of retreating vehicles.

In Yekaterinodar, I stayed overnight at the Kubanoil factory. Its name had been Sedova under the Bolsheviks. I was then put on a bus with non-commissioned officers from our units. On the 28th or 29th, we stopped overnight at Slavyanskaya Stanitsa. At this time Host Starshin [Cossack rank equivalent to lieutenant colonel—*trans.*] Borzik died from wounds received in a Red bombardment of the stanitsa. We arrived at Kurchanskaya Stanitsa, where I stayed all of February and half of March. On March 20, I moved with my group to Akhanizovskaya Stanitsa, in which I stayed until September 1943, that is, almost until the Germans abandoned their fortifications in the Kuban. I heard nothing about the organized departure of Cossacks from the Kuban. At that time, I was working very hard to free Cossacks from prisoner-of-war camps. These Cossacks trusted me and I often happened to hear:

"Ech! If only they gave us weapons, we could take care of the Bolsheviks ourselves!"

In Melitopol, there was already a Cossack staff formed of Kuban, Terek, and Don Cossacks. Colonel Georgi Pavlovich Tarasenko was its Chief of Staff.

From Melitopol, I went to Proskurov. For a while, I settled in Grechana (six kilometers from Proskurov). I became an interpreter for railroad matters.

At this time, there were already various organizations of Cossack units being formed: in Mlawa, Warsaw, on Volyn, and elsewhere.

The fleeing masses—women, children, the elderly, retreated spontaneously, on their own means. Only in December of 1943 did Colonel Pavlov receive permission and the means to organize all the masses of Cossacks. The place where the Cossachi Stan was born— the village of Grechana—a Cossack military town. The Commandant of this town—Don Cossack Yesaul T., a former military engineer. His assistant was Kuban Cossack Yesaul K. (He died of typhus at Lesnoy Station near Baranovich.)

The Chief of Staff at Proskurov was Colonel O. The Chief of the Propaganda Section was Yesaul—or Sotnik—D.

Domanov at this time was in the Kamenets-Podolsk area, Pavlov—in Proskurov.

We had to leave Proskurov-Grechana in the following order: family echelon; Cossacks, horses, wagons—that was the order of march. But God judged differently.

Bolsheviks approached us much sooner than we expected.

January 6th, 1944, on our Christmas Eve, we were given *marchbefels*—one for every thirty people and their goods and told that on the 7th, in the morning, we would have to leave on any given train, but only 30 people at a time, so as not to be left on the road without our goods.

The station of our departure was Baranovich-Lesnaya. And here, masses driven by their panicked emotions gushed forth toward the railroad (Grechana).

What went on there is difficult for me to relate. There were German and Russian officers present, but dealing with people losing their minds was difficult. One woman threw three children onto the platform of a slowing departing train, and herself slipped from the steps of the platform and fell between adjacent rails. A passing train went over her while we all stood and in one voice, as if singing: "Steady … steady … don't move … stretch out!"

Even now, it is painful to remember that moment.

My husband was the elder for our group. He held the *marchbefel*. In it were: engineers, physicians, a priest with his son, and others.

Our path from Proskurov-Grechana lay across Volochisk, Tarnopol, a three-day stay at Peremyshl, Cracow, also a three-day stop. Here we were met and shown to our accommodations by a duty officer from the staff of Dukhopelnikov. Farther—a week's stay in Warsaw, Brest-Litovsk, Baranovich, and Lesnaya. There, we were quarantined in camp for three weeks. Beyond Novo-Yolnaya Station, where we were moved on peasant carts in a heavily armed German convoy, we were redistributed: Kuban Cossacks in the village of Zaroye, Terek—Kozmichakh, while Don Cossacks—I do not remember. Staff—in Novogrudok.

We left Novogrudok hurriedly, pressed on all sides by Bolsheviks and partisans. We often went along mined roads, captured partisans being led at the front of the column. This was a frightful trip with masses of blown-apart people and horses … I give you the words of our song:

Heat and cold, inclement weather

All this we learned…

We walk along a road through heavy sand and woods. Vehicles of all sorts and appearance pass us. I do not know their makes. The vehicles sputter to a halt. Our column is cut across and stopped (leader of the column, Colonel Bedakov).

A young Don lad steps out from the first vehicle. Born in Yugoslavia, he is the driver of the vehicle. He looks to see why it was stopped. He stepped on a mine. A horrible and frightening spectacle. The Germans shot the unfortunate youth, since all of this flesh was spread in different directions: there an arm, here another, there a leg…

We went to Belostok entirely on back roads. (We were carrying the body of Field Ataman Pavlov.) We went without supplies, with brief over-nights, and often without. Horses fell from hunger and fatigue. What strongly reverberated through the souls of the people, calling up, more than pity, was the incredible fear of falling behind the column. This fright did not leave me the entire way, and my nerves became terribly frayed. It became especially difficult for me, the family of Doctor Sh., engineer A. and family, and engineer T., with family. We were not adaptable: we did not know how to approach horses and carts, were pitiable, comical, and constantly heard from the *babas*—"Ah, a jurist, even, but he does not know how to hitch a horse," and other comments of that ilk. We rode using towels and torn up dresses instead of reins, often on three, and even on two wheels.

A terrible trip! An unforgettable journey.

We rolled through Poland, passing through Belostock Gubernia, Grodenskaya, Kalyshkaya, Lomzhinskaya, and Lublin. I remember the cities: Lodz, Keltz, Ostrow, Petrokov, many villages, and places. We touched a piece of eastern Germany, came anew to Poland, and stayed about three months near Zdunska Wola.

Twenty kilometers farther, again on horse carts, to some sort of Polish railway station. We board a train with Czech railway men.

Then Vienna, Salzburg, Villach, and, in the end, into Italy, at Carnic Station.

The staff of the field ataman settled in Gemona and Cossacks in surrounding villages, based on their host and stanitsa.

Then our accommodations were moved to the area of Tolmezzo. From there, we crossed in May over the Alps to the valley of death of the River Drau.

T. S.

•

Events on the Kuban from 21 January 1943

On January 21, 1943, the Field Commandant had a meeting with regional atamans, police chiefs, financial managers, and agronomists from the Umansky, Starominsky, Novominsky, Kanevsky, Krilovsky, and Pavlovsky Districts at No. 810, Uspenskaya Stanitsa.

At ten in the morning at this meeting, Colonel von Kohler (Field Commandant) announced that the situation on the front required evacuation of part of the Kuban and that the Umansky District fell within the sphere of evacuation. As with the military, so for the civilian sector, full arrangements for evacuation were in place.

At the same meeting, Colonel von Kohler passed on the *bulava* of ataman to the ataman of the 1st Model Umansky Section, T. I. Gorb, that is, to me. With my agreement, he named as Field Ataman, Host Starshin I. I. Solomakh, the Assistant Ataman of the Office on Military Affairs.

The evacuation of civilians from the Umansky District was intended to be across the Sea of Azov to Taganrog and its environs, while police and Cossack volunteers were to meet at gathering points at Kanevskaya Stanitsa. The Field Commandant's offices and the Gestapo had already been moved there from Umanskaya. General von Kleist came to Kanevskaya.

I left Umanskaya Stanitsa for Starominskaya Stanitsa on the night of January 23rd, arriving in Starominskaya at midnight. That morning I went to the stanitsa offices, the *selkhoz* [agricultural sector —trans.] commandant's office, and the police. I gave the order to evacuate and that same day left Starominskaya for Novominskaya. With me was my second assistant, Yesaul L. F. [Ф.—*trans*.] Mitla. After spending the night in Novominskaya Stanitsa at Regional Ataman R. G. Andross's, I set off with Mitla for Kanevskaya Stanitsa, giving Ataman Andross orders to have every transport available to local residents for evacuation. It was his responsibility to give out the transports. This order became necessary when the police chief of Novominskaya, Tcherneg, took a transport, filled it with goods and, in contact with speculators having no ties to the stanitsa, as was also true of Tcherneg, left for parts unknown.

We got to Kanevsky in the evening. A heavy rain was falling. We had to wait at the dam as a column of German heavy trucks, weapons, tanks, and mobile kitchens, etc., passed, stretching for some eight kilometers. The entire column was moving to the front, that is, east.

In Kanevsksaya, we found only police and its chief, Yesaul Gretchy. Ataman Tchernish had already evacuated with his offices in the direction of Rogovskaya Stanitsa. He had not exactly fulfilled the directive: "Ataman and police leave last."

January 25th, the Field Commandant offices of Host Starshin Solomakh, got to Kanevskaya from Umanskaya, along with the police chief of Pavlograd, I. V. The commander of the southern front, von Kleist, arrived January 26th.

That same day, General von Kleist brought a written form to me and Field Ataman Solomakh, requesting that we remove all the Cossacks who did not wish to fall into the hands of the Bolsheviks in the Kuban.

There, Solomakh was named Field Ataman, not only of the Umansky Sector, but also of the entire Kuban Host.

Almost every Cossack wanted to leave, but some, fearing for others in their families, who could not be evacuated in the time available, requested that we mobilize them, so that they would not appear to have "volunteered," which, to their thinking, would bring special vengeance on their families from the Bolsheviks.

January 27th, the Field Ataman had several copies of the mobilization order typed up, but this order never even reached the Umansky Sector, let alone the entire Cossack Host.

The situation at the front required rapid evacuation from Kanevskaya so as not to be cut off in Kagalnik, Azov, etc.

January 29, at 7 o'clock in the morning, the Field Commandant left Kanevskaya in an automobile and, with him, so did I. Our journey went through Novominskaya, Starominskaya, Azov, and Taganrog. Starting especially from Starominskaya and farther, roads were completely filled with evacuees and retreating Rumanian units. In these units there were especially many saddled horses. Wet snow fell.

In Starominskaya, on January 29th, there was no one from the administration left. It was without authority. We passed through Starominskaya without stopping and reached Azov toward evening, where we spent the night.

January 29th, even Field Ataman Solomakh left Kanevskaya, with the police and Cossack volunteers. He spent a night in Starominskaya.

We went across the Sea of Azov on the morning of January 30. There was a frost, which strengthened the ice, so we crossed without incident, although we arrived in Taganrog late in the evening, since we went by the mouth of the Don, where great care had been required.

In Taganrog, I learned that two days before our arrival, Bolsheviks had bombed the city, and that a certain evacuating officer had had a leg torn off. Later, in Berdyansk, I learned that this was E. I. Us, who had been the ataman of Starominskaya Stanitsa even before the First World War.

February 2nd, I left with my command staff in an automobile for Taganrog-Zaporozhye. The journey was very difficult. Often, it became necessary to travel over graded roads. There were huge snowdrifts.

In Taganrog and through the Ukraine, I noticed that there were still people with sympathy for the Bolsheviks within the populace, even if not many. In Taganrog, this was particularly characterized by the many who were readily exchanging German marks for denominations of Soviet currency.

February 10th, in Semenovka Stanitsa, I learned of a meeting of Kuban Cossacks, to be held in the city of Berdyansk, where General von Kleist was staying.

February 11th, I left the Field Commandant's offices in Semenovka and went by train to the city of Berdyansk. I spent February 12th in Berdyansk, where I saw Colonel Joseph Ivanovich Belovo for the first time. He told me that General Kleist had named him as the Military Ataman of the Kuban Cossack Host. Colonel Belovo had already formed a staff. The head of his staff was Lieutenant Colonel G. P. Tarasenko, his adjutant, Korshenko, and his clerk, Kharitonov, in charge of his domestic staff.

I stayed in Belovo's quarters (in the house of the deputy to the city's head), while he moved to different quarters, with a woman who was not known to me, whom he called his wife.

I liked the Colonel very much, and I was very pleased that we had in the Kuban Host a man with the capability to unite and properly lead Cossacks into battle against Bolshevism. General von Kleist showed great deference to Belovo, which I also considered a big plus for his effectiveness as Host Ataman.

February 12th, I also spent some time at Berdyansk in the village of Novospasskoye with Host Starshin Salamakh, his adjutant V. I. Pavlogradsky, sixty Cossack men, and their guests. There, in Novospasskoye, the 1st Kuban regiment was being formed.

February 19th, I drove from Berdyansk to Novospasskoye in an automobile. By this time, the regiment numbered about eight hundred men. But there, I learned from the Cossacks that many Cossack evacuees and police, especially, had gone to Zaporozhye, Krivoy Rog, and elsewhere. In general, all had moved to beyond the Dnieper.

Considering all this, and given the situations at the front and in the rear, I advised in written form that Colonel Belovo move beyond the Dnieper and there put together a center for the formation of Kuban units.

Both Colonel Belovo and General von Kleist agreed with my proposal.

February 22nd, the staff of the Host Ataman left Berdyansk. I too left with them, on a cart and horse. That same day, the 1st Kuban

Regiment also marched out under the command of Host Starshin Solomakh. Their march route was: Kakhovka, Beryslavl, and Kherson.

I stayed at different times in Kherson, but in particular: with Colonel Bely and staff, March 7th; on the staff baggage train, March 10th; and with Host Starshin Solomakh March, 13th, at the same time that the regiment went through Kherson and settled into the villages of Muzikovka, Viseltsy, and Zelenika, seven-to-twelve kilometers from Kherson.

Full details were recorded at various times by the former ataman of the Umansky District, Cornet Gorb (as follows, signed in his own hand).

30-12-44

We have edited these writings of T. I. Gorb for print, as, farther on, he writes of personal details, his designation as Kuban Ataman, and Colonel Belovo, which do not have a direct bearing on the given topic.

In brief, this part of his writings is as follows:

The 2nd Kuban Infantry Regiment, consisting of more than one thousand men under the command of Colonel Malovik, soon arrived in the region of Muzikovka. After this, both regiments were considerably reorganized.

In view of the inaction of Colonel Belovo, the German Cavalry Captain Lehman led them with great enthusiasm.

Colonel Bely, under the pretense of a call from Berlin, had abandoned the Cossacks and later, when they had been transferred to Mlawa, where the 1st Cossack Division was being formed under Colonel von Pannwitz, he came to Mlawa and told the Cossacks that he had been received by Hitler and designated to be the Kuban Host Ataman. The Cossacks believed him and passed on the *bulava* in a solemn ceremony.

Soon it became clear that Colonel Bely had fooled the Cossacks. Hitler had not received him. Neither had he been named ataman.

The *bulava* was taken from him.

•

Departure West

By the end of July 1942, the Germans began their attack on the North Caucasus.

Cossacks who had been mobilized into the Red Army, dispersed to their homes on its retreat, having "fallen behind" their units.

Soviet authorities tried to evacuate the populace and drive livestock into remote areas of the country, but still it was difficult, since the people did not went to leave. As for the directive to drive off the stock, they gave only the impression of driving them to the east. This was when some unrecognized superior came to them, since the local leader charged one of the older herdsmen with the responsibility, while he himself whirled off ahead.

At the beginning of August—I do not know the date, 2nd or 3rd —at seven in the morning, the Soviet Information Bureau announced on the radio, "In the direction of Kushchevsky, the enemy succeeded in coming close to our forces," but at four o'clock the same day, German tanks cruised through Stavropol.

In the territory that the Germans took, they organized local authorities and police and tried to make life normal once again, as this made it easier for them to supply the army, etc.

I worked in territory occupied by the Germans registering labor for a water brigade in the "Millionaire" Kolhoz and only once saw a Cossack squad (not a sotnya), formed by the Germans from prisoners-of-war. All were dressed in German uniforms with German insignias. They counted the Cossack squad as part of the German Army. Commanding the squad was a Caucasian Highlander. This was in the rear, and the squad rode around the steppe as if on an outing, obviously to show that, besides the German units, there was also a Russian military presence.

At the end of December 1942, the carts of evacuees stretched west from the Kalmyk Steppe. The Red Army began to attack. To our regret, the first attack by Soviet units broke through where there were no Germans.

January 1, 1943, I went to work, as always, preparing a report on the previous ten days, since the yearly report had been submitted December 20.

About ten in the morning, one of my acquaintances came into the office and asked:

"Have you heard nothing?"

"No!"

"Let's go outside,"

Stepping out of the office, we heard weapon fire and the resounding reports of drum rolls of machine-gun fire.

The front!

We took a horse cart and went into the village. This was an area, not far from Manych, that had been resettled by those sent there in 1930.

German units drifted around the edges of the village. Carts and evacuees went farther away from the front, stopping only to catch their breath.

There was no pattern to the evacuation. We passed German units intent on holding the front, at which they succeeded, although not for long.

No work was being done in main offices of the kolhoz. Everyone was listening to the gunfire.

The local police went from door to door, looking for horses and carts with which to evacuate their own families. Motive power was insufficient for all who were leaving. To leave on foot was possible only for those people who were strong in body and soul.

Paying no attention to orders given for the evacuation, people began to load supplies needed for several days onto carts as soon as it became dark, and they dragged themselves west.

This was the night of January 1, 1943.

In the village of Petrovsky, police stopped evacuees, confined them to quarters, and, several days later, ordered them to go back.

One group of Cossacks, twelve men in number, with myself in that count, instead of returning, rode off to visit our old stanitsa, from which we had been expelled as kulaks in 1930.

The situation on the front did not improve. It was broken through once more. On January 19th, *Kreshcheniye* [Russian religious holiday—*trans*.], our group of twelve Cossacks left Philomonovskaya and rode west on horse carts as part of the general flow of evacuees through the stanitsa. Here are notes from my diary:

20-1-43—Novo-Troitskaya, 21-1—Krasny Partizan Khutor (not far from Uspenskaya Stanitsa). 23-1—Amansky Khutor, 24—kolhoz brigade out on the steppe, 25—Pavlovskaya Stanitsa, 26—Kushchevskaya, 27—a khutor, the name of which I do not remember, 28 and 29—the village of Golovatovo, on the shores of the Sea of Azov, 30—crossing the ice from Azov and spending the night on the other shore, in Sinyavke.

Our weapons were taken away from us in Sinyavke, and we continued father on equal terms with the others.

31-1-43—the village of Troitskoye, 1 & 2 February—a German column, 3&4—rest at the village of Fyodorovka, from 5 to 8 —under a strong blizzard, left for Peredovoy Khutor, 9&10 February —Ostheim [spelling could not be verified, but the author certainly could not have met the French city—*trans*.], 11—Novaya Koran (a Greek village), 12—a village whose name I did not write down, 13&14—Neihoff [spelling could not be verified—*trans*.], 15—Kuibyshev, 16-17—Konskiye Razdory, 18—Shevchenko, Pology, 19 —Orekhov (a small city), 20—Yulyevka, 21&22—Grigoreyvka, 23&24—Zaporozhye.

In Zaporozhye, we obtained permission to cross the Dnieper. Until our arrival at Zaporozhye, young men of the Cossack Army directed those evacuated. (The first I saw were two officers with Russian shoulder boards—one was in a *cherkesska* [long coat—*trans*.], the other in a black greatcoat and a Don cap. They were taking Cossacks into the army.) Not wishing to join the army, I was assigned to work in Germany, while the elderly were given permission to cross the Dnieper.

Starting from Atamanskaya (not far from Kavkaskaya Stanitsa) all the way to Zaporozhye, from dawn to dusk, one could not see the beginning or end of the carts of evacuees. All had been told to first go to Azov, then farther on to Zaporozhye.

Crossing over on the ice of the Dnieper, we continued our trek west: 24 February—a German column, 25—Preobrazhenskoye, 26—Petryankivka, 27&28—Tokmakivka, 1, 2 & 3 March—

Yevreyskoye Selo, 4 & 5—Dolgievka (120 kilometers west of Zaporozhye).

Here was given the order to end farther travel. We—twelve men and eight horses—stopped to work in a kolhoz. Other columns of evacuees were directed on to Nikolaev through Taganrog and crossed the Dnieper as we did, while some, ordered to stop their evacuation in mid-trip, settled into the Ukraine.

On April 30th, the kolhoz elder announced to us:

—"By orders from the German Command, all evacuees must be sent to their regional commandant offices."

We—twelve men—were driven to the regional commandant offices. There, a representative of the staff of the Kuban-Terek Volunteer Host met us, with an order to form Cossack units. Colonel Bely had signed the order.

From our group of twelve, the representative let seven go based on their age, while the five of us, he added to a group of possibly a hundred men. On that night of the 1st to the 2nd of May, he directed us to the city of Krivoy Rog. On the morning of May 2nd, we went through registration by representatives of the staff of the Kuban-Terek Volunteer Host, at No. 22 Pochtevaya Street.

The representatives introduced: head, Yesaul Novikov, his assistant, Cornet Nemtsov, head clerk, Junior Cornet Striga.

In those premises, at the first table on the right, there sat an old clerk. He asked everyone who passed him for proof of identity. All who qualified, he entered into a book and directed them in groups to the barracks on the outskirts of town.

Instead of a passport, I submitted my discharge from the Red Army. The clerk looked it over and told me that, based on that document, I could not join the Cossack Army.

They gave me a certificate freeing me from military service, gave it the official stamp of the Southern Staff, with a notation on the back in German, and I returned to the elderly, while those mobilized were probably sent to Mlawa.

Those who were not registered in May, but two-three months later, were not relieved from duty, but were sent to guard mines and factories in the region of Krivoy Rog. They carried out guard duties, stayed in separate platoons, and on the whole made up the 1st Infantry Regiment, which was commanded by Host Starshin Lobysevich.

Representatives of the Don Host were on the same street, on the odd-numbered side. I do not remember the number of the building.

The staff of Field Ataman Pavlov was situated some 120 kilometers from Krivoy Rog. (I can not remember the name of the city or village.)

At the time of evacuation from the Kuban to the city of Azov, there was no authority anywhere. Evacuees came into a kolhoz, helped themselves to provisions, and went on farther.

Crossing the Don, starting at Sinyavke, provisions could be obtained from kolhozes by permission from the commandant's office.

In September 1943, units of the Red Army crossed the Dnieper. Again, an evacuation was begun. Evacuees were directed to Nikolaev.

The organized 1st Infantry Regiment rode from Krivoy Rog on horse carts, with Cossacks who were not in the regiment following them.

The representatives of the Cossack staff organized and directed families of evacuees along march routes. Subsequently, the 8th and 9th regiments were formed *en route*.

The 1st Infantry Regiment, and those Cossack families evacuating with them, stayed in the area of the city of Pervomayskaya (Nikolaevskaya district) until December 20th, then—a new march route. December 20—Sophievka, 21—Olshanka, 22—Golovinskoye. 23—the small city of Grushka. Farther: Graivoron, Zhuravka, Gaisin, Maryanovka, Vinnitsa, Pogoreloye, Olochentsy, Nezhin, Davidkovtsi, Proskurov, Tchaban, Biryunivka [spelling could not be verified—*trans.*]. (Farther in my notebook, written in pencil, the writing has faded away.) This was our route to Brest-Litovsk, and, after, by way of Berezov Kartuz, to the area of the city of Novogrudok.

The 8th and 9th Regiments went by way of Rumania.[*]

---

[*]   The 1st Regiment, and 8th and 9th, as given in the notes of Alekseyevich, should not be confused with the 1st Cossack Division, which was formed in Mlawa. Those three regiments belonged to the Cossachi Stan and were under Field

Alekseyevich

•

Cossachi Stan

Much has been written about the Cossachi Stan in the foreign Russian-language press, but mostly of its tragic end and almost nothing about the reasons for its appearance.

I will try to tell about this, as much as brevity allows, on the basis of testimony received from the deceased General P. N. Krasnov and the first Field Ataman during that time, General S. V. Pavlov.[1] Then it will be more understandable what the reasons were that called for the creation of the tragic Cossachi Stan.

I myself, sent by General Krasnov to the staff of the German Southern Front as his trusted functionary, was a participant in and witness to the organization and life of the Cossachi Stan. Later, as District Ataman of Don Stanitsas, I was a member of the staff of the Central Administration of the Cossacks.

As the Germans invaded our native land, Cossacks took heart —so said Pavlov. It was already not possible to see those dejected Cossacks, who had started organizing surreptitiously. Communist officials must have noticed, but lacking the protection of the NKVD, they somehow quieted and everywhere, as they had even in the cities, slowly began to hide somewhere.

There began a payback with one or another for former offenses.

And about the time that defeated Red units began to flee in disorder from the attacking Germans, Cossacks dug up hidden weapons from the time of the White battles and, arming themselves with whatever was at hand, began to attack small groups of Reds and their transports, taking their weapons.

As the front neared, several small armed units organized in stanitsas and khutors, carried out night ambushes and created panic among the disordered Red units. If they succeeded in capturing

---

[1] Ataman Pavlov.

active party workers, they quickly liquidated them, while they took the weapons of Red Army soldiers and released them.

All these units acted independently. There was no communication between them.

Still, from the capture of Novocherkassk, when the front moved farther, the Don stirred up and slowly began to organize, as it had in 1918.

Analogous movements took place on the Kuban and Terek.

Cossacks, according to Pavlov, were not as strong as they had been a quarter century before: physical and moral hardships had undermined the past might of Cossacks. But still, even those remaining Cossacks represented a force to be reckoned with.

Pavlov himself organized sufficiently large units to take into battle against Reds.

On the liberation of Novocherkassk, the remaining Cossacks elected him Field Ataman of the Don Cossacks.

Pavlov—rooted in the Don, completed the Don Cadet Corps, then the Cavalry Military School. By the First World War, he had the George Weaponry, Vladimir with Swords, and other medals. He was a reconnaissance pilot in the Civil War and was the first to make a connection by airplane with the Upper Don District, as it arose in rebellion in the Red rear. As did most Cossacks, he missed the Novorossisk evacuation, but hid his past in the USSR and succeeded in obtaining a position as an engineer.

To our regret, the Germans did not make the hopes of Cossacks come true. They forbade armed units, allowing only police and some kinds of small, local militias to carry arms. It was thanks only to the German commandant of the city of Novocherkassk, General N., conducting himself with great sympathy for the Cossack movement and for Pavlov as an individual, that the latter succeeded in keeping his unit armed.

This unit, in fact, served as the foundation of the Cossachi Stan.

On the surrender of Vinnitsa, this unit arrived well armed, consisting of sixty mounted Cossacks.

After the liberation of a large part of the province, Cossacks began to return to their former lives. They elected atamans for stanitsas and khutors, opened churches, etc.

The Don Cossacks remembered their popular Ataman, General P. N. Krasnov. Cossacks from the Don came to him with a request that he come to his native province and take its leadership into his hands.

General Krasnov could not go, but he sent some sorts of advisories and an article of his for the Novocherkassk newspaper. This way, ties were knotted with Cossacks in the homeland and continued through the retreat of Cossacks from the district.

During the retreat of the Germans, disorganized masses and Cossack refugees went on the move, perishing from partisans, Red Army units, and its aviation.

But there were even organized columns. Grushevskaya Stanitsa (Near Novocherkassk) was lead by the military ataman of the stanitsa, Starshin Grekov, who took them in full marching order to the city of Proskurov, where there was a gathering point for Cossacks. This stanitsa had also led away with it the stanitsa's horned livestock. On orders from Pavlov, at the last moment, the entire Provalsky horse stables were secreted out, with all of its brood mares, sires, and colts.

Obtaining agreement, General Krasnov created a Cossack Administration of the Don, Kuban, and Terek, which later became the Central Administration of the Cossack Hosts. The masses of fleeing refugees (Cossacks, Highlanders, Ukrainians, and ordinary Russians), not having any administrative structure or basic leadership, suffered terrible disorder, especially after crossing the Dnieper, where the refugees suffered horribly.

How the Reds took revenge on refugees, those who lived through it know. Red tanks overtook carts and refugees with cries of "Squash the German kolhozniks," driving straight into columns, killing people and livestock.

The next day, I had to speak with wonder about what the Cossacks salvaged: carts, mostly of Caucasian Highlander—it was simply terrible.

Staff from the front stopped at Vinnitsa to organize the fleeing masses. At the end of December 1943, all Cossacks were transferred to the leadership of the German, Major Mueller, an officer on the Front Staff from the Eastern Ministry. Highlanders, meanwhile, were placed under the leadership of Captain T.

At this time, I visited Major Mueller, representing General Krasnov on certain tasks that served as the beginnings of the future Cossachi Stan.

In general, the administrative leadership of the Cossacks at that time appeared to be as follows:

At the head stood P. N. Krasnov with his staff, having received the necessary sanctions from the Eastern Ministry. For convenience in dealings between Krasnov and the ministry, the latter was designated to be in the service of Dr. N. A. Himpel and his Central Administration of the Cossack Host—on the whole a decent man. A native of Russia, he was educated there and always displayed great sympathy in dealing with Cossackdom and questions about Russia. I personally had a chance to be convinced of this in conversations with him when I was named to the staff of the Southern Front and during later meetings with him. He treated General Krasnov with great respect.

In the area of the Southern Front, Cossacks were under the leadership of Major Mueller. I think that every Cossack had a good word for him. What he did for Cossacks is supported by the fact that Pavlov, who hated Germans, singled out Mueller with gratitude for his work for Cossacks, ceremonially offering him his grandfather's sword and a Cossack hat.

It was a pleasure for me personally to see that Major Mueller put great value on the authority of P. N. Krasnov and considered him to have a truly first-rate mind. He brought all of General Krasnov's directions to life with absolute precision.

As part of the staff at the front, Mueller was at one time the representative of the Eastern Ministry. Under him was the representative of General Krasnov (the author of these lines) and the representative of Dr. N. N. Himpel, the German Russian, E. E. Rathke [English spelling could not be verified—*trans.*], Mueller's adjutant, and another official.

Before deciding on questions concerning Cossacks, Major Mueller always asked Field Ataman Pavlov, E. E. Rathke, and General Krasnov's representative.

Since in the rear of the retreating Germans, in territories of the Ukraine, several arbitrary Cossack staffs appeared before the German Army Command, introducing confusion in the columns through their own directives, then it clearly felt the necessity of uniting the Cossacks under a single authority. For example, I can verify that in the region of Nikolaev, a Cossack staff announced itself with a Colonel Tarasenko at its head, who by his orders created no little trouble among refugees.

The unification of all Cossacks by Mueller did not successfully start until the beginning of 1944, in the city of Proskurov, where the staff of the Southern Front was. After an announcement on the 3rd or 4th of January, election fell to Pavlov, who used the great authority he had in all the retreating columns of Cossacks.

General Krasnov's consent and approval were obtained by telephone.

The staff of the Field Ataman was based in Proskurov, which had already been designated as the gathering point for all Cossack refugees.

The staff of the Southern Front took upon itself the task of providing for Cossacks and their families, as they had done with provisions and forage for horses. From them were given out orders to all local commandants and field gendarmes to give *marchbefels* for Proskurov. With them, refugees received rations from commissary stores on even terms with German soldiers, and forage, too.

After being designated Field Ataman, Pavlov immediately went to the front with representatives of General Krasnov, organized transports for Cossacks he encountered, naming elders for their columns, and giving directions.

Cossack resettlement points were established in several cities and boroughs (Odessa, Nikolaev, Mogilov, Kamenets-Podolsk, Vinnitsa, etc.) Columns accidentally happening into the Rumanian sector met with bad treatment: Rumanians took horses, horned livestock, weapons, and even all their goods away from Cossacks, then put them behind barbed wire.

General Krasnov's representative, on instructions from Major Mueller, served on the staff of the General-Governor of Trans-Istria (Odessa and its neighboring territories), as it was called. After his discussions with the Rumanians, they freed the last Cossacks and gave out orders to send columns that happened upon them into the German sector, and to give necessary directions by radio when columns crossed larger roads.

Soon Proskurov was overflowing with refugees, and the Front Staff gave permission to relieve the burden. In deliberations on the question, Colonel Pavlov asked that Cossacks be given the area of Kamenets-Podolsk for temporary settlement, or, at the outside, Galicia, to which there were blood ties for us.

Mueller agreed, the Front Staff did not object, and all that was needed was the sanction of the Eastern Ministry. Krasnov was informed of the decision, which he approved and made a presentation on it to the Eastern Ministry.

At the same time, Pavlov succeeded in getting permission to obtain Russian rifles and machine guns from stockpiles.

Pavlov thought to organize a cavalry unit, during which time he would train it, leave Cossack lands in the rear, and move to the front with the goal of breaking through to the rear of the Reds and raising a rebellion there. He was convinced that, with Russian-only forces, he would not only raise the man on the street, but also entice Red Army soldiers away with him. Going from Novocherkassk to Proskurov, he was certain of future success.

The wealthy and large village of Balino was chosen for the urgent relief of Proskurov, where more columns of Cossack refugees arrived daily.

A great need was discovered for experienced officers, which were lacking. Pavlov asked to be sent volunteers from the White Army emigrants. The Front Staff and Mueller agreed and turned Pavlov's request over to General Krasnov.

Soon, several officers arrived from France.

Totally unexpected was the receipt from Berlin of orders to immediately transfer the Cossacks to Belorus, in the area of Novogrudok.

It became clear that such an order arrived through the insistence of the War Command, so as to settle Cossacks in Novogrudok and nearby villages to guard them and the railroad into Eastern Prussia against partisans in the rear.

Considering the question of resettling Cossacks still undecided, if Novogrudok was to be only a temporary accommodation for Cossacks, Mueller decided to send the greater part of the Cossacks there, armed and trained, with Colonel M. in charge, in echelons by train and marches across Volochisk, Tarnopol, Sokal, and Brest-Litovsk, to which leaders for the points were sent in advance, with the task of gathering supplies, provisions, and forage. The staff of the Field Ataman was left in Proskurov, since an influx of lines of refugees still waited there, as warned by field gendarmes. There was a Cossack sotnya in Balino. The chief of staff of Field Ataman Domanov was sent to prepare for the arrival of refugees.

Making a tally of all the Cossacks who left their native regions was impossible.

As the Reds neared, Cossacks, almost to a man, abandoned their long-occupied homes and rushed west. From the testimony of authoritative Kuban and Terek Cossacks, and Pavlov himself, it can roughly be estimated at a significant number—greater than 100,000 Cossacks were to be found in route with their families. Bolsheviks captured no small fraction in their home areas. Others, having learned the horrors of retreating under frequent air attacks, returned on their own or stayed in place.

In this way, as recommended by the Front Staff, approximately 100,000 refugees came to Krivoy Rog and Zaporozhye from their home regions. Among them were Caucasian Highlanders, Ukrainians, and others.

On crossing the Dnieper, the wave of refugees was sent to Pervomaysk (Voznesensk). Here, fewer turned up, and it was possible to make an exact count, more or less, although the Cossacks dispersed in varying directions: some went to Nikolaev and Odessa (Rumanian Sector), others to Vinnitsa-Proskurov and, in general to

Podolia. Many wandered not far from the front, hoping to return home with a German advance.

However that may have been, to Pavlov, Cossacks seemed very weakly connected at the time. Dukhopelnikov and several others who recruited Cossacks into German units played no small role in this.* Mueller had to struggle with them a great deal.

Having received the first news of the arrival of advanced units in Novogrudok, Pavlov went there by automobile, following the route of refugee cart trains, with the goal of examining the orderliness of their line of march.

The first absolute attempt on his life was there on the road to Sokal. He was shot at from a distance—missed.

After the front had been quiet for some time, the Reds mounted a strong attack with large forces. Now knowing the location of the Field Ataman, Cossacks rushed *en mass* to Proskurov. The village of Balino soon emptied.

At this time (the end of February 1944), Red tanks broke through to Starokonstantinov, threatening Proskurov and sweeping around Balino. Domanov was ordered to go to Galicia immediately. A mechanized column and a housekeeping unit managed to get off in time. Domanov, though, was delayed with housekeeping matters and was surrounded by the Reds. Obviously, after several critical weeks, he succeeded to break out and reach Fellstien [English spelling could not be verified—*trans.*] with insignificant losses.

Pavlov returned from Novogrudok about this time. He based himself in Lvov, where the staff of the Southern Front had moved.

P. N. Krasnov's chief of staff, Colonel S. Krasnov, and Dr. N. N Himpel came to Lvov. This was their first meeting with Pavlov and the Cossack refugees. Orders from Berlin to send all Cossacks as soon as possible to settle Novogrudok, along with the Field Ataman, were received in Lvov.

Major Mueller designated Sandomir-Peremysl as the gathering point for converging Cossacks. All Cossacks were to be dispatched from there to Novogrudok.

Here, in Peremysl, conflicts with agents of Dukhopelnikov and others took place. Marvelously dressed in Don and Kuban officer

---

* Dukhopelnikov recruited Cossacks for Pannwitz's division.

and sergeant uniforms, they appeared in refugee barracks and, offering inducements, recruited Cossacks into German units. Contending with them was difficult, because they had Wehrmacht papers. It got to the point that some recruiters stopped an echelon of Cossacks in Taganrog, forcibly removed the more able-looking Cossacks, and sent their families farther along. Then Mueller contacted Berlin and received instructions that, on the grounds of the agreement with General Krasnov, Cossacks were allowed to form armed units and were to come under the direction of Field Ataman Pavlov. On this basis, Major Mueller and the representative of General Krasnov traveled to the Taganrog area and freed the Cossacks held there, to their great joy.

A second attempt on the life of Pavlov, survived miraculously, occurred in Lvov. Pavlov, as usual, went to the Cossack point on one of the out-of-the-way streets of the city. When Pavlov rose to climb out of the automobile, suddenly, unexpectedly, he was shot at from almost point blank range from the lower floor of a house opposite. His bodyguard kept his wits and, risking his own life, rushed it, firing his automatic at the window from which the gunfire had come. The assassin jumped out into the street and, returning fire, began to run. The Cossack caught up with and shot him. That same Cossack also survived miraculously.

I was a witness to this, as I was walking to the point. Hearing gunfire, I ran there and learned what had happened from Pavlov, who had not yet recovered from the experience.

Mueller awarded the Ataman's bodyguard a medal.

Now, after the second attempt, it was clear that Pavlov was very dangerous to the Reds, and that they had decided to liquidate him.

Loading of Cossacks to be sent by train to Novogrudok began at the very beginning of March 1944.

In view of the fact that a large number of Cossacks had still not joined the Field Ataman and that Red attacks liquidated Cossack resettlement points before contact with the Field Ataman could be made successfully, refugees scattered through all of Galicia and even turned up in Poland. There were incidents when commandants and gendarmes loaded Cossacks into railroad coaches and, for some reason or other, sent them either to Hungary, Croatia, or Serbia. General Krasnov's representative had to travel there in order to have Cossacks be allowed to leave for Novogrudok and to force railroad commandants in Hungary and Croatia to send all arriving Cossacks to Novogrudok without delay. That was where the staff of the Field Ataman had moved, while Mueller, continuing to represent the Eastern Ministry on Cossack affairs, remained in Galicia. That was where the representative of General Krasnov was, too, collecting Cossacks, and according to their inclination, directing them to Novogrudok.

Novogrudok—this small Polish city located in a forested area suitable for use for the activities of partisans, which they did.

Before the arrival there of the staff of the Field Ataman, the first party of Cossacks, functioning from the end of January 1944, was organized into a large detachment by Colonel M. and occupied Novogrudok and a row of adjoining villages within a radius of 80 kilometers. An armed sotnya was found in each village there, keeping guard of families and transports, and watching all the sectors in which attack by partisans could be expected from the woods.

Beginning with the presence in Novogrudok of the Field Ataman with a second party of Cossacks, two regiments were formed that firmly took over defense, occasionally combing the woods in large battues against partisans.

At times, partisans fired at the villages occupied by Cossacks, but they were always repulsed.

Based in Novogrudok, Pavlov set to putting the settlements in good order. He brought order to the columns of refugees, then turned his attention to the formation of regiments. He obtained good results, as was evident from a parade review he held of his units. The review was written about in both Russian and German newspapers.

In the beginning of June, when Vilnius seemed to be the target of the Red advance, local partisans began to stir.

The situation became worrisome and dangerous to Cossack settlers in the area of Novogrudok. Pavlov brought all his units to battle readiness, occupied the more obliging places, and ordered refugees to be ready in case of retreat.

June 17th, on an official trip south of Novogrudok, the Field Ataman perished tragically.

Afterwards, Cossacks stayed in the area of Novogrudok for about two more weeks, then they were ordered to move southwest to the city of Bialystok under the command of the new Field Ataman, Colonel Domanov.

The 2nd Regiment served as the rear guard, covering departing refugee columns, but it fell into a difficult situation, was surrounded, and only with great effort got itself free of encirclement.

At the end of June and the beginning of July, refugee columns began to gather in relatively good order at Zdunska Wola (Poland), where they stayed for more than a month, putting themselves in order and adjusting to new lives.

Pavlov's death caught everyone by surprise. All that went before among Cossacks under the tutelage of Mueller was reported first of all to him. In answer to his telegram about Pavlov's death, General Krasnov answered that he named Domanov the Field Ataman.

A few words about him, since the last days of the Cossachi Stan are tied directly to him. Had he been an officer in Tsarist times, as some insisted, it is difficult to say. That he was a member of the White Movement at an officer's rank is without question. He called himself a village "semi-intellectual," that is, from a prosperous Cossack family. His education did not extend beyond four classes of a city school: he wrote ungrammatically. Like all Cossacks, he participated in the Great War. At the rank of junior officer, he gained a knack for tactical understanding of small-scale situations, read maps, and wrote tolerable dispatches. Of his past, we only know that he was a sergeant in a Don Cossack regiment, as verified by an old émigré who served with him. It must be granted that he completed a four-month or an eight-month accelerated course at the Novocherkassk Military School before the revolution, in the time of Kerensky.[*]

His outward appearance was such: greater than average height, fairly thickset, with streaks of gray, clean shaven, and

---

[*] As verified by one of the Kuban Cossacks, who finished the Yekaterinodar Cadet School during the war, with Domanov finishing it along with him.

wearing glasses. His eyes were colorless and gave the impression of a good nature. He spoke much, quietly, and in an engaging voice. When he spoke of something disturbing, he often let his tears flow. Those he first met, he simply charmed with his courtesy, obsequiousness, and attention. And it took much time to learn how much falsehood there was to him. He stubbornly went toward goals set, using every means possible. How he behaved toward General P. N. Krasnov—was shown later.

At Zdunska Wola, where Cossack columns converged, and settled in complete disarray on fields and forest openings, it became obvious that they required reorganization.

There were regional atamans for the columns along the route of withdrawal from Novogrudok. They commanded a system of columns in which Cossacks from all hosts were mixed together This created disorder in the masses of refugees, and made it difficult at times for column leaders to deal with the uneducated Cossacks.

Now, after eighteen years, distance lets it be told how earlier it had been possible to harm General Krasnov's plans for the rebirth of Russia, and it can be shown once more how much he loved Russia and how devoted he was to it.

At the front staff (Ожечев), I was told that General Krasnov had urgently requested by telegram to see me.

I left for Berlin fully bewildered. Arriving at Krasnov's, I was utterly stunned by his words:

—On the request of the Cossacks and by my own wishes, I name you the Regional Ataman of the Don stanitsas. Do not linger here, but go to Novogrudok within the next two days.

He did not know yet, as I did, that on this day the Cossacks had abandoned Novogrudok. Seeing my confusion, and even embarrassment, and apparently taking as a refusal my answer that there were Don Cossacks more experienced and knowledgeable than I, he said that after tea he would speak with me in private.

This is what I heard:

—How even in 1918, I put a stake on the Germans, and then, as God wills. What the Germans think, having declared unmerciful war on Communism, I do not know.

I only know that there can be nothing more fearsome than Communism, for it will without a doubt destroy Russia not only physically, but also spiritually.

The Germans now count on us, as before, to share their goal to divide Russia, creating a Don, Kuban, and Terek. But this is Utopian, and it is simply mindless to consider our Don outside of its common homeland. We, Cossacks—are Russian people, proud of it and wish to help somehow in bringing about a rebirth of our homeland.

In the past, the Germans believed us and made use of this. My wish is to free at least a corner of Russia from Communism and return it to its former Russian life, so that this corner should shine like a beacon, drawing Russian people and bringing them hope of freedom. We all are Orthodox and the children of one mother, and I hope that others will gradually join us. But if they do not understand this—let God be their judge! We will for now use the "protection" of the Germans, but the future will tell. The Germans do not frighten us. History has shown that the Russian nation will not tolerate domination by aliens. So, go with God and gather together under the umbrella of Cossacks all Russian anticommunists. Try to organize cadres of future leaders on the Don, so that on our return we do not have to take up the work at once. These are my instructions—this is Order No. 1, which you will take for guidance.

Arriving in the Cossack columns with the instructions, I passed them on to the regional atamans at Zdunska Wola, and there the atamans addressed Domanov with a request that he give permission to reorganize the columns. Domanov asked for them to wait. After several days, the request was repeated. The same answer. The atamans saw that they could not continue so any longer and, taking advantage of Domanov being called to Berlin by Krasnov, gave orders to their columns. All Don, Kuban, and Terek Cossacks and foreigners were to gather at designated gathering points. The result was unexpected— everything was ready by evening. Now regional atamans could attack their own work. In that same short day, khutors and stanitsas were organized, with elected atamans. In the end, we succeeded in making an almost exact census of all our people. There were more than 3,000 Don Cossacks, about 1,500 Kuban, 800 Terek, and more than 300 non-Cossacks. This did not include the staff of the Field Ataman and his convoy, fleet of automobiles, and housekeeping units, or the regiments.

More arrived with each day. As they fell behind en route, so did Mueller send them here. Life in the stanitsas came into full swing. After a twenty-five-year interruption, assemblies were held in stanitsas and khutors that decided their own affairs. Stanitsa and khutor administrations appeared, elders regained their prestige, etc.

Here also, something unexpected surfaced: within the columns were hidden activists and even party bosses. Finding themselves among fellow khutor mates and stanishniks [members of same stanitsa—*trans.*], they were identified and ran away. I relate the following as a curiosity: the Cossacks identified one young Cossack as a follower of Communism, but not of having done anything bad himself in the stanitsa or homeland, it was resolved to flog him for the edification of the others. The flogging was executed, to the great pleasure of Cossack men and women, by the very elderly only.

Also clearly emerging was the presence of rather great cultural ability: there were many clergy, schoolteachers of various levels, physicians, surgeon's assistants, choristers, etc.

A trumpet chorus came from the Don in its full composition, a choir, and marvelous artists. Now they had the opportunity to organize in order to apply their talents. At the Don Regional Administration, where there was a tolerable facility, a gathering of clergy was started under the leadership of Archpresbyter G. They formed a diocese of the Don, Kuban, and Terek and resolved to begin worship services, even if under the open sky.[*]

Following them, teachers began to gather there, resolved to open schools, and chose P. for their inspector.

---

[*]   Cossack life began to return to normal even in Novogrudok.

In the stanitsas, under the eye of quartermasters and sergeants, young Cossacks began lessons. They were told of former Cossack life and taught to sing Cossack songs.

Tailors went to work, causing epaulets, caps, trouser stripes, and even *cherkesskas* to appear.

Cossack settlements went from looking like gypsy camps to well-organized stanitsas and khutors. They put an end to all manners of excesses taking place in the columns. In this service were the stanitsa and khutor atamans and their assemblies.

And here is where the name Cossachi Stan appeared. It was not so decreed by anyone, but in Italy, it somehow became official.

In Zdunska Wola, several officers arrived, old emigrants who greatly assisted in the formation of the Stan.

Approximately after a month's stay, it was announced that the entire Stan was to be transferred to northern Italy. Billeting parties were sent there. The loading of echelons onto railroad trains went with great interruptions.

The Cossachi Stan gathered itself together in Italy in mid-September. Staff of the Field Ataman settled into the city of Gemona, while stanitsas set up camps in fields surrounding Osoppo. Here, the Cossachi Stan was put under the charge of the SS, commanded by General Globochnik. It became clear that Cossacks were to be responsible for guarding railroad routes from Gemona to Udino.

It was vital to have battle-ready regiments available here. Apparently for this purpose, there was an improvement in Cossack provisions. Every individual Cossack was even given money in Italian currency.

Concerning forage for more than 3,000 horses, horned livestock, and camels, the situation was catastrophic. If we could now feed our livestock only in fields on poor grass, we would soon not even have that. Regiments could still somehow obtain forage, but stanitsas were left to fend for themselves.

Mueller, having come to Italy, was very concerned by all this. He saw that the Cossacks were under the control of Globochnik here. Domanov no longer paid attention to him the way he had previously.

He asked me to present a plan of his at a coming conference of regional atamans. The plan consisted of the following: to remain in Italy was impossible without forage. The Cossacks would soon be transferred farther north into the hills and their ravines, where it would be even worse. Besides this, there were growing numbers of partisans there who would not be without danger to us. He was correct, as we all soon learned. For this reason, he suggested that all stanitsas be settled according to host in Bavaria at sugar beet facilities, where there was a great need for people, especially those having draft animals. His plan was such: in the center, at the factory, would be found the regional ataman with his administration, while in neighboring villages—stanitsas, where we could open churches, schools, etc. Apparently, Mueller had scouted all this out.[*]

With regret, when I spoke of this at the meeting, Domanov interrupted me, making it understood that Mueller's venture was a worthless one. I am very sorry that we had not listened to him, for finding ourselves not in a camp, but among Germans, many would have escaped having a part in Lienz.

Why Domanov declined it remains a mystery. In general, here in Italy, he began to manifest great independence, reckoning only with Globochnik.

Toward the end of September, having been left in Zdunska Wola for some reason or other, the remaining regiments arrived.

Only the Kalmyks did not appear. They got permission at Zdunska Wola to join with their own kinsmen, old emigrants with whom they had established a correspondence. There were a hundred of them. They went, it seems to me, to Germany. They had recounted how the Bolsheviks had subjected them to great repression after the Civil War.

At the beginning of October, the staff of the Field Ataman and the Cossachi Stan were both moved north of Gemona.

In accord with Globochnik's plan, Cossack regiments, in battles, cleaned out partisan units from settlement points in the hills and ravines. The operation dragged out for a long time, since there was a nest of partisans there.

The staff of the Field Ataman stayed in the city of Tolmezzo. The Don stanitsas were thirty kilometers to the south in the small city

---

[*]   We must posit that Major Mueller depended on the ability to bring the plan to fruition through the Eastern Ministry.

of Alesso and four neighboring villages. Kuban Cossacks were in two-three villages midway on the route Alesso-Tolmezzo, while the Terek Cossacks were approximately two kilometers west of Tolmezzo, in hilly woods, apparently to guard a large bridge and the approaches to Tolmezzo from partisans.

It has been falsely stated that Cossacks removed all residents from these places. In accord with the orders of the Italian governor (he had visited the stanitsas) the area that was cleared out was in close proximity to the railroad. That was where the Don stanitsas had settled. Kuban and Terek Cossacks lived with Italians.

It turned out, in general, that the arrangement between General Krasnov and the Germans to form squads to guard stanitsas was good only on paper.

What of the Cossacks, when the fate of Hitler's Germany was at stake! Globochnik controlled Cossack regiments. The Cossachi Stan was seen as a reserve to replenish general losses.

In what follows, I speak only of Don stanitsas. Having settled into new places, Cossacks once more started to bring their lives back to normal. They opened churches, schools, a hospital, a home for invalids, a vocational school, workshops, and stores. A cadet corps was organized, while in the staff offices of the Field Ataman—a school for *junkers* [Cossack ensigns or cadets—*trans*.]. All this was in the face of the serious situation on the front. The allies were on the attack, rushing toward Austria.

The stanitsas became agitated when they noticed a face in Domonov's staff that was well known to them from work in the USSR…

Grushevskaya Stanitsa presented a petition through their Regional Ataman requesting that the editor of the Cossack newspaper, "Yesaul" Boldyrev, be removed from duty. He had been the chairman of the Communist Peasantry (Kombed) [Committee of the Poor—*trans*.] and had dealt harshly with Cossacks. This was brought out by a family that had suffered because of him. Domanov did not answer the petition and Boldyrev remained as editor. One day, a delegation of the elderly from Don stanitsas came to the Regional Ataman and anew insisted that the request be repeated, presenting this time the names of six individuals with descriptions of their positions of responsibility in the USSR. They came to convey how upset Cossacks were by their presence in the staff. The Regional Ataman went to Domanov and had a very long talk with him, warning that if measures were not taken, he would have to submit his resignation. Domanov was upset by this, promised to take steps, and asked that the request for resignation not be given to General Krasnov. Once more, though, nothing was done. The Regional Ataman waited for the arrival of General Krasnov's assistant, General S. N. Krasnov.

The work of agents-Soviet partisans to disrupt morale at stanitsas and contaminate their regiments began to increase.

Wanting to avert this, Novocherkasskaya Stanitsa began to send out patrols and set up ambushes at night. Having a man killed one night and hung on another, they stepped up the ambushes. Finally, they succeeded in catching an agent with important papers and leaflets. They forwarded them to Domanov's staff and awaited further developments. What bewilderment and indignation there were among Cossacks when they learned that the agent had been released. When questioned by the Regional Ataman about why they had acted so, staff answered: "We do not have the time or room to concern ourselves with it." Meanwhile, the guardhouse was full of officers and Cossacks from General von Pannwitz's divisions who had come to visit kin. General Shkuro, arriving at that time, visited the guardhouse with the permission of the chief of staff and was indignant at what he saw and heard. As a result of his visit, he was forbidden to come to the region of the Cossachi Stan in the future without permission.

But soon the partisans went from word to deed. At the end of September, they made an air raid on the Svodno-Cossachye Stanitsa in the aviation city in Osoppo. In fifteen minutes, more than a hundred people were killed and even more wounded, mostly women, children, and the elderly. It was said these were English planes on their way to Vienna that bombarded us. As if a squadron would take time to bomb some sort of group of people in the hills. Subsequently, partisans more than once bombarded stanitsas and even Tolmezzo. Then the partisans began to shoot lone Cossacks away from their stanitsas and variously terrorized the populace.

During the middle days of October, partisans made a strong offensive on Alesso—the center of the Don stanitsas. By a previous order of the Field Ataman, all those in the stanitsas who were capable of advancing were taken into the regiments. They did not touch the trumpet band or the singers. The stanitsas were left almost without guard. All who were left were police and men sixty-five years and older, who were in charge of internal defense. This became obvious to the partisans. They attacked the stanitsas at night from three directions.

Their attack was betrayed accidentally to the sentry of the police guards by the noise of falling rocks. The watch post opened fire. On the alarm, the Regional Ataman gathered trumpeters, singers, and the old men of the guard, gave them individual defensive positions, and began a firefight.

The partisans had prepared their attack in advance, cutting telephone lines to Tolmezzo and Gemona, from which help could have come.

The city of Alesso was located in a ravine between hills. A mountain stream flowed along the western part of it, while marshy country was to the east. The only escape route was across a bridge in the southern end of the city, to where, by the partisans' reckoning, the residents would have to rush, bunching up on the square to the bridge. That was where they concentrated the full strength of their bomb launchers.

The Cossacks answered the partisans' volleys and returned machine gun fire, the latter unexpectedly. The battle lasted around an hour, then gradually subsided. Since the most danger could be expected from the north, in which direction there were no natural barriers, that was where the most defenders were concentrated. Thanks to a stone defense on the outskirts of Osoppo, we avoided losses. There were only a few who were wounded by shards from grenades and stones.

Not expecting such a rebuff, the partisans withdrew. Reconnaissance sent into the hills at dawn discovered traces of blood, bloody rags, and piles of cartridges.

An Italian priest reported that the partisans suffered significant losses before withdrawing.

The SS Command became convinced that the stanitsas were assets. This was an extra plus for the Field Ataman, raising his prestige even more in Globochnik's eyes.

In addition, the regiments carried out a spectacular operation, just as he wanted.

Domanov was necessary to the SS. He understood this perfectly and felt himself less tied to the Central Cossack Administration. Not consulting the regional atamans, he removed those not useful to him from their posts, naming others. In the Don stanitsas, he removed the ataman of the Sallskoy Stanitsa, a former participant in the White Movement, replacing him with some Professor P. He also changed the chief of the police there, replacing him with someone Cossacks identified as a former Chekist. Finally, after a conference with regional atamans and commanders of military detachments, called to it specially, along with other higher ranks having responsible positions, he asked them to give their opinions of the Cossachi Stan. It seems that the next day, a notice from the staff to relinquish their duties and immediately leave the Cossachi Stan was received by General Borodin, commander of a military detachment, by the valiant Terek, V. Vertepov, who in his time had been nominated for the post of Field Ataman after the death of Colonel Pavlov, and by someone else. Meanwhile, several regimental commanders were removed. They did not touch, for a time, those who had been individually named to their posts by General P. N. Krasnov himself. The position of assistant to the Field Ataman, later to be a general, Vassiliev, and the Regional Ataman of the Terek stanitsas, became unimportant. Domanov raised some sort of charges against them, but then dropped them. Vassiliev, in private conversations, offered to let General P. N. Krasnov know about everything in a letter. But all mail went through the staff of the Field Ataman, so for this reason we waited for a visit from S. N. Krasnov. He came, but regrettably, for only two days. He visited the Don stanitsas and was informed by the regional atamans of the abnormal situation that prevailed, affirmed by witnesses and documents.

General S. N. Krasnov, knowing about the Cossachi Stan only through reports by Domanov to General Krasnov and having seen only the outward appearance of life in it, which was incomparably better than in Belorus, simply refused to believe. Still, he was very perturbed by the revelations. And he said that the next day he would return to Berlin, where he would present everything to General P. N. Krasnov. Concerning the resignation that the Regional Ataman asked to submit, he did not want to hear of it and asked him to continue to work for the benefit of Cossacks, promising to return soon.

But by this time, life in the Cossachi Stan took on a rather strange character. Unexpectedly, as if on command, a bouquet of Soviet "toadyism" blossomed in print. Domanov was praised to the heavens by word and in the newspapers. Poems were written in his honor and essays lauded him in columns as the Cossacks' savior, having brought them out of the USSR. It was forbidden to pronounce Pavlov's name aloud, etc. Promotion to general turned the head of the former quartermaster. It now became impossible to approach him and flatterers filled the ranks of the staff. On the day of his promotion, the newspapers reached the heights of toadyism.

Some "pen pusher" wrote almost exactly these words in the newspaper of the Stan:

—"Not only did the residents of the Stan rejoice at the occurrence of this promotion, sharing their joy with one another, but joyous smiles also were sent in greetings to the worthy general-ataman for a month after."

Especially surpassing all others in praising Domanov was E. E. Rathke. Staying in the Stan after Major Mueller had been recalled, he became friendly with Domanov and considered himself the second official below him. He did not know that a month later Domanov would simply throw him out of the Stan, taking away his cow and several of his things. With bitterness, when he was in Salzburg, Rathke defamed Domanov, almost accusing him of having ties with the NKVD.

On General S. N. Krasnov's second visit, Domanov was at the obvious zenith of his glory and it was already impossible to touch him, since it was necessary to deal with Globochnik.

Greeting S. Krasnov with a full dress dinner, Domanov was unusually courteous and attentive to him. After the dinner, the Don Regional Ataman had a discussion with Krasnov in his hotel room.

After listening to him, he became agitated. He said that he would present all of it to General Krasnov for his consideration.

—"The situation is such now—he said—that time and great care are required." He casually let it drop that it might be that we were making a mountain out of a molehill. All of it might not be so serious.

The Regional Ataman, mildly annoyed, started to answer him. Almost thirty years of service together with S. Krasnov during times of war and beyond our borders had brought them almost as close together as relatives. But at this time there came a knock on the door and S. N. Krasnov's nephew, Captain N. N. Krasnov, the younger, came in and said:

"Uncle Syoma! Mikhael Mikhaelovich has told you only part of what is happening here as a matter of fact. I have been here for less than two weeks and have seen enough of this situation. I don't trust Domanov. I accidentally overheard portions of your conversation from my room next door and came to you. I ask your forgiveness."

Semyon Nikolaevich was overwhelmed by this and was silent.

—"Once more, I am going back to Berlin and will see General P. N. Krasnov, and once more, I will relay your words to him."

He left and I never saw him again.

But the situation on the front threatened Berlin itself. The Cossachi Stan and its life were temporarily on the back burner.

In the beginning of February 1945, we awaited the transfer of General P. N. Krasnov and the Central Administration of the Cossack Hosts to the Cossachi Stan. A part of the staff arrived earlier. General Krasnov, it seems to me, arrived on February 12.

Domanov greeted him with great respect, warmly welcoming his arrival. They exchanged kisses on greeting each other. Touched by the reception, General Krasnov said that he was a guest here and would not interfere with the directives of the Field Ataman.

Domanov took what was said from simple politeness as an affirmation of his full powers.

After several hours, the Don Regional Ataman and the Commander of the 1st Cavalry Regiment, Colonel Kravchenko, received notice of their resignations with the suggestion that they quit the Stan within a period of two days. This is what the Regional Ataman received:—"According to the directive of General Krasnov, Head of the Central Administration, You are required to surrender your post to the Ataman and the Assistant Administrator of the Central Administration, General Fetisov. You are requested to leave the Stan within 2 days and to go to…"

This is remarkable, as but a week before, he had received a letter from General S. N. Krasnov with a request to work quietly and not to worry about things.

The Regional Ataman sent a letter by courier to General P. N. Krasnov and asked for a meeting prior to his leaving.

This was the answer:—"My greatly esteemed M. M. Some sort of mistake has been made. I gave no orders of any kind. Remain in place, as You are needed here. See me."

I went to the "Villa Rosa Martina," where General Krasnov was staying in a separate house.

Before reaching this village, I was stopped by a patrol. I asked to see the head of the patrol. He turned out to be a former Cossack in my regiment, whom I had trained as a new recruit.

He told me that by a directive from Domanov, he was ordered not to allow anyone to see General Krasnov without his consent and that this especially referred to me.

"But since General Krasnov has called for you—he continued,—I will on my own responsibility and risk let You pass. But if anyone asks You, tell them that you saw neither me nor the patrol."

This was to be my last conversation with General Krasnov. I left him my report with several documents. We decided that under the current situation between Domanov and myself, it would be better for me to leave.

I am deeply convinced that General P. K. [error in original—*trans.*] Krasnov understood that his role had ended and he was but an honored prisoner here. He attended to the Cossacks only in the company of Domanov. Each step of his was controlled, while all approaches to him were closed. A convoy from General Domanov's regiment guarded him.

Who then was Domanov, I cannot say, since my prognostications might be greatly mistaken. But his name will go down in the history of this terrible period of Cossack life during the time of the 2nd World War. He is being written about and will continue to be written about.

M. Rotov

•

The Death of Field Ataman Colonel S. V. Pavlov

On May 27, 1944, while temporarily fulfilling the duties of Head of the Central Administration of the Cossack Hosts in place of General P. N. Krasnov, who had fallen ill, I left Berlin for Novogrudok (Belorus), in the area in which Cossacks and their families were gathering in the group of Field Ataman Pavlov.

I went there with General Krasnov's approval in order to become familiar with the condition of this large group of Cossacks. I stayed there until July 2.

During this period of time Cossack groups left in route during the move were scattered through the area mentioned.

Cossack echelons and their families arrived with their goods by train at the Forest Station, near Baranovich, then continued farther in marching order.

The staff of the Field Ataman and several of his officials were located in the city of Novogrudok itself, while refugees and regiments occupied the villages nearest the city.

The environs of the area of Novogrudok were forested, perfect for the activities of partisans. The latter were not notable for great activity, but nonetheless occasionally dared to approach villages occupied by Cossacks and shoot at them. They also mined roads.

The guard for the area occupied by families served only the Cossack regiments that had been formed. The Field Ataman had to occasionally organize small expeditions to clean out the surrounding woods of partisans.

The head of the German forces in Novogrudok turned out to be the Head of the District (Gebietskommissar) Doctor Gilly (artillery lieutenant colonel) [English spelling could not be verified—*trans.*].

Aside from him, there was a German Major Mueller found in Novogrudok, serving on the staff of the Southern German Group as the representative of the Eastern Ministry. In December 1943, serving in Vinnitsa with the staff mentioned, he was charged with the task of managing all the Cossacks who were retreating with German forces.

As with Doctor Gilly, so did Major Mueller understand the situation well. They always conducted themselves toward Cossacks with kindness. They rendered all possible assistance to the Field Ataman and worried about the Cossacks, but did not interfere with Cossack internal affairs. In his activities, Pavlov was completely free. They required of him only that he keep the indicated officials well informed.

At the command of the Gebietskommissar were small police squads, German and Belorussian, under German leadership. Their duties included the safekeeping of the region from partisan attacks.

Doctor Gilly asked the Field Ataman to keep him posted on all Cossack movements, without exception, so that he could notify his own subordinates and avoid having major misunderstandings.

Field Ataman Pavlov, receiving a dispatch that one echelon was setting out in the morning from Lesna, decided to go out to meet them in the large village of Gorodishche, lying southeast of Novogrudok, within a thirty-five kilometer distance from it (in a straight line).

The day before he left, we were with him and his chief of staff, Lieutenant-Colonel [Host Starshin—*trans.*] Domanov, for a long time, discussing tomorrow's operation. To my question whether Doctor Gilly had been informed of the coming operation, Pavlov answered affirmatively.

Early on the morning of June 17, along with Lieutenant-Colonel Domanov, Colonel Silkin, Lieutenant-Colonel Lyukyanenko, and his adjutant, Captain Bogachev, he set out from Novogrudok with a convoy company, making a detour through an area of villages occupied by Cossacks southwest of the city. He took one company with him on the trip.

They rode along a very large road. Pavlov was at the head of the column with the people who accompanied him. Three Cossacks were sent ahead on advanced point, led by the Don Cornet Krysin.

At around eight o'clock in the evening, when the head of the column passed the hamlet of Omnyevich, eight kilometers to the west of Gorodishche, and went up a small pass east of the hamlet, white rockets were fired ahead and gunfire opened up almost immediately.

Pavlov shouted for a rocket launcher in order to return the rocket fire. The rocket launcher did not appear. It was with Bogachev's orderly, who was at the tail of the column, just then dragging up to Omnyevich.

Several Cossacks rushed into the pass, but Pavlov ordered them to withdraw. The orderly and Cornet Bogachev with him, he remained on horseback going off to the right of the road by which they had come up.

Meanwhile, as soon as gunfire opened up, Domanov turned the column around to the left and headed for the village through which they had just passed. He stopped at its outskirts.

The shooting continued. Pavlov, apparently wishing to rejoin the column, headed at a trot along a small rise toward it. Light gunfire continued from the right.

Meanwhile, Domanov and the other officers with him determined from the gunfire that it was not partisans leading him on, but a trained unit. They sent a scout with a wind flag to determine who was shooting and, if our own, to let them know that Cossacks were coming. Watching the progress of the Ataman, they noticed that approximately 150 meters from the village and from them, his body began to lean, then fell off his horse. People rushing up to him found him dying.

A small bullet hole could be seen on the left side of his cheekbone, while a larger one (exit wound) was behind his right ear. It was eight o'clock in the evening.

Almost on the traces of Pavlov's mortal wound, the shooting ended. The returning scout told us that it was Belorussian police who had been shooting

---

It turns out that several days before, partisans had attacked the village of Gorodishche and were repulsed, suffering several deaths. On retreat, they threatened to return soon and settle accounts with the villagers.

Anticipating a new attack from the bandits, appropriate measures were taken. Among them, west of Obnyevich, beyond a small rise, on low hillocks, foxholes were put in to safeguard that direction on both sides of the road and manned by Belorussian pickets with machine guns. The foxholes were located in a way that put in crossfire a small pass along which the head of the Cossack column appeared.

When Cornet Krysin topped the rise with his patrol, the aforementioned white rocket was launched from the Belorussian pickets. An answering rocket did not follow. The Belorussians opened fire. Krysin, with his Cossacks, charged the left picket and was mortally wounded.

Just at that time, Pavlov appeared on the pass, along with the people nearest to him.

Almost from the moment of Pavlov's death, rumors began to spread that his own men had killed him. What served as the basis for this is the circumstance that during his passage the gunfire came from the right, but a bullet striking the left side of his face killed him.

On the day after the Field Ataman's death, Doctor Gilly personally went to the site of the tragedy. Most of the responsibility of carrying out a detailed investigation was entrusted to Colonel Golovko. I personally questioned the ranks of the witnesses to Colonel Pavlov's demise.

It was established that the fundamental and major reason for the Field Ataman's death was that he did not inform the "Gebietskommissar" of his departure.

Why, ignoring a reminder, he did not do this—is not known.

Not knowing of his movements, Doctor Gilly could not warn his subordinates.

The Belorussian pickets, not expecting the arrival of Cossacks and awaiting partisans, nevertheless unquestionably launched identifying rockets. They received no reply and opened fire.

It must be noted that after their protracted trek, during which Cossacks generally wore out clothing, most were variously dressed, and the Belorussians found it difficult to tell them from partisans. The circumstance that several Cossacks had caps and wore trouser stripes, and others, German battle uniforms did not change matters. A number of the partisans also wore such clothes.

The tragedy was enabled by the circumstance that Colonel Pavlov, having sent an advance patrol, went, as the saying goes, right on its tail. Without this, if the column had followed the patrol at a reasonable distance, then Pavlov would have had time to figure out the situation and to take needed steps.

All military men who take part in battle know that even the bravest man might be killed from behind while attacking.

It is very probable that when Colonel Pavlov trotted to rejoin the head of the column, he turned back over his right shoulder at the moment that a bullet struck him, on the left side of his face.

Considering all the facts received during the conduct of the investigation and from interrogation of eyewitnesses to the tragedy, there is no doubt remaining that a bullet from a Belorussian picket killed Field Ataman Pavlov.

The cargo vehicle by which Pavlov's body was transported from the site of the tragedy to Novogrudok was left on the outskirts of the city until the time that everything necessary to receive him was ready.

I went there to give my respects to the remains of the departed.

On the truck, guarded by Cossack sentries, lay the body of Colonel Pavlov, completely covered with live flowers. A white cloth covered his face.

When they lifted him, I saw the completely peaceful face of the tragically perished Ataman. On his left cheekbone, close to his nose, a small wound could be seen from the entry bullet hole.

I wish to note that at almost the same time as the Field Ataman, Cornet Krysin also perished, attacking the Belorussian trench from which the firing had begun. Having been wounded several minutes before the Ataman, he died several days later.

Four Krysin brothers left the Don. Three of them perished en route on the withdrawal from the Don, as the fourth, a brother-Cornet left among the living, related to me in tears. But the fate of his brothers befell him, too, when he threw himself with selfless bravery into the trench works of an alleged enemy.

V. Naumenko

•

The Appointment of Field Ataman Domanov

On the day of Field Ataman Pavlov's death, Lieutenant Colonel Domanov was his chief of staff. Just on the evening of his own death, Pavlov, in my presence and completely surprising me, and even Domanov himself, it seems, promoted him from yesaul to lieutenant colonel.

After Pavlov's death, an alarming mood grew in his group of Cossacks in connection with various rumors and malicious propaganda. It became necessary to name a new ataman immediately.

The nomination to replace Pavlov as Field Ataman and member of the Central Administration of Cossack Hosts could have been done through selection and recommendation by General Krasnov, but there was not enough time for this. Conditions in

Novogrudok required the immediate, even if temporary, designation of a leader for this group of Cossacks.

At the time, Colonels Kravchenko, Vertopov, Silkin, and others who were completely suitable for this by their education, duties, and length of service in command, were available, but they were old emigrants. Taking into account certain cautious attitudes of General Krasnov toward old emigrants, I named Domanov as the temporary replacement Field Ataman. Through his position as chief of staff, he was already well informed on matters.

On the next day, an order for his appointment came from Major Mueller, who left Novogrudok for several days the day after Pavlov's death, leaving Oberlieutenant Schatz as his replacement.

On June 25, a telegram was received from General Krasnov regarding Domanov's promotion to colonel and his appointment to Field Ataman and member of the Central Administration of Cossack Hosts.

V. Naumenko

•

Rregarding the Interrelationship in the Cossachi Stan of General Krasnov with Domanov

That on my arrival in Italy, the Head of the Central Administration of Cossack Hosts, General P. N. Krasnov, truly turned over all of his duties in the organization of the Cossachi Stan to the Field Ataman, General Domanov, as supported by a letter of February 18, 1945, *No. 74* (Villa beside Kuyalis) from General Krasnov.

Here are excerpts from this letter:
Your Excellency
Dear
Vyacheslav Grigorievich
....

Such an attitude has built up here, under which double leadership must not be permitted. It creates mental agitation, which in the given time especially should not be permitted. The Ataman of All Cossack Hosts found here is one—Major General Domanov.

....

From my order *No. 4*, given here on February 14, you can see that I conferred even the Central Administration entirely to the Field Ataman, so as not to create an unhealthy double leadership that would slow work on Cossacks Lands,

There are all sorts of things interfering with this work, all the more making criticism of it impermissible.

....

I ask you to accept my assurance of my complete good will, with which I remain, P. Krasnov.

•

General Domanov's "Cossachi Stan"

Cossachi Stan, under the leadership of Field Ataman, General Timofey Ivanovich Domanov, came to be based in northern Italy in the summer of 1944. The city of Tolmezzo became the center of the Stan. Cossack families and single Cossacks, who for various reasons did not serve in combat units, settled in surrounding villages. The latter came to be called "Cossack stanitsas."

At first, Italian partisans showed the newcomers energetic opposition, but then life on the stanitsas continued in absolute peace.

Only Cossack regiments doing guard duty in the Udine-Trieste region occasionally had mild skirmishes with partisans.

The residents of the stanitsas lived in the role of tenants with Italians, and only in the Don stanitsas had the local residents been displaced and their land given to Cossacks to cultivate. This caused resentment not only in Italians, but also in most Cossacks (the order for removal was given by the Germans).

Thus, life went on in the stanitsas in relative peace and quiet, and to this "quiet haven" came an endless flow of Russian refugees from Germany, especially Berlin.

Cossacks and non-Cossacks who somehow managed to receive the necessary papers came to Italy.

The percentage of the non-Cossack element in the Stan was in general not high, but it rose especially sharply in the first months of 1945. Officially, all were counted as Cossacks, nonetheless.

There was almost no social-political effort in regiments and stanitsas: that which could be in that category stayed at an extremely low, miserable level. The ROD press was forbidden by decree. Issues that came accidentally to Cossacks were confiscated.

Still, the "quiet haven" became troubled in March-April of 1945. This occurred in connection with the arrival in Italy of the head of the Central Cossack Administration, P. N. Krasnov, on one side, and the representative of the staff of ROA, Colonel A, M. Bocharev, on the other.

This was a time of significant and long-awaited organizational hopes for ROA, and active proponents of rapid union with ROA appeared.

P. N. Krasnov, as is clear, was the most decisive and influential opponent of such a union. One of General Krasnov's countermeasures was the organization in the Stan of propaganda schools. (Officially they called it "union schools.")

The program of studies consisted of people close to General Krasnov and in agreement with him. At the ceremonial openings of the schools, General Krasnov set forth his political views in an extensive speech. He gave his primary attention, as could be expected, to questions around unification that were troubling all: characteristics of the Vlasov movement and General Vlasov himself. His views were about as follows:

1.—In his time, there was a Greater Russia, which he came to serve. It fell in 1917, infected by the incurable, or almost incurable, disease of Bolshevism.

2.—But this was true, however, only in respect to properly Russian provinces. In the South (in particular in Cossack provinces), people turned out to be almost immune to the "Bolshevik disease."

3.—It follows that it is necessary to sacrifice the incurably ill to save the healthy. Yet there is the danger that the more numerous "sick element" might stifle the healthy element, that is, northern Russians—Cossacks.

4.—In order to avoid this, it is necessary to find an ally-protector, and that can only be Germany, for Germans are the sole "healthy nation," producing in itself immunity against Bolshevism and Masonry.

5.—It does not follow to join in the Vlasov movement: if it turns out that Vlasovites are absolutely committed to Hitler's Germany, then it might be possible to talk about a union with them. But for now, we should count only on the armed might of the Germans.

––––––––––

Soon the notorious letter from General Krasnov to General Vlasov appeared. Then the Stan learned of General Naumenko's decree to Kuban Cossacks to accept the command of Vlasov, which General Krasnov answered likewise with a decree not to obey General Naumenko's decree.

Cornet N. S. Davidenkov took part in editing the letter to General Vlasov prior to taking up service in the ROA. In his own words, he had great success in avoiding "sharp edges" in Krasnov's letter, that is, making it less defiant. The entire Cossachi Stan became greatly disturbed, Kuban Cossacks more so than others. Spokespersons were sent to them with the goal of "undressing General Naumenko." Among them was General Solamakhin—a Kuban Cossack. He was almost assaulted in an assembly of Cossack stanitsas. The same story took place even with the more skillful and temperate spokesperson—Cornet Davidenkov.

General Naumenko became the symbol of the long-awaited reunification with General Vlasov.

K.

•

Valley of Death

There is a valley in the Tyrol
And in that valley, the river Drau
But remember—and shudder with pain
As from the hidden wound of a small blade.

There, where the hills were deep in thought
Clustered about a heavenly mirror
The wind carried such grief and shame
Never to be repeated for ages.

You, poet, your bitter stanzas
Hurry so to break free from
Beneath the knife of a new Golgotha
Go down on your knees, do not breathe!

Somewhere the Drau weeps inconsolably,
Struck against its banks as if on its breast,
Lamenting over the lives of Cossacks
Coldly thrown into the hands of the enemy.

They outwitted laws and defenses
Questions could not touch the dead …
Innocent blood on the ground
Wails, cries out, of perfidy.

Gonfalons fluttered like specters …
And in the hot flow of prayers
Wickedly gushed destruction
Drowning all your verses!

On shoulders, heads, and icons
Trampled hundreds of shod legs …
Far and high their groans swept
But no one came—no one helped!

Only the heartbroken Drau

Reflecting the firmness of youth
Covered with a wave of blood
Escaping out of fright into death ...

The hills frowned more sternly,
Tremors resounded in a long echo, —
Not from the clanks of steel wonders,
Was flesh torn and dragged?

Cossack men and women and children
The bright light of the last Cossack land,
Forgotten by all on earth
Not for nothing did they fall into a trap ...

So go down on your knees, O poet
And cry, and pray, and ask
That at least late news of treason
Like fire spreads through Russia.

May the memory of those sacrificed tremble
In the heartbeat of Russia always!
But for now ... let the Tyrolian mountains
Fill with the color of shame!

— Maria Volkova

•

A Short Description of the Departure Route of Cossacks from Northern Italy to Austria and Their Disposition Along the Drau River

Toward the time of German surrender, Cossack refugees with their families, along with combat units organized for their protection, were located in northern Italy, under the leadership of Field Ataman General Domanov. This Cossachi Stan, as it was called, occupied a row of villages near the city of Tolmezzo, approximately twenty-five miles in a straight line from the Austro-Italian border.

General P. N. Krasnov, Head of the Central Administration of Cossack Hosts was found there.

The Austro-Italian border ran along the crests of the spine of the Alps, going from west to east with a slight tilt to the south.

The entire multi-thousand Cossack mass left for Austria along the only paved road heading into the valley. This route ran along the banks of a small mountain stream, the Buth, which flowed through the pass.

Rising slowly and passing through the settlements of Paluzza and Timau, at which a curvy paved road that is ten kilometers in length begins, the route was very difficult for exhausted people on foot: a heavy rain fell, later changing to snow. Large snowdrifts built up along both sides of the road and the edges of deep ravines, becoming the graves of several people and a number of horses.

This route led to the Plöcken Pass, approximately three thousand meters in height.

From the pass there is a descent into the village of Mauthen and farther, through the village of Kötschach, once more rises up a small mountain shoulder, then descends into the Drau River Valley.

Here, on orders from the English Command, Cossacks and Highlanders were settled from Oberdrauburg to Lienz along a stretch of twenty-one kilometers.

Craggy peaks border the Drau River Valley, which is two to three kilometers in width. It is covered with meadows, thin forest, and shrubs. Along the left (northern) bank of the river is a railroad line from Lienz to Oberdrauburg and farther to Spittal.

The Issel, a feeder stream of the Drau, transects the city of Lienz. It divides the city into two parts, north and south, and flows into the Drau southeast of the city,

Domanov's staff settled in the northern part, while the English in the southern. That was also where the burgomaster of the city was.

General P. N. Krasnov was allotted a villa some four kilometers from the city.

The city of Lienz is six hundred fifty meters above sea level.

Cossack family households were settled in Camp Peggetz, about two and one half kilometers outside Lienz. Others bivouacked

in tents, various types of huts, or under carts on both banks of the
Drau. On the right bank, above they city, stood the Cossack military
school; below it, the cavalry regiment. Farther down were stanitsas
and combat regiments.

The easternmost settlement, Nikolsdorf—and farther,
Oberdrauburg, were occupied by Highlanders.

V. Naumenko

•

Crossing the Plöcken Pass, May 3, 1945

> This short article was submitted by one of the
> main collaborators of General P. N. Krasnov
> when he was the Head of the Central
> Administration of Cossack Hosts.

When the English 8th Army began to near the position of the
Cossachi Stan, rather than let that happen, Cossack combat units that
were south and west of Cossack "stanitsas" around the city of
Tolmezzo, in Italy, decided to leave Italian territory and go toward
Germany, that is, into Austria, which at that time belonged to
Germany.

The German main commander of the Trieste region (to the
southern slopes of the Alps, right up to the Austrian border),
Obergruppenfuhrer Globochnik, did not want this change. In all
probability, he counted on Cossack regiments to bear the onslaught of
the English and the attacks of Italian partisans, while at the same
time assisting the final, hopeless German military actions in the
region.

There were the very closest of ties between the Cossack
regiments and the Cossachi Stan: husbands, sons, and other relatives
stood "on the front," their families lived in stanitsas.

A more or less disorganized movement of the populace to the
north began, and Domanov, forced by a losing position, could do
nothing else, regardless of Globochkin's wishes, but organize a move
north to avoid total chaos.

Caucasian Highlanders were north of the Cossacks. When the Cossacks passed their settlement, they were all in the middle of preparations to go north.

People walked or rode carts. For the elderly, automobiles were "arranged" somewhere. Everyone carried or took what they could in their carts.

A large autobus moved through groups of civilian Cossacks with part of the staff and wives of staff members.

There was also a light automobile, a Fiat, set aside by the staff for Peter Nikolaevich Krasnov. The Cossack chauffeur sat on the left, Peter Nikolaevich was on his right, and Lydia Fyodorovna* sat behind him, next to me.

They stopped overnight at Piana D'Arta, a small village in the foothills.

Gunfire was heard everywhere that night. We awaited an attack by partisans. Guards were placed everywhere and we passed the night with heavy trepidation.

On the next day (May 3), the most difficult part of the journey began. The road rose steeply in switchbacks all the way to the Plöcken Pass. Horses fell and perished. People abandoned their worldly goods and moved ahead listlessly, like robots, without hope, into an unknown future.

Peter Nikolaevich's auto broke down. It was tied to the bus. That is how we went over the Plöcken Pass, reaching the village of Kötschach-Mauthen at around 10:30 on the evening of May 3rd.

Semyon Nikolaevich** and I went to the local commandant, the very kind and sympathetic Obersturmbannführer (I forgot his name), who arranged to let us have the hotel "Bahnhof," close to the railroad station to Hermagor-Villach.

It was not possible to accommodate the masses of Cossacks in Kötschach-Mauthen. Besides which, snow had fallen and there was neither pasture nor dry feed for horses. To their disbelief, the tired people and horses had to continue their trip toward Oberdrauburg-Lienz at night.

---

* Lydia Fyodorovna—wife of General P. N. Krasnov.
** General Semyon Nikolaevich, brother of Gen. P. N. Krasnov and Chief of Staff of the Cent. Admin. of Cossack Hosts.

Those who could do so found places along the route to spend the night. Many succeeded in finding hiding places in Kötschach-Mauthen, and several of them remained there after the Cossack combat units passed through and, after them, the English.

Cossack combat units began to appear the next day, similarly heading north. Field Ataman Domanov and his staff came with the rear guard and also settled into the hotel "Bahnhof."

Peter Nikolaevich expressed his wish to greet the passing Cossack regiments. He had never before had a chance to see them when they were stationed in their stanitsas in Italy. Only now did he see that these regiments did not have the appearance of troops by any concept of our time. This was a rag-tag group dressed in various uniforms, many in civilian clothes, with household junk on their carts, and pigs and sheep along with them.

I can see it as if it was happening today—Peter Nikolaevich waved his arm and returned to his modest room in the hotel, completely disillusioned. He spoke little, merely telling me that he had had a different impression of Domanov's military units.

Peter Nikolaevich realized that the war was over. He saw how German military units, in groups and individuals, moved through Mauthen to the north, with the same look of hopelessness as the Cossacks.

An unpleasant incident occurred: Cossacks attacked German soldiers to rob them. This was a single incident, but it caused Peter Nikolaevich great suffering.

The first time that I ever saw his uncontrolled anger was when a representative of General Vlasov, Cossack Colonel B., who was seen taking part in the robbery, came to Peter Nikolaevich.

—"The Germans are our allies. Those who have fallen should not be beaten. You bring shame to the very name of Russia. Get out of my sight!"—he shouted.

On the 5th or 6th day of May, Domanov sent a delegation with a white flag back across the Plöcken Pass to meet the English.

The delegation returned bearing the happy news that the Brigadier General said that it was unclear for the time being what would be done with the Cossacks, **but that under no circumstances would they be turned over to the Soviets.**

Domanov's staff celebrated the news with champagne that evening.

Peter Nikolaevich did not step down from his command at this party. On May 7th, along the road down from Kötschach-Mauthen, long rows of English tankettes dragged through, and both villages were quickly occupied in full order.

Communication between Domanov's staff and the English were quickly established.

When, on the 8th of May, the English ordered us to vacate Kötschach-Mauthen, the hotel "Bahnhof," not the least, and move to Lienz, Peter Nikolaevich wanted to remain there.

I met with the English commandant's adjutant and asked if Peter Nikolaevich's request could be allowed. I was refused, and on May 9th, Peter Nikolaevich and Lydia Fydorovna left in a light auto that belonged to the English staff.

On Domanov's wishes, I did not leave with Peter Nikolaevich.

Domanov's entire staff and Domanov, himself, moved to Lienz soon after General P. N. Krasnov.

This ended my connection with the Cossacks, with the exception of those few who remained secretly in Kötschach-Mauthen. There was no mail. The English prohibited moving from one place to another. Going out on the street in the evening was not allowed. There were individual instances when the English gave passes or some Cossack got through without permission; but in Kötschach-Mauthen, there was no trustworthy news from the Cossachi Stan.

The horror of the betrayal of the Cossacks only slowly reached us, and weeks went by before the entire nightmare became known in detail in Kötschach-Mauthen.

N. G.

•

The Area of the Cossack Betrayal in Austria

Many do not clearly present where the betrayal took place or all the rest of it that goes by the name of the **Lienz or Lienzists' Tragedy**.

The Cossacks were turned over in southern Austria, in the province of Kärnten (Carinthia), but in two places separated by a distance of approximately 120 kilometers.

The group led by Field Ataman Domanov, named the Cossachi Stan, left Italy before the end of the war and, on orders from the English command, settled along the River Drau between the cities of Lienz and Oberdrauburg. The Highlanders were at this latter point.

Lienz became the military-administrative center of this area. In it were the Eastern Command offices and the Staff of the Field Ataman. Camp Peggetz, in which the bloody events that were connected with the forced repatriation of Cossacks and their families on June 1st were played out, was close to this city. Cossack stanitsas and military units stayed along both banks of the Drau in eastern Lienz. They were called out from the places in which they had settled to be turned over. Officers and officials were removed on the 1st of June from the city of Lienz, itself, with General P. N. Krasnov at the head, along with the staff of the Field Ataman and the command ranks who were staying in the city.

The area in which the Cossachi Stan was located was approximately 30 kilometers west of Spittal. The units of the Cossack Corps were found 70 kilometers (as indicated by a straight line) northeast of it, near the village of Altgofen. From there to Klagenfurt, lying to the south, was about 25 kilometers.

From this region, the commander of the corps, the German General von Pannwitz, was turned over, along with his staff, Cossacks, and the officers of the corps.

Both turnovers were carried out according to plans made in advance by the English command. Officers of the Cossachi Stan, Highlanders, and the Cossack Corps were separated from the Cossacks and taken away to be turned over to the Bolsheviks in one day—May 28, 1945.

During the following days, the forced removal of Cossacks and families of the Cossachi Stan and Cossack Corps took place.

At the time of the betrayal, there had been no communications whatever between the two Cossack groups. They did not even know where each other was found and what happened to them.

V. Naumenko

M. N. Leontieva's Address to Those Gathered in the Russian Camp Kellerberg, May 31, 1949, for the Blessing of the Monument to the Victims of Lienz, on the Fourth Anniversary of the Tragedy of Lienz, May 28-June 1, 1945

Four years ago, in these mournful May days, had been read, it seems to me, the final sentence to the history of Russian Cossacks.

The nightmare that was lived through erased the minutia of the past: dates and many details have been forgotten, but one huge monstrous grief burns even on this day in the soul of every Cossack, but especially in women Cossacks left single and unfortunate, having spent four years already here in a camp in a western land alien to them, with the difficult and unneeded title of DP.

What happened to those who as Stalin's winnings in the game at Yalta, fell into the Soviet meat grinder, is to this time one of the many secrets behind the "Iron Curtain."

The joyful life that appeared for us from that irresistible impetuosity of Cossacks for individual freedom, when they, still bleeding from 1918, persisted in a struggle against the Communist power they hated by them. In this fight and in the sacrifices of Cossacks through their unbridled bravery in devotion to the White idea and their native land, we saw the "powerful breath of ancient epics," as one German journalist wrote in the article, "The End of the Volunteer Corps," printed in the newspaper "Wochen Post," *No.* 48/1948.

And here, heart wrung with pain, a cold analytical thought whispers:—was it all in vain? Did we not make a fatal mistake?

M. N. Leontieva's Address to Those Gathered in the Russian Camp Kellerberg, May 31, 1949, for the Blessing of the Monument to the Victims of Lienz, on the Fourth Anniversary of the Tragedy of Lienz, May 28-June 1, 1945

But life then had been full of hope, buried in work. There was not time for "analysis," and belief in the victory of good obscured our central reality and deafened the sound of the triumphal march of coming evil.

Cossack volunteers, leaving in 1942 for the west, went across Ukraine and Belorus with the song:

> Under the banner of freedom
> Regiments of volunteers
> From the Terek, Kuban, and Don
> Marched the Cossack tiers
> On fields of battles fearful
> Their blades aglitter—
> With songs loud and prayerful
> Dashed the Cossacks into battle
> Not to heed the Kremlin's call—
> Those parasite wretches all—
> But for the people will Cossack picks
> Be raised to strike down Bolsheviks
> For their insults to churches
> For our executed fathers
> For those who perished in '33
> All Kuban and Don Cossacks
> For burning our Cossack regions
> For stanitsas and farmhouses that were ours
> And for sending us to frigid regions
> For revenge, has come the hour
> For our final dying deed
> We have gathered in our ranks
> Orthodox sons indeed
> From the Don, Terek, and Kuban banks

The first blow to their combat service for their homelands was the order to go to Italy. It seemed an inconceivable offense to curtail our fight and go somewhere into an empty space. Our hearts pulled east... And such a bleak and slow trip it had been west...

Not frightful and somehow inconsequential were the horrors of the route we traveled—death and destruction. But the thousands of deserters and the chaos prevailing in the German army, so recently mighty-as-steel, brought forth repugnance. At least, on occasion, when we met individual Cossack compatriots who were searching for the mythical ROA, we believed then that it was true that the Russian cause, in the end, would be crowned with victory. The clear ray of hope that all had not yet perished lit the depths of our souls.

The journey into Italy brings to mind a kind of gray fog. After that, the half-starving and pointless existence of a chaotic camp, where not people, but shades moved among the window dressing of a Cossack existence. All wished to fool themselves and believe that here a great Russian cause was in the making, and that everything still pointed to hope for better days, as had so strengthened Cossack spirits in 1942.

But a catastrophe approached with snowy flakes, ever enlarging in their own swift race. Domanov's army, with its Cossachi Stan, left Italy in a hurry to get over the pass into Austria. Cold alpine rain and sticking flakes of snow covered the poorly dressed people, women and invalids, who had been thrown from the pleasant banks of the Don, Kuban, and Terek into a harsh fate in the spectacular and overly luxurious Alpine beauty. Only sudden temporary breakthroughs by the sun, blinding in reflection off the drifted snow, and hot Alpine beams warmed the shivering souls of orphaned Cossack children. In those moments it seemed that something great was taking place, that Cossacks were witnessing their turn to move into the history of Russia, and perhaps of all humanity. It seemed that somewhere there at the top of the pass, Suvorov himself was leading them to some noble victory.

Austria met the Cossacks with a bright spring. The Lienz Valley shined. The Drau carried its water tumultuously. A stand of pines spread its resinous aroma. But the flights of fighter planes were oppressive, whistling terribly in single low flights over the columns of Cossack *kibitkas* [hooded carts—*trans.*] that were drawn out on the gray-blue asphalt of Austrian roads. In fright, children jumped into the bushes and roadside gullies.

M. N. Leontieva's Address to Those Gathered in the Russian Camp Kellerberg, May 31, 1949, for the Blessing of the Monument to the Victims of Lienz, on the Fourth Anniversary of the Tragedy of Lienz, May 28-June 1, 1945

The first news of surrender did not register on our minds. Motorized columns of American and English military units, boring ahead from Lienz, testified, however, to an accomplished fact.

An order came to give up arms. People dragged themselves from roadside woods and meadows to the highway. Silently, not looking one another in the eye, they lay their weapons in a pile, as if tearing from their hearts the dearest thing and burying it in a cold, black grave. Officers were allowed to keep their revolvers and swords.

In the middle of all this, the joyful holiday of spring approached—Easter. On a field beside a pine forest, beneath steep mountain cliffs, a field church was built out of greenery—spruce and pine. Two elderly priests performed the sacred matins. Their singing echoed a harmonious choir of Cossack men and women. Just as dawn brightened, a joy for life answered from our souls: "Christ has arisen!" Feelings of spring and the beauty of God's world chased off thoughts of coming failures. We paid the victors little mind, since, for example, each soul was given ¼ kilogram of flour and officers had been allowed to keep their weapons. This created hope that we would find them to be good friends, who would help us create the conditions for our victorious return to the banks of our native rivers —the Free-flowing Kuban, the Quiet Don, and the Stormy Terek. Evil would be destroyed and a resurrected Christ would return our Holy Russia,

Over 2-3 weeks, all Cossacks were pulled toward Lienz. Regiments began to bivouac in the woods and fields. Cossack families settled in nearby Camp Peggetz. The staff of the Cossachi Stan situated itself in the city, working in full contact with the English staff, which was located in another part of the city, beyond the river. A liaison was sent to the Cossack staff, Major Davies. Officers and Cossacks were given new uniforms to replace the German uniforms worn by many Cossack volunteers. Food rations were almost level with those of English soldiers. Gendarmes made up of Cossacks were formed to keep discipline and order. They were given weapons.

All this calmed Cossacks and quelled various fears.

But then, early on the morning of May 27, the supply units of the Cossack staff were ordered by Major Davies to confiscate revolvers and swords from officers and rifles from gendarmes. It was hinted somewhat obscurely that this was being done in order to exchange the weapons on hand for newer ones.

At eleven o'clock on May 28th, an order was received for all officers to gather at the offices of the Cossack staff at thirteen o'clock, when some sort of a decree by the British forces would be announced.

At thirteen o'clock, trucks and a large bus were driven up to the staff building. Major Davies arrived. Using an interpreter, he asked the officers to take places in the vehicles in order to go to a "conference."

General Salamakhin, as chief of the Cossack staff, ordered the officers: "To the vehicles!" Several English soldiers who had arrived earlier with automatics vanished.

The officers boarded peacefully. Old General P. N. Krasnov, frail and ill, arrived.

On a sign from Major Davies, the column darted off through the streets of Lienz to the east, in the direction of Oberdrauburg.

Families saw off their loved ones: husbands, fathers, and brothers.

A tormenting, frightening premonition pressed not just one woman's heart...

Major Davies, staying behind with the crowd of women, was amiable and courteous even on difficult questions: where and why were their kin taken away. He assured them that they would return, that they had gone to a nearby village, and that all would definitely return by 4-5 o'clock that evening, so that there was no reason for concern. He told them to return to their homes and await their people toward evening tea.

The day ended in tormented waiting. Cossacks, even if unarmed, guarded the staff building.

And here, worrisome rumors and suppositions crept about. The sun set. Most of the women rushed at Davies to learn the truth. He, as always, was amiable and friendly. Looking right into the eyes of each Cossack woman with his gentle, gentle, smiling eyes, he tried to calm them.

On the morning of May 29, Major Davies announced that the officers would not return to Lienz, but that they were in a very good place, although, exactly where—a military secret. It was right at the time that the officers were being taken from a camp in Spittal, where they had spent the night, and on that very day were being turned over to the Bolsheviks. Sending them any provisions was unnecessary, Major Davies added, as they were well fed, but if someone wanted to send anything, he would send it on in an English car.

Toward evening, rumor that all of the officers had been turned over to the Soviets began to spread. Major Davies categorically denied it. He remained as friendly as before. But when it was no longer possible to hide the truth, with tears in his eyes, he began to assure us that he, too, had been fooled by his own superiors. The role of a liar had been difficult for him in front of the remaining Cossack men and women, whom he had already had time to come to love, but he could not disobey, since…he would then have been sent to the Japanese front.

A miserable, sleepless night passed. Thoughts and souls shuddered from the horror of betrayal.

On the morning of May 30, Major Davies told the Cossacks and remaining families that on the 1st of June, all Cossacks—and in general all Russians—found in the valley of Lienz, were to be sent to the Soviet Union.

He stood, suddenly dry and completely unfriendly. In his eyes sparkled the fires of triumphant and cruel evil.

People began to rush about. The leaderless Cossacks could find no way out of the situation that had arisen. They knew only one thing—return "home" was tantamount to either physical or spiritual death.

And then, in these minutes of terrible confusion, some young Cossack sergeant loudly announced himself to be the Host Ataman. With the passion of youth and an irrepressible impetuosity to save Cossacks from a Soviet hell, he energetically began to organize the confused people and instill in them the fortitude to resist. It was he who brought Major Davies the piles of petitions from organized groups and individual Cossack men and women. They were addressed to King George of England, the Archbishop of Canterbury, English and American parliaments, and, in the name of King Peter the Second of Serbia, to commanders-in-chief and marshals of the western allies. Major Davies took the petitions, but, apparently, these entreaties, written in blood, did not move beyond his basket of useless papers. Major Davies did not step back an iota from the orders he was given.

The Cossacks made a decision to hold a hunger strike. The majority of Cossacks accepted it, especially the women, for it amounted to a great Lent before their prospective suffering. Cossack women did not allow even their children to eat. No one unloaded the provisions brought by the English, so the food was dumped from their trucks onto a field inside the camp. But no one touched the food and atop the pile of bread and canned food, a black flag, stuck there by Cossacks, blew about.

Black flags fluttered on all the barracks of Camp Peggetz, along the roads, and even on individual tents of Cossack bivouacs, and in many places placards were posted with the English words: **"Better death here, than sending back to the Soviet Union!"**

The sergeant, taking the role of Host Ataman on himself, gave Major Davies the Cossack's decision: not to obey the order and not to board the conveyances voluntarily.

People bunched together into groups and even throngs. All day, there was noise, as if from a swarm of alarmed bees. Women cried. Children held onto their mothers' skirts in fright. Cossacks with pained faces were animatedly telling each other that forced removal could not happen. "These are democratic people!" But whatever was to be, it would all in all be better to die than to go!

Late in the evening, Major Davies came to camp with an interpreter and announced to the gathered crowd that the next day, June 1st, at eight o'clock in the morning, vehicles would be provided and all would have to board them. The trucks would drop them off at the railroad station. From there, a train would deliver them to the USSR.

About the Ataman's announcement that no Cossack would leave voluntarily, Major Davies advised against resistance, or else the British command would use force.

Under shouts, curses, and hysterical cries from women and children, Major Davies drove off to the city.

Right there, a general meeting of Cossacks was organized. Their decision: to firmly maintain passive resistance and avoid all incidents that might take on the characteristics of a riot.

People spent all night in churches in the fields, where Holy Services continued without interruption. Many took last rites.

At five o'clock on the morning of June 1, priests led a religious procession out onto the camp square. Cossacks in drill formation approached from the Oberdrauburg side with a cross at the head of their procession. The *junkers* of the military school arrived. Cossacks and *junkers* locked in the elderly, women, children, and invalids with a tight circle.

A solemn service was held to the Lord God. Several Cossack choirs sang.

The multi-thousand crowd raised their arms into the air during the prayers and prayed for Holy Russia and for their native lands. They were ready to fulfill the debt of faith before them and, if necessary, to accept death. Several women lifted their children up into the air from fanatic belief in God's mercy.

The words of the prayer—"Holy Mother of God, save us!"— rose to the heavens.

At eight o'clock in the morning, English trucks, covered in yellow canvass, began to roll out, making eerie wheezing noises. The crowd fell back like a cornfield before a sudden gust of wind. The Holy Service continued. The choirs sang.

But through the crowd went:—"Pray to God! Do not fear! The Mother of God will save us—they will not take us by force!…"

And, once again, enthusiastically rose to the heavens:

"Holy Mother of God, save us!"

The Cossack circle surrounding their kin, elderly, and invalids, squeezed even tighter.

English soldiers armed with automatics and clubs began to come out of the trucks, which had stopped lengthwise across the square. They started to walk around the crowd, encircling it.

The priests continued reading the liturgy. At the moment that people began to take communion, soldiers, cursing rudely in English and Russian, attacked the crowd. With blows from clubs and rifle butts, they tried to break apart the tightly linked arms of the circle of Cossacks. The rattle of machine guns rang out. Blood flowed. Dead and wounded fell. "The Valley of Death"—that is how the place was called in Suvorov's time—resounded with the terrible screams of women and children, blending with the inspired singing of prayers.

When, under the onslaught of soldiers, the crowd began to move back, it knocked down the camp's fence and ran out on the field beyond it. But here, tanks surrounded it.

The loud voice of the sergeant ataman commanded "Tighter in a circle! Off with your headgear! On your knees! Sing the prayer to the Holy Mother!"

Pressing against each other, all fell to their knees, and, once more, with even more fervor, prayers went out from thousands of mouths.

The hot summer sun burned the bare heads in the kneeling crowd unbearably. Lips dried and darkened from internal fire and terrible thirst. Exhausted faces became flooded with sweat, but people sang one prayer after another addressed to the Mother of God. Priests with crosses elbowed through the crowd, raising the spirits and firming the faith of their people.

A breeze passed occasionally through the valley and fluttered the gonfalons.

English tanks died some 50-100 meters from the crowd. Trucks were lurking in a long column behind the camp's barracks. Their yellow-brown tarpaulins could only be seen from the square here and there in the spaces between barracks.

And here, on someone's orders, a change in loading occurred. Automatic gunfire could still be heard only beyond the Drau, in the woods, on hillsides. This gave hope for escape. Later, corpses of those killed or having taken their own lives were found in those woods.

M. N. Leontieva's Address to Those Gathered in the Russian Camp Kellerberg, May 31, 1949, for the Blessing of the Monument to the Victims of Lienz, on the Fourth Anniversary of the Tragedy of Lienz, May 28-June 1, 1945

Even the Drau took victims: Cossack women tied children to their bodies and threw themselves into its turbulent waters in order not to give themselves and their children into the suffering and humiliation of Soviet torture chambers.

In this way, the "Democratic West" met and conducted the Cossacks "home," those Cossacks who had fought against Communism to save the world, who had completed thousands of miles in their *kibitkas* and on foot, who had hoped to find support for themselves in the free nations. They left the places in their native lands that were flooded with human blood and the evil of the Bolsheviks. They ran away from the coercion of satanic authority, from the horrors of the NKVD. They had gone in search of friends who could help them in their fight to free their Homeland and to defend other nations from Communism, which over the course of twenty-five years had slain souls and bodies in multitude.

The will of the Cossacks, their physical hardiness, in spite of having endured famines and long sentences in the prisons and labor camps of the USSR, was their stronghold.

They were not broken even by the extraordinary hardships of the long march from the banks of the Don, Kuban, and Terek to the Alps and the banks of the Drau. The Cossacks searched for truth. They searched for friends and allies in their fight for their Homeland. They made mistakes but did not despair. And when they happened upon the western allies, they placed their full trust in them, believing that the free nations would understand them better and help them. The Cossacks who were left in safety dispersed over Austria and Germany, settling in the camps of the occupiers—England, USA, and France, harboring their sorrow and working to restore a Europe that was alien, hungry, and cold to them.

Hearts mending, they accepted the news that the sentence given by Soviet authorities to execute their old Ataman, General P. N. Krasnov, along with their military commanders was carried out.

M. N. Leontieva

**

M. N. Leontieva's account, completed above, covered May 28 and June 1, when the forcible removal and turning over of the Cossacks began.

In days that followed, the same was continued in the stanitsa*s*, combat units, and with the Highlanders.

In addition to the account of M. N. Leontieva, there are letters from the survivors of the Tragedy of Lienz, brought in August 1945 by the Kuban Cossack I. K. Z., along with reports communicated to him, which are printed below.

•

Excerpts from the Letters of Terek Cossack A. V. F.

April 26, German units in Italy stopped fighting.

27th, insurgents arrested Mussolini.

28th, in Tolmezzo, three officers of the Italian National Militia arrived at Domanov's staff headquarters and demanded immediate removal of all Cossacks from Italy, first having turned over their weapons.

Domanov refused to give up weapons, but promised to take the Cossacks out of Italy.

May 1st, Cossack units stretched in a march from Italy to Austria.

What happened here is difficult to write about. Almost every Cossack had his own horse and cart or trap, brought from home—some obtained in Poland—while those who could manage it, took them from Italians. But all those families who were brought to Italy, individually or in groups, had nothing at all for transportation. People took wheelbarrows from Italians, two wheelers, and even baby carriages, hitched themselves to them, and towed their goods themselves.

The route was dangerous! Ten thousand people walked, rode, passed one another, and all pointed north—into Austria.

It was impossible to get anything to eat, for those who were in front, who had better-stronger horses, so having greater endurance, like locusts, destroyed everything along their route.

I went 62 kilometers on foot before I got a chance to rest.

Our route was as follows: Tolmezzo, Paluzza, Mauthen, Oberdrauburg, and Lienz.

All units stopped to bivouac along the line Oberdrauburg-Lienz, 21 kilometers in length. All spent the night under open sky or in a tent.

I arrived at Oberdrauburg May 4.

The English Red Cross took on the responsibility of feeding all the Cossacks. Gradually, units situated themselves in fields and woods, more or less fairly well.

Every day, newer and newer groups were added.

May 16, they began to disarm Cossacks, but weapons were not taken from officers.

May 23, the last unit arrived—this was the 5th Reserve Regiment from Svetlya.

May 27, weapons were taken from officers.

May 28, the English invited all officers to prepare for participation in a conference.

Having gathered all officers, even those on guard duty, they took them away in trucks, in the direction of Klagenfurt.

May 29-30, Soviet agitators visited the Cossack camp, calling on them to go home or be moved by force, otherwise. About the officers, they said that they had been given to Stalin.

Panic arose among the Cossacks.

31st of May, several men in English uniforms arrived and said that tomorrow, June 1, vehicles would arrive to take the Cossacks to the USSR. Those who resisted would be punished.

On the night of May 31 to June 1, many left for the hills.

Early on the morning of June 1st, all women and children gathered on the camp square. An iconostasis was set up. In the center (apparently in error, the author of the letter meant the platform with the iconostasis, on which the Holy services were carried out. Ed.), inside which the priests and choir placed themselves. Cossacks stood around them, and a unit of *junkers* arrived, having made the decision to protect the women and children from being forced to board.

Holy Services started.

About eight o'clock, trucks and tanks arrived with soldiers, among whom were many Russian speakers.

Tanks surrounded the praying crowd and gradually tightened their circle, pressing the people into the center. Much foul language was heard from them.

Without a single cry, people silently squeezed against each other.

When they had pressed together all they could, the first sounds of women screaming and children crying were heard. At this same time, the iconostasis (platform. Ed.) cracked and collapsed. The gonfalons fell...

English soldiers attacked the Cossacks and, stunning them with clubs and rifle butts to their heads, grabbed those who fell unconscious and threw them into trucks, then transported them to the station and locked them inside freight cars.

Here, something happened that was unbelievable: women threw their children under tank treads, then themselves after them. There were instances of suicide.

Several English soldiers became unnerved.

Then some sort of fat soldier wearing the uniform of an English sergeant stepped out and started to say that there was nothing to fear, that nothing would be done to anyone, that they needed to go home, for there was not enough food anyway, etc.

While he spoke, people became aroused and suddenly, with a cry, took off for the woods, breaking through the cordon and running. Several women tied children to themselves and jumped into the river and drowned. One—with two small children.

Many Cossacks went into the woods and there hung themselves.

In the following days, almost the same thing happened with each regiment.

When they came to take the 3rd Kuban Regiment, the Cossacks fell to their knees and sang "Christ has Arisen!" They were shot at.

When all was over, long lines of Cossack transports were left standing, stretching 21 kilometers from Lienz to Oberdrauburg. Thousands of horses wandered in the hills.

Residents started to catch the horses, and they began to rob the Cossack camps.

Over the course of a month, I watched as local residents dragged off suitcases, baskets, and sacks, and wheeled bicycles, carts, two-wheelers, etc.

Every day, Catholic priests gave sermons that upbraided residents for the robbery and called on them not to touch the Cossack camps, which were still covered with not-yet-dried blood.

Still, this did not help. Residents continued to drag off goods from morning until night.

The camps presented a sad picture over the entire distance from Lienz to Oberdrauburg.

Abandoned *kibitkas* and tents stood in silent rows along the highway. Thin, dirty, abandoned horses wandered through them, dejectedly looking at each passing automobile.

Piles of broken, torn, and broken-open suitcases, packages, and cases littered the ground between carts and *shatrams* [square Cossack tents—*trans*.], from which everything had been removed and what was of value taken. But dirty linen, caps with cockades, trouser stripes, military uniforms, worn boots, letters, albums, photographs, dishes of various kinds that were blackened by cook fires, Russian yokes and harnesses, all were thrown about in piles on fields and in woods.

This was all that was left of Cossachi Stan, which so shortly before had lived a feverish existence.

Here, in the Valley of the Drau, near Lienz, the English finished off the last of the Cossacks.

A. V. F

●

From the Letter of the Daughter of Colonel Z.

This letter was written spontaneously after the days of the handovers.

If You only knew how much grief, how much horror, we all lived through during this time.

But I will begin at the beginning, so that You will have a clear picture of everything that happened to our unfortunate Cossachi Stan.

When we arrived in Italy, it was the first time in twenty-five years that we felt that we were in a stanitsa—among our own.

Of course, all this was clearly only outward appearance, that is *papakhas* [tall sheepskin hats—*trans.*] everywhere, Cossack speech, trumpeters at dawn, and the singing of "Oh Kuban, you are our Homeland"... But within, everything was rotting, thoroughly dysfunctional by any concept of organization or leadership.

You remember, Papa was ill. We brought him in that condition to Italy and put him into a hospital in Tolmezzo, while we went to Covazzo—in the area of the Kuban stanitsa*s*.

They treated us reasonably well, that is, gave us a room, while others lived much worse, but this is understandable—the numbers of people gathering together was huge, and there was no place for them to stay.

And then... came the days of leaving Italy. Father had just returned from the hospital.

The entire trip was one continuous horror, which some day will get into our chronicles.

Horsemen left first, while the rest trudged along on foot, abandoning their things.

It was horrible! People came to complete despair, fearful of falling behind. Natasha and I completed the entire way over the pass and farther, almost 100 kilometers, on foot, having abandoned all our goods. Mama and Papa also walked a lot, and Papa was still ill. And in this way, thousands of people...

Coming into Austria, we settled into the camp near Lienz.

Some kind of inappropriate giddiness was felt by all.

Andrey Grigorievich Shkuro behaved very properly and with dignity, but they did not let him go anywhere, and even old Krasnov was put into some sort of apartment and forgotten.

The first blow was the arrest of Andrey Grigorievich, May 26.

The 28th, they gathered the officers, as if for a conference. Father had only the day before returned from the hospital, having relapsed into pneumonia after the crossing. We urged him not to go, but, obedient as always, he answered that, since all officers had been ordered to go, he must also.

They loaded them into automobiles and took them off in an unknown direction. Then they came for officers for another three days.

Few remained. They took away close to 2000 men. They took them from everywhere—from stanitsas and regiments.

Then we learned that they had been taken to the small city of Spittal, but there, we lost all trace of them.

Rumors flew extensively. My hair stood on end from the thought that they might have been sent to the Soviets.

For this, all blame Domanov. He either gave up the Cossacks carelessly or on purpose—God only knows.

June 1st, we were forced to go to the Soviets. What we lived through is probably known to You. Many of us carry scars from this shipment to this day, Mama numbering among them.

Then they took away the regiments. The same thing took place with them.

L. Z.

•

The Letter of Yesaul V. N. M.

—This officer behaved with great circumspection toward all that took place in Italy, on the route, and on the Drau. He refrained from the trip of May 28 to the "conference," which saved him.

Poorly dressed, ill, hungry, we walked the entire route from Tolmezzo to Lienz. Many shot themselves. Others fell into despair and perished from the cold.

When we arrived in Austria, it was clear to me that we had been given up.

And so it was. Under the guise of a conference, they irretrievably took away our best officers. In all our attempts at tracing them down, we have failed up to now.

June 1st and there were more nightmarish days which are difficult to write about. Mothers threw themselves into the Drau with their children. Entire families shot themselves in the woods and hung themselves. May the Lord rest their souls, so innocently and prematurely perished.

V. N. M.

•

The Account of Cossack I. K. Z., From Baysugskoy St.

—Cossack I. K. Z. lived through and witnessed all that took place on the banks of the Drau on June 1st and in the days that followed. Much of what he related has already been given in the letters printed above and, therefore, appears as confirmation of the aforementioned.

April 27, Italian partisans gave the Cossacks their second and final demand to give up their weapons.

Domanov and Lukyanenko (Colonel, leading the Kuban Cossacks in the Cossachi Stan.—Ed.) carried on negotiations with them, with the result that they obtained the right to leave Italian territory in three days with their weapons in hand.

At this time, partisans approached Covazzo, occupying the commanding heights above it.

At 12 o'clock on the night of April 28, the withdrawal began, from Covazzo toward Paluzza, and farther to the Austrian border.

We went in this order: Staff of the Field Ataman, workshops, stanitsas—first Don, behind them Kuban, and Terek in the rear.

Domanov stayed in Tolmezzo with Lukyanenko and a regimental convoy, awaiting the arrival of the combat units (which were located in the area of the city of Udino and farther north.—Ed.).

Of General P. N. Krasnov, Z. could say nothing. He had heard that he had left by automobile in advance, but how credible this was —he could not say.

In view of the fact that there was not enough transportation, from three to five hundred families, Don and Kuban, stayed behind in Covazzo. Cossack combat units, who arrived the next day, rescued them. The partisans went off into the hills, leaving the village.

The Cossack families who had been left behind in this village recounted how on the morning of that same day, firing rifles into the air, partisans had entered, searched for weapons, and took away some valuables. Then they chased everyone into the school and placed a guard around it.

Those Cossacks moved farther, to Tolmezzo, taking their families with them.

The stanitsas left, but not without avoiding partisan attacks. Units of Badoglio's army pressed the rears of our combat units.

April 30 and May 1, stanitsas and units crossed over the pass, as they crossed the Austro-Italian border and on May 1 descended to the village of Kötschach. They stayed there until May 5. On that day, crossing over a small pass, they descended into the valley of the River Drau and headed toward Lienz.

They came to this city May 6 and stopped east of it, camping in fields and woods, according to Hosts and sections. Kuban Cossacks were some four *versts* [one *verst* is two-thirds of a mile—*trans.*] from the city.

They fed in those days on whatever they could find.

May 9, units of the English army came to Lienz. They paid the Cossacks no mind.

The Caucasian Legions (Cherkess, Kabardine, Karachaev, and others), who had left Italy a little ahead of the Cossacks, had positioned their camps closer to Oberdrauburg.

May 10, the Cossack Command approached the English with a request that provisions be given out. The answer was that nothing would be given out for the time being.

On the 15th, the Red Cross began to provide food. The first week, it was little: 150 grams of hardtack, canned goods, sugar, and other staples. After a week, they started to provide 400 grams hardtack and, daily, 110 grams of sugar, and increased the number of canned meats, butter, and lard.

The camps lived without interference. No English were seen in them.

During the time of our stay in the camp in Lienz, Brigade Commander General Tikhotsky visited the 4th Terek-Stavropol Regiment, in which Cossack Z. was at that time.

The commander of the sotnya asked him about the attitude of the English toward the Cossacks. Tikhotsky answered that the English had said that Cossacks should continue their activities, that they would soon be useful.

May 25, the English ordered Cossacks to give up their weapons, explaining that, since the weapons had become obsolete, they would be replaced with new, up-to-date ones.

They left officers their weapons, but on May 27, took them away even from them.

May 28, all officers were called "to a conference" in Spittal, as it was called, to decide questions of reorganization of the Cossack army.

Vehicles were provided that took away more than 2000 Cossack officers and Caucasian legionaries, whether combat or living with families. Only an unknown number of officers did not go. In the main, they were those living in stanitsas and not wearing military uniforms.

Further on, I. K. Z. writes about what took place after the officers had been taken away, right up to June 1st.

Since all this falls into what has already been published earlier, this part of his account has been skipped in order to avoid repetition. Further on, he says that on that day of June 1st, when the Cossacks and their families were being taken away in the area of Camp Peggetz, the same occurred in the Terek stanitsas, which were located farther from Lienz. In Z's impression, it was easier to escape from there. Approximately 10% of their total did.

The place in which this was carried out was two to three kilometers in width and covered in meadows, sparse woods, and bushes.

There were no English guards immediately in place, but English posts occupied all exits from the valley, so that the majority of escapees fell into their hands.

On the 1st of June, the 1st and 2nd Don Regiments were loaded to be sent to the Soviets. They refused to board. Machine gun fire was opened up on them. Many were killed and injured. (Removal of the Cossacks of the 1st and 2nd Don Regiments did not take place on the 1st, but the 3rd or 4th, of June.—Ed.)

As in the stanitsas, armored cars were aimed at them. There were incidents of crushing and stabbing. Cossacks were driven to wagons and loaded on them.

As Z. heard later, the 1st and 2nd of June took place also with the Highlanders.

The morning of the 2nd, the 3rd Kuban Regiment, the Artillery Division, and the Reserve Regiment began to be loaded (at 5 o'clock in the morning.)

Again, the same picture…

On this day, Z. escaped from camp and watched what was going on in the valley from the cliffs, using binoculars. A small group of Cossacks was with him.

He saw the Terek-Stavropol Regiment taken to trucks. Shaken by all that took place, the Cossacks had offered almost no resistance. Half the regiment was taken away that day. It was announced that the rest would be taken away the next day.

During the course of the evening, the majority of them ran away.

June 3, the rest of the regiment was loaded, and on the 4th, the escapees. The English had caught them with the help of aviation, which had opened fire on those trying to leave.

Local residents took the Cossack's goods. The English— horses. Cossacks were designated to watch and pasture them, one Cossacks per twenty horses. The horses grazed in meadows. Cossacks stayed in all manner of huts with them and without any guard. Several of them took off.

After June 4, there were no more removals, but all the captured Cossacks and Highlanders were accommodated in a camp near Lienz, first in a field, but then barbed wire was strung.

They had English guards. Leaving this camp was easy enough, but it was difficult to get out of the valley.

Z., with a group of Cossacks, got out through the mountains to the south. Along the way, the group steadily increased—to sixty men. They turned back at the Italian border and headed toward Innsbruck.

Going around English posts, they mainly went above the snow line and occasionally crossed glaciers.

June 11th, during one of the crossings, they were surrounded by English airplanes and fired at, with one Cossack wounded.

The Cossacks hid themselves in the mountains. The airplanes flew away, but when they resumed their journey and crossed over the pass, aerial reconnaissance arrived anew and followed them farther. When the Cossacks finally came down from the snow line, they stumbled into a large English post and had to surrender.

The English brought them down from the mountains, put them in trucks, and delivered them to Lienz.

After having been locked in the camp to which even a "*sotov*," someone who wanted to return to his homeland, had been brought, Z. left the camp after a few days and successfully got to Salzburg.

Written from the words of **I. K. Z.**

•

The Tragedy of Cossack Forces

Under this heading, in the pages of several numbers of the journal, "The Sentinel," there was a series of articles in 1948 and 1949 on the Cossack tragedy on the River Drau in Southern Austria.

The editor and publisher of "The Sentinel," V. V. Orekhov, kindly gave us permission to reprint all the articles in this book as excerpts or in full. Two are included here.

The first, under the signature—Colonel Steppenoy (a pseudonym) was published in "The Sentinel," *No* 284/4, in April 1949.

In it is characterized, to a certain extent, the attitude toward the Cossacks of the leaders of the English Command during the handovers.

The second article gives, in the main, statistical details on the officers turned over, the means of transportation used in taking them out, and the English armed guards.

A former staff officer, commissioned under Field Ataman General Domanov, who was with him until 1 o'clock on the tragic day of May 28, 1945, asks us to report the following eye-witness account, based on his personal observations:

The regiments of Field Ataman General Domanov arriving in the Austrian Tyrol numbered around thirty-two thousand men in all, having with them a collection of Cossack families and a large line of carts with Russian refugees. Regiments situated in full order in the narrow valley along the River Drau in the region of Ober-Lienz.[*] Refugees similarly threw in their own lots with the combat units and stopped beneath the open sky. Only a small portion occupied the later-to-be-famous Camp Peggetz. Several establishments were situated in the area, too. The staff of the Field Ataman stayed in Kotschan (Kötschach.—Ed.) the first five days of May 1945, but then relocated to Lienz, where General P. N. Krasnov was also, with his wife Lydia Fyodorovna. They settled into a villa that had been allotted by the English to General Domanov, but the latter yielded it to General Krasnov.

General Krasnov and General Domanov often hosted one another and were very friendly toward each other. There was never heard to be any disagreement between them. Quite the opposite, General Domanov coordinated all his important decisions with P. N. Krasnov.

General Krasnov no longer had an official position in Austria, but it was only by his own wishes that he did not maintain any contacts with the English. This did not mean that P. N. Krasnov had no interest in what affected Cossack affairs. It was this interest that caused him to write his first letter to British Field Marshal Alexander

_____

[*] —Apparently a typographical error slipped through. It should be "in the region of Oberdrauburg-Lienz."

137

(Commander-in-Chief of the army), pointing out to him the particular situation of the Cossack Hosts; he received no reply to the letter.

The conduct of the English was somewhat mysterious. It did not then call forth any suspicions. They left the Cossacks alone. Order and discipline were maintained in the regiments. Later, not too much before the horrible day of May 28, 1945, a British lieutenant-general inspected the Cossack military school and was surprised by its orderliness, joked, smiled, spoke of the future of Russia, tasted the Cossacks' food, and ordered that rations be increased. Suddenly, four days after that visit, their attitude changed sharply. In response to General Domanov's complaint that English soldiers were taking Cossack horses without permission, that general proclaimed: —"There are no Cossack horses here. They belong to the King of England, along with the Cossack prisoners... Until that time, the term, "prisoners," had never been used for Cossacks by the English.

Having been informed of this by General Domanov, P. N. Krasnov immediately wrote a second letter to Field Marshal Alexander, who from the time that he was a young officer was known as a friend of the Russian Army, which he earlier considered himself to be—with a request to save the Cossacks. This letter, too, received no reply.

Instead of an answer, there came an order: "All officers carrying arms should give them up at 12 o'clock on the 27th of May, 1945, according to the areas of their units." The weapons were quickly turned in.

On the next day, that is, May 28, 1945, the English Major Davies came to General Domanov and ordered him in the name of the British Command to come with all his officers at one o'clock in the afternoon to "the place at which weapons had been turned in" in order to go to Spittal for a conference. Captain Butlerov was the interpreter for this conversation. Seeing the military official ext. ad. [надв. сов.—*trans.*] to D. standing there in narrow officer's stripes, Davies unexpectedly added in Russian—"and officials."

The order to come to the place where the weapons had been turned in had the aim of catching all officers, for which there had been prepared a list of those present.

The Field Ataman immediately sent out to all k-ram units and regional atamans an order to come to his staff offices at 11 o'clock the morning of May 28. After this, a tall English general arrived at General Domanov's lodgings and once more repeated the order given by Major Davies, adding: "Please do not forget to convey my request to old Krasnov. I particularly ask you to do so." Who would have thought then that behind this request from a British general, such a cruel trap was hidden, moreover that the general then would express his gratitude to General Domanov, in most flattering terms, for the impeccable order of the Cossack units. No Russian officer, taught along the noble traditions of the Imperial Army, would think about any betrayal at that moment.

At 11 o'clock on the morning of May 28, 1945, all unit commanders and regional atamans gathered at the staff headquarters. General Domanov, outwardly calm, presented the order from the British Command with an even, impassive voice. Silence first ruled, then there began a rain of questions. Here are a few: "Can we take our things?"—"No."—"What about those officers who are skeptical and set off into the hills?" General Domanov looked at the colonel who had asked the question and, in the same even voice, without change of expression to his face, answered:

—"You command your regiment. You understand me."—

"Exactly, General sir."—"And what awaits us?—asked Kuban General T-o."—Nothing good. Probably—barbed wire,"—the ataman answered. So, they went off, with few exceptions. Not just the officers, priests: Father Alexander and Father Ioann (they were turned over, too.) Journalist Tarussky, having lived in the Stan as a civilian, went in order to share the lot of his brother-officers.

At 1 o'clock in the afternoon, English autos were brought to the staff, in one of which sat Generals Krasnov and Domanov. An English officer requested to join them; they cordially invited him in. —"I believe in God and his kindness," Krasnov whispered as he left.

Only officers who were ill, invalid, or on guard duty were left in the Stan. They were captured the following day (searches in quarters) and sent in addition. It was absolutely clear that the English had decided to capture and turn over all without exception, for within five days, they began to round up every defenseless person, regardless of gender or age. That the Bolsheviks needed General Krasnov and that they pressured the English for him, there is no doubt. This is confirmed by the phrase of the English general: "Do not forget to tell old Krasnov."

––––––

"The Tragedy of Cossack Forces," as it was titled in "The Sentinel" is now in the past. Of those who perished, we can only pray; they perished for us and perhaps saved us, we who remain. Even in our mean age, this vile deed has created such a storm that to carry on farther in the same spirit was already impossible.

But may it be of service to the Russian people, so easily appeased and forgiving—still one more lesson and one more chance to establish that one must depend only on **personal** strength and believe only in **one's own** words.

Colonel B. Steppenoy

**
*

> This article is reprinted in full, with the exception of the list of officers given over, from the journal "The Sentinel" *No* 275/6, July 1, 1948.

To this day, events ending in a bloody tragedy for a thirty-thousand mass of Cossacks and Russian nationals during the first days of the end of the Second World War, in Austrian territory, in the city of Lienz and its surroundings, along the valley of the Drau, have yet to be examined fully in print.

And now, in the days of the three-year observance of this tragic end of implacable anticommunists, the days of May 28 and June 1, 1945, have entered the history not just of Cossackdom, but of the Russian people, as memorials of sorrow, grief, and mourning.

Drawn below in cold, impartial ciphers and covered in black crepe, the names of those gone to never return, perished and tortured, will freshen the memory of that tragic day.

At the bloody cost of many millions, beginning with the foul deed of slaying the Tsar's Family, carried on to the measureless venom of Yalta—unending forced repatriation.

Capable of all things, applying the points of the Yalta agreement, slyly and cleverly using the naiveté of the allies, the Bolsheviks brought to a bloody insult this number of former enemies —the participants in the White movement.

————

These were old enemies, pursued for almost three decades, having earlier escaped from the hands of the CHEKA. It was absolutely necessary that retribution be taken on them. The enemies were inveterate, irreconcilable counterrevolutionaries from the years of 1917-1922. They were White Guards of every "color" of white army. They were: Denikinists, Mamotovites, Krasnovites, Shkurists, Kolchakovists, Hetmanovites, Petlyurists, Makhnovites, and Kutepovists. All had followed the difficult path of emigrant life starting on the deadly isles of Lemnos, Cyprus, and the Princes' Islands. They went through and endured it all with tenacity. Seeking kindness, but bitter over their reception by the foreign governments and kingdoms that welcomed them to the heat of colonial islands and the cold of northern dominions. All went through school, starting as porters, boot blacks, peddlers, elevator boys, and chauffeurs, and ending up as professors, performers, physicians, inventors—hard living in strange lands. And as much as they hated those temporary jobs, they all loved their homeland, which now, on the brink of death, they would meet again, but not in open battle, but defenseless, surrendered to the scandalous injustice of Yalta.

All the horrors of their own deaths paled before the fear of torture and questioning, agony, and torment.

The Soviet commanders rejoiced at meeting up with them. It promised not just the flow of a sea of new and fresh, long awaited blood, but even more. That blood bath would reward them with special privileges, medals, ribbons, and awards, given out by their leadership.

For the true flower of counterrevolutionaries, genuine, implacable, constant foes of Soviet power, now stood before the Soviet commanders.

On the basis of an agreement between the leaders of the allied commands, signed in Vienna, May 23, 1945, in fulfillment of the Yalta agreement, the entire population of the refugee camp, "Cossachi Stan," was subject to being turned over by force to the Soviet commanders. The refugee camp, "Cossachi Stan," had fled from northern Italy and the approaching Red Army and had temporarily settled in the valley of the raging Drau River.

Based on false information, the allies took those in the camp in the area of Lienz into custody, interring the entire population as a special part of the German SS.

On May 28, 1945, all officers, as "leaders of squadrons of German SS-partisans, composed of counterrevolutionaries and White Bandit Cossacks, having gone over permanently into service for the Germans after having deserted from the Red Army as traitors to their countries," were subject to transport to the city of Spittal.

The entire officer complement was required without exception to go to a "conference," also in the city of Spittal. Those in reserve, on leave, or on guard duty were also included in the list of officers that was provided earlier to the allied command by the staff of the Field Ataman, in fulfillment of an order from the commandant, Major Davies,

The order of the Field Ataman, requiring presence without exception at the "conference," in the main applied to 2756 people (according to the staff list.)

Among them were the following Cossack ranks:

Generals—35, colonels—167, host starshins—283, yesauls—375, under-yesauls—460, sotniks—526, cornets—756, military officials—124, medical personnel—15, military photographers—2, field priests—2, interpreters—2, liaison officers to ROA—5.

Loaded into automobiles arranged by order of the Ataman to drive them to a "conference," with the instructions that "toward evening, they would return again and not to take any things with them, not even their overcoats,"—2201 men.

Freed while still in Lienz and under house arrest, the English-speaking interpreter (Sotnik Yakovenko)—an old emigrant, having lived in Japan—1 man.

Announced as escaped *en route* from Lienz to Oberdrauburg —5 men.

Jumping out of moving automobiles before reaching the city of Spittal—3 men.

Freed by the allies from the camp in the city of Spittal: priests —1, military officials—2, medical personnel and military physicians —12 men (in that number were Prof. Tikhomirov, Verbitsky, and others.)

Freed juvenile Cossack, special parachute-jumper of group "Ataman" of the Cossack school, nicknamed "Red" and "Transrussian"—1 man.

Escaping from the concentration camp in Spittal—5 men.

Ending his life in camp (shooting himself)—General Silkin.

Ending in suicide: Colonel Mikhailov, Yevgeny Tarussky, and Kharmalov—3 men.

Escaping while under guard, jumping from a moving automobile during transfer from camp in the city of Spittal to Graz, at that time occupied by Russian forces (in this number of escapees: photographer, military official, and liaison officer to the ROA)—4 men.

Shot trying to escape near Graz by allied guards—15 men.

Found prior to automobiles being unloaded during the handover to the Soviet Command, poisoned *en route*—2 men.

Turned over to specially designated units, 2146 officers; from which the Soviet leader, Colonel Lysym freed 3 men as officers of the Soviet military intelligence service.[*]

On May 31, General Shkuro and his adjutant, Sotnik Alexander Polovinym were taken from the city of Spittal in a special light automobile.

---

[*] The data on the numbers of officers turned over cannot be considered as absolutely accurate. Already in the following number of the "Sentinel," there is a correction. There are other inaccuracies. For example, there is evidence that Colonel Mikhailov was taken down from a noose.

Sent on the staff bus for special questioning and delivery to Moscow, former generals of Russian and White Armies—12 men.

The fate of the remaining 2133 offices appears to be as follows:

Shot by Soviet convoy on the road to Vienna—120 men.

Disappeared during repeated questioning (in fulfillment of agreements) during transfer from Graz to Vienna—1030 men.

Disappeared and removed for questioning in Vienna—983 men.

The complement of the officers given over to the Soviets stood as:

Cossacks: Greater Don Host—870, Kuban Host—233, Terek Host—203, Russians—176, Ukrainians—63, Belorus—5, "Folksdeutch" [Russian-born Germans—*trans*.]—3, Poles—2, Kalmyks—3, Armenians—2, Georgians—3, gypsy—1, Ossetians—7, Tatars—3, Azerbaijani—3, Kabardines—3, Cherkess—4, and additional nationalities—8.

Of all the officers and command staff given over to the Soviets, former Soviet citizens turned out to be only 32 percent. Under strict terms of the Yalta agreement, the others should not have been subject to compulsory handover. Here, once more, it became clear who was needed there for their turn for reprisals.

During transportation of officers from Spittal to Vienna, the strictest of measures were taken against escape attempts. The military transports provided by the allies and the numerous mechanized guards underlined once more that it was not a "return to the homeland," but the fulfillment of the Yalta act of forced repatriation. In hindsight, the commissions on repatriations appear to be the extraordinary ones of the nineteen twenties. ["Extraordinary" commissions were the basis for the CHEKA—*trans*.]

Means of transport provided:

Passenger buses, including the staff bus—4, trucks, covered in taut canvass—58, military all-terrain vehicles of closed type—8, light automobiles—3, "first aid" vehicle (with dead and injured officers, found earlier in field hospitals and also subject to being turned over to the Soviets)—2.

The guard, armed as before an attack with newer automatic weapons, for the two thousand unarmed officers who had given up their weapons back in Lienz, consisted of:

Chauffeurs and assistants, having the newest release of automatics—140 men, 25 tankettes with typical crews—70 men, 105 motorcycles with side cars—110 men, with automatics on roofs and in the cabins of each automobile—70 men, special trucks at the head of the column with 30 men, two special trucks at the rear of the column of autos, fitted with tear gas and radio receivers—30 men, commanders with adjutants and interpreters—15 men. In all, 465 men.

Aside from the two fighter planes patrolling the air, additional weaponry consisted of automatics—310, machine guns—125, and cannon—21.

… The dust swirled sorrow along that road on which the transports carried off the sentenced. They rode into unquestionable peril, preferring death from the bullets of the allied guards to a return to life in the Soviet "heaven" that thirty years before had not been on the map of Imperial Russia, the countless concentration-"correctional" and "labor" camps.

The dust had not yet settled when, echelon after echelon, a new load of human lives rolled on steel rails *en route* to the east. It was a load made up of ranks of residents of refugee camps—of Cossacks, from distinguished, destroyed families, of old women and young maidens, the elderly and the *junker, djigits* and invalids. All of them, finding themselves becoming part of an unfolding bloody tragedy, futilely appealed to the Bishop of Canterbury, to Churchill, King George… The poison of Yalta—forced repatriation—had already poisoned the collecting points, the places where refugees gathered, and the prisoner-of-war camps.

After the complement of officers had been turned over, the thirty thousand-refugee population of Camp Peggetz was treated to sharp reprisals. And, like an echo, answered by ominous bloody events at Kempton, Farely [spelling could not be verified—*trans.*], Gessen, Manheim, Dachau, Plattling, Salzburg, Daggendorf, Badvas, Hof [spelling for previous two entries could not be verified—*trans.*], and a whole row of unknown stamps of the occurrence of forcible return to the "homeland." Then began endless torture by the suffering souls and the hypocritical calls of "the Homeland awaits."

And a distant, inaccessible, frozen, ice-covered cruelty, jumping and whipping by Stakhanovism in piling up "middle-progressive" norms—the Homeland awaits.

Vasyuta Serdyukova

•

More on the Handover of Officers of the Cossachi Stan, May 28, 1945

With the aim of leaving Cossacks leaderless in order to turn them over more easily to the Bolsheviks, the technical side of removing the officers was worked out thoroughly by the English Command.

The success of this "operation" resulted from lies and speed.

The officers were fooled, being told that they were invited to a "conference," while their actual removal was being carried out at the same time at all the camps stretching from Lienz to Oberdrauburg

We are often asked: How could the officers of the Cossachi Stan let themselves be fooled so easily, and almost to a man leave for this imaginary conference?

We can only hypothesize about their conduct based on a study of the available material.

It must be supposed that the main reasons were:

Thorough preparation of the betrayal of the Cossacks by the English Command and its skillful execution in actuality by Major Davies, the immediate dbbirector of the removal of officers and Cossacks of the Cossachi Stan

Russian officers were accustomed to trusting the word of an officer and did not allow a thought of the possibility of betrayal by the English officers.

In connection with the trust of the officers taken away, tbhere arises another question: Were there armed English guards on the cars provided for the officers' trip to the "conference?"

Witness testimony diverges on this question. Some say that there was no kind of guard, others insist the opposite, but give its composition differently.

As can be seen from what follows, there were guards, but organized in such a way that it did not jump out at the eyes of those being taken away.

1. Excerpt from the Letter of a Cossack Mother on the Removal of Officers From Peggetz

... They were evacuated (she says of her own son) over the pass with the Cossacks at the end of April 1945, into the valley of the River Drau, near Lienz.

The situation was troubling and uncertain. There were morning and evening roll calls daily, and strict orders not to remove shoulder tabs.

They held continuous watches in the staff of the Kuban Cossack Ataman, Colonel L. (head of Kuban Cossacks in the Cossachi Stan—Ed.) Various rumors went around. People began to leave—went into the hills, woods, and took off shoulder tabs.

In the end, May 27, weapons were taken away from officers, after which, the mood fell into hopelessness, but May 28, an order was given to go to a "conference" in Spittal.

At noon, on the square of the camp, Don, Kuban, and Terek Cossacks formed up into separate groups. Each column had its ataman at the head. Most were in military uniform, with Cossack shoulder tabs and sleeve patches—"Don," "Kuban," and "Terek."

They were told: "Do not take your things," since they would return to camp by evening, but their loved ones, as they said farewell to their kin, felt trouble in their hearts and slipped them what was allowed: warm things, tobacco, food…

The columns formed up as if for a last parade. They went out through the gates of the camp to where the English trucks stood—there seemed to be forty or fifty.

On each, beside a chauffeur, there were two with sub-machine gunners in the cabin.

They loaded. For this, some of the officers had to sit on the knees of others.

Then they closed the walls (lowered the canvass), and we became quite alarmed by this reinforced guard and all that was uncertain ahead.

Suddenly—the terrible shriek of a young girl saying farewell to her father, so frightened, heart-breaking… She tore herself away from her mother and ran to the truck her father was in. She felt that she would never see him again.

All were shaken by her childish despair…

At last, farewell salutes, and the trucks moved down the road.

On the first day, we knew nothing. They took those who for some reason did not leave on the 28th of May to Spittal.

Of course, there were various rumors that they had been held up several days.

We all gave, in our way, the things that they might need. The English took them. No one told anything. (Then, as is said, those things burned up in Spittal.)

For a long time, we did not know how cleverly the trap had been set for our close ones.

About 1949, I received word that my son was in exile, somewhere beyond the Arctic Circle. Since that time I know nothing about him.

A Mother

2. From a Letter About Being Taken from the Same Place

Concerning how the loading of officers into automobiles took place, I will at the same time write about the entire situation for several days before and after the removal of officers.

For now, I can say that there was no special convoy, but there were at least two armed soldiers in every truck.

Most officers were blindly obedient to directions from the staff and gave in to herd instincts, unaware of their own actions and consequences. They formed into columns and followed the one who took command, ordering them to form up, go, and take seats in the automobiles.

For them, going in columns, this convoy was not evident, and if anyone had noticed it while taking a seat, already in the automobile —it was too late.

To a man standing on the side and watching what was happening, it was clear that the armed soldiers were a convoy, even if not very substantial. I add that the automobiles were covered with canvass, so that even I could not determine the number of soldiers, but I saw those sitting near the officers as the columns approached. Their heads could be seen inside the cabins.

Cunning Englishmen and their friends, the Soviet agents who had slipped into our ranks several days before, did preparation for this "convoy."

When I have time, I will write a full account of those "naïve souls" (among them the sculptor shaping a monument to the union of Cossacks and Englishmen) who believed in the possibility of some sort of conference.

People had simply been blinded... Yes, and that is somewhat understandable. Such baseness is not known in the history of all the wars on earth.

Few expected it.

In addition, I give two examples: one, herd instinct; the other, belief in a conference.

1—When the last row of a column of officers passed us to be loaded into trucks, Host Starshin L., standing next to me, made a giddy attempt to get into line. But I stopped him firmly by the hand

and dragged him into an emptied barrack, from which we continued to watch the loading and departure of the automobiles.

2—When I returned again with him to the strings of carts of Pashkovskoy Stanitsa, immediately after the departure of the automobiles and on the same highway (we had come by a different road), L. rubbed his leg, stopped, and began to take off his boots.

At this time we see some kind of two-horse cart catching up to us. The man on it was excitedly urging on his horses.

I stopped it. It turns to be Yesaul Z., going for provisions from the commissary supply.

Knowing him from the 1ˢᵗ Kuban Campaign, I ask:

—"Why are you hurrying so?"—He answers.

—"I am hurrying so that I will have time to return and distribute the goods and still make it to the conference in the extra automobile that is coming for those left behind for various reasons."

He gave us a ride for a little way. Parting, I suggested that he would do better not to hurry and to miss the automobile, but he gave the horses a flick and rushed off.

Half a year later, I met his younger brother (now living in England) and asked him how was his yesaul brother—did he make it to the conference?

—"Yes," he said—"he made it and did not return, leaving a wife and three grown daughters."

Two of them, forgetting what the English had done to their father, married English soldiers. The third is with her mother and to this day awaits her father. (Until 1950, she lived in Austria, in the city of Villach.)

G. S.

3. From the Letter of a Former *Junker* of the Cossack School Concerning the Removal of Officers of the School from the Village of Amlach (near Lienz)

About the departure of our officers, I can offer the following, to which I am myself a witness.

On the day that followed our (*junkers* and officers) weapons being taken, several English trucks and two tankettes came to us in the village of Amlach, where the school was and the teaching command stayed...

The loading of officers began.

We all had slept in the square in front of the church and began to give our farewells to those leaving.

There was not a special convoy in the generally accepted sense—bayonets attached, etc.

They all load as if voluntarily, as instructed by the staff of the Field Ataman.

An armed soldier sat beside the chauffeur of each truck. Several men were in each tankette.

The mood of the officers was divided: some were pessimistic, others, lulled by belief in the conference, increased rations, and new clothing, were perfectly calm and accepted the convoy as a necessity. There were places along the way to the conference, they said, with large numbers of Yugoslavian partisans.

I must conclude from the words and actions of the head of the school, Colonel M., that he saw nothing good coming from the journey.

Giving us a word in farewell, he could not hide his tears, even though he was a brave and steadfast man.

Just before loading, he changed the officer who was on guard, naming Host Starshin Sh., since the English, certainly just to put to sleep any vigilance, were allowing one guard officer to remain at the school and one at the teaching command.

On leaving Colonel Sh., Colonel M. said to him:

—"You remain to guard—you have small children."

Obviously, he anticipated something wrong and wanted to save H. Sta. Sh., whom he greatly valued, for the sake his large family.

I remember the depressed attitude of Sotnik Kh., who said, while seating himself in the auto:

—"Farewell brothers! Think kindly of me."

The rest, trusting the English, were calm.

They left in this order: tankette in front, then the autos, tankette in back.

After the officers left, many of us realized that something was wrong and urged Host Starshin Sh. to change into a *junker's* uniform. But he refused.

After two hours, a car came again, with a young English officer, and took the three who remained: Colonel V. (Terek), who lay ill, as a few days before, he had hurt himself falling off his bicycle, Host Starshin Sh., and one other officer from the Teaching Command.

Of interest was the conversation through interpreter P. between Sh. and the English lieutenant. Sh., obviously suspecting something wrong, asked, as one officer to another, that he be left alone for five minutes (apparently thinking to shoot himself). But the lieutenant began insisting on "the honor of an English officer" that they were only going to a conference and would return in several hours.

Host Starshin Sh. accepted his word.

The next day, an English officer came to us in a tankette with the interpreter for Domanov's staff, Ya. (living now in England).

The Englishman announced that we all were to be repatriated, but to our cavalry sergeant's question about what would happen if we did not want to go to our Homeland, he answered that, in such a case, force would be applied.

May 30, considering passive resistance to be useless, I went to the stanitsa for my father, who similarly had avoided going to the "conference." We went into the woods together.

V. S.

To this letter was appended a list of officers removed from the Military School, twenty-one in all, among whom was the father of the interpreter, Colonel P. (The interpreter was not turned over himself and is now found in the USA.) Those turned over were: Don —12, Kuban—6, Terek—3.

Among the officers of the school who were accidentally spared: Don Host Sotnik S. and Kuban Cornet Ch. The doctor for the Military School, Kh. L., and the doctor's assistant, Kuban Cossack S., were also spared.

4. From the Letter of Col. L. "On Muddled Minds"

To this day, I cannot make out the psychological condition of the officers when told about the "conference."

Seemingly, even if not believing, they nonetheless obediently seated themselves in the trucks.

You remember N. A. Sh. He was a careful, practical man. He believed in something only when he could convince himself that it was something that must be believed.

He came to Lienz from a Viennese hospital, where he had been recovering from wounds. At the time of the handovers, he was entirely capable of walking freely and had almost recovered fully.

In the words of an eyewitness, on the day after the removal of the officers, he was sitting out in the sun near the premises in which he lived.

An English truck pulled up and stopped near him.

—"What's with you—were you wounded?" he was asked from the vehicle.

—"Yes,"—answered Sh.

—"Then have a seat. We're going for a ride, there, at least, you will be treated and cared for."

Sh. took his bundle and sat down in the vehicle.

Subsequently, he shared the fate of the officers of the Cossachi Stan.

Meanwhile, a month before, I had spoken with him in Vienna, as it happened, about the possibility of a catastrophe, in general. He told me that in such an occurrence, one had to head into the hills and even farther. And, suddenly, such submissiveness, and only days after General Krasnov and the officers were taken away.

L.

5. The Story of Oly P.—An Old Emigrant

Friday, June 1, we were all supposed to gather on the square of the camp for prayers. Mama's leg pained her (erysipelas of the knees). She could not stand for long, but I was afraid to leave her by herself in the barrack. All that happened around us was such a nightmare that I decided to run away from the camp into the hills. I took a basket of provisions and two blankets—all our worldly goods. We had no other things, because they had all been stolen in Covazzo by passing "good people" while we were hiding from an air raid.

We crossed over the river on the bridge and took the road into the hills. But Mama could no longer walk, so we had to hide behind bushes in the foothills.

Soon we heard shots and the noise of automobiles on the road.

We spent two nights and three days there.

When it was quiet, I looked out from the bushes, but as soon as I saw an English patrol or automobile, empty or loaded with people, I hid.

The sound of a man's voice or footsteps close to us made us tremble, and our hearts filled with horror.

In two days, we ate all that we had. On the third day, I reached such a condition that I no longer cared where I wound up—in heaven or in hell.

Mama felt very poorly. She had a fever.

On the third day, toward evening, we heard steps approaching us, along with English words.

What we went through in that moment—only the Lord God knows.

The bushes spread apart and… In front of us stood English soldiers.

They looked us over, discussed something, then one of them offered in broken German:

—Can your mother walk?

I explained to him that we were old emigrants, that Mama's leg hurt, and that she could no longer walk.

Probably I looked totally dejected—I was so distressed that I could not speak, as in what follows.

The soldier patted me on the shoulder and said that we had nothing to fear, that he would take Mama to the dispensary.

With the help of the English soldier, Mama was led close to the barracks that housed invalids. The next day, she was taken to a hospital in Lienz.

I found gray hairs on me after those days, even though I was only thirty years old.

O. P.

6. Two Instances During the Removal of Officers of the Cossachi Stan

—Excerpt from an article in the journal, "Our News," [Наши Вести—*trans.*] *No* 53/2190, from April 15, 1954.

On the street in Lienz, I stumble on a stanishnik. He is a typical, thickset, Kuban Cossack.

—"Come on here, I want to tell you something"—he calls to me—"we'll drink some tea, have a chat about... I stayed here when they gave our officers up,"—he said as we drank tea—"and here I live. They were gathered for a conference. Several young people understood that here was danger and ran away, hiding in the woods, while the others went into the trucks and were immediately surrounded by machine guns. My generals—I was near the generals —told me: "Prepare dinner for us. We will return toward evening." This is how they returned! One woman did get her husband released. She must have been some Cossack woman. She runs, jumps across machine guns, searching for her husband among the trucks, yelling in French. I hid behind a tree, looking at it all, thinking: How did they not kill her? She pushed one soldier. He did nothing. "OK" he shouted. And they all began to yell "OK" at her as she jumped across more machine guns. She rescued her husband, found him in the last truck. For a long time, she and the sergeant muttered something to one another, then he pulled her husband from the truck. Saved the man. Another *baba* cried all the while—to no purpose."...

———————————

I crossed the ocean, got to know the commander of the 1st Engineering Regiment of the old Russian Army, Colonel L. I. V.

How many times I drank tea, how many times I ate at his hospitable home, and only accidentally did I learn that, born to luxury, from childhood raised like a princess—the colonel's wife is that marvelous, selfless woman about whose exploits the Cossack had told me, and that L. I. V. is the very person who was the only one saved from being sent away in trucks with the command staff of the Cossack Division.*

K. Gr.

On the day of the removal of the officers of the Cossachi Stan from Lienz, a man from the Kuban was there accidentally with his wife. He had no relation to the Stan and had moved to Lienz a few days before.

When the order was given to go to the "conference," not listening to his wife's pleas not to do so, he also sat down in one of the trucks.

She turned to the English sergeant, explaining to him what the matter was and asked him to take her husband out of the vehicle.

The sergeant fulfilled her request, but this Kuban man, learning that he had been taken from the vehicle at the request of his wife, grew indignant and jumped anew into the vehicle.

His wife could only say to him:

—If you do not understand that you are climbing into a noose —then go!

He went and would up in a concentration camp in Siberia.

V. N.

7. From the Letter of Lydia Fyodorovna Krasnova of Novemer 1947

This happened that horrible day of May 28.

Peter Nikolaevich had turned in his resignation several days before, and we took a small house near Lienz. As we moved in, P. N. said sadly: "Of course! Nothing is left for me..." I told him—"Not at all! You have in this time seen and experienced so much that you now have great new material for a novel."

After losing himself in thought, he said—"Maybe..."

I had people carry his trunk with his things, certificates of membership, and portraits into his room, and he arranged them all in

---

*   —There is an inaccuracy here. The events took place in the Cossachi Stan, where there were no divisions, but only separate Cossack units.

his own way on the table and in the table, as if he had already started gathering the materials he needed in his mind.

He is so strong of spirit that, even in the most difficult of times, he has always found a suitable way out. Toward evening, with people's help, we put the room in order. It turned out to be a small, but very comfortable apartment.

The next day, some acquaintances came to visit. It was a marvelous and quiet day. Everything was so beautiful, nature so good. We decided to restrict ourselves to this little corner. P. N. would start to write something large and excellent, and I, at last, would calm down from all of life's travails, living only for P. N. and protecting his peace.

The next morning, an adjutant arrived from D.* with D.'s request to go to a "conference" in Lienz at one in the afternoon.

P. N. grumbled a little that they do not let him write in peace, but I felt that something big and terrible was coming. Such a tortured, unfathomable despair lay on my heart.

We were told that a carriage had been provided.

P. N. put his arms around me, made the sign of the cross over me, looked me in the face, and said:

—"Do not be sad!"

I smiled, put my arms around him, made the sign of the cross over him, and accompanied him to the carriage. When he started off, he shouted to me:—I will return between six and eight o'clock this evening." And he never returned…

It was the first time ever that he had promised and did not come, but without warning me that he would be late. After forty-five years, the first time that he did not keep that promise. I understood that trouble had suddenly arrived…

L. Krasnova

•

---

* —The letter "D" stands for the name of Field Ataman Domanov.

On the Banks of the Drau

The events at the end of May and in June of 1945 we call the Tragedy of Lienz and speak of it as a betrayal by the English. Was it? The betrayal was through the treachery of allies, friends, and others. Who are and were then the English to us, with Churchill at their head, we learned well in the years of the World War.

Friends in need, it is said, are friends indeed, and we accepted them as such.

In the days when the entire Russian nation and we were on the eve of liberation, Churchill made a pact with Stalin. His Yalta, Potsdam, and Tehran agreements with Stalin dispossessed not just us, but all Russian people, and sold into the sphere of Soviet influence the people of Yugoslavia and other lands formerly found only in weak association.

In this article, I will not even start to analyze the pathological block-headedness of Churchill's personality. Criminologists will have words about him in the future.

In the events that we have come to call Lienz, there are many blank spots left still, and our generation is obviously not destined to know all that took place in those frightening days. We, the survivors, now found outside the borders of our native land, know only what happened here. The rest—what happened to our fathers and brothers who were returned to the Soviet Union—is known there only, in that native land. It will take many years before both halves are connected and we get a complete picture of Churchill's evil.

Most of all wrapped in the darkness of uncertainty is the fate of the officers taken to the "conference." For many, to this day, it remains unclear how the English managed to seduce the flower of Cossackdom in so simple a snare as a trip to a "conference."

Yes! By our simple-hearted nature, we are very trustful—this is one reason. The second—we were accustomed to trust in the word of an officer, and in our minds did not fully put together a complete understanding of officer and villain that, as we see, quite normally, begins with the common English soldier and goes all the way to their commander in chief.

This snare for the Cossack and Highlander officer complement was carefully nurtured over the course of almost an entire month.

And how did Cossackdom react?

In different ways, to be sure.

To describe the range of individual opinions, explanations, and discussions has little value, because all these ideas were built on guesses and suppositions. They have varied without pause, changed, and, of course, most of all reflected the deciding moment—the call to the "conference."

So, the minds of the officers were analyzed most of all and in the most definite form on this short slice of time, several hours. I also want to focus attention on this and, as much as I am able, give an explanation why the Cossack and Highlander officers went to a man to the "conference."

The announcement of the order to quickly assemble and depart for the "conference" became known to me a little later than to others who were notified, because, that entire morning, I had been with my wife, who lay in the hospital.

The weather remained changeable from the morning on— now misty and barely noticeable rain, now the sun broke through and the meadows became silvery from billions of iridescent drops.

As soon as I was notified of the call to the "conference," I quickly sought out some officers with whom I was acquainted, but not catching any of them at "home"—in their tents and *kibitkas*—I set off straight to the gathering place, which was located on the other side of the Drau from us. The place specified was on the road beyond Dölsach, where Camp *No* 2 (command) had been set up in our first days there. I caught up with a group of six to seven officers, who were also late, and attached myself to them.

Along the way, we discussed the suddenness of the call to the "conference." It all seemed plausible to us. It should be noted that long before that day, throughout the Cossachi Stan, from *kibitka* to *kibitka*, a rumor from "the most credible sources" went around that the English had led us into this canyon with the aim of hiding us from the eyes of the Bolsheviks, and that we would stay here only long enough for ships to arrive somewhere and take us to the "black" continent (to Africa) to carry out guard duties, and that our families would be sent to England, etc., etc. Rumors similarly flew that the entire officer staff would have to go through a short course to familiarize themselves with new English weapons and the structure of the English Army... We spoke of the coming inter-ally training, and of the American and English ambassadors leaving Moscow, which clearly spoke for that day of the inevitable clash and campaign against Stalin that would come soon.

It was clear that no one among us allowed the thought that we could indiscriminately be turned over to the Bolsheviks. All agreed, of course, on the possibility that all of us, like German officers, could be put behind barbed wire, where Soviet representatives would seek out perpetrators of war crimes.

In such discussion, we arrived at the indicated gathering spot, where trucks covered with canvass stood ready to take us away.

I walked into the columns, looking for friends with whom to sit in the same vehicle. I soon found my acquaintance from Kherson, Yesaul Ilyass Tchatchukh (Cherkess), in one of them. In the same vehicle was Major General Ye., with whom I had had suitably good relations in Tolmezzo. But after what took place inside the Kuban stanitsas in Covazzo-Carnico in connection with the publication of Order *No* 12 to the Kuban Host and Cossachi Stan on March 23, 1945, when Kuban Cossacks openly refused to accept the order of the Supreme Command, and similarly refused to follow the decision of the "Kuban Host Leaders," in which Major General Ye. was a member (as head of the Cossachi Stan Court), caused our relationship to change sharply, even if we did not have a falling out between us after all that happened. But he was well informed of my negative attitude toward the "Kuban Host Leaders" and my non-recognition of its authority, arising as it did through the dispensation of the Supreme Command, rather than by election by Kuban Cossacks. Ignoring that, I still considered that now was not the time to remember personal internecine conflicts, as we stood on the threshold of a new existence, which might turn out to be decisive for all of Cossackdom. It was better to fully go over our unclear present situation, so full of uncertainties.

General Ye. answered my greeting correctly, but very coldly. When I noted that the presence of English soldiers with automatic weapons made me doubt more strongly that we were going to some sort of "conference," and that our journey might end in some sort of isolation camp surrounded by barbed wire, General Ye. said:

—"You misunderstand the new situation, Sotnik, and the present organization of democratic armies, but for your concern over our relation to sub-machine gunners that you note, they are simply our guard. Obviously, somewhere along the route we are to follow, there are partisan groups."

—"But for that, Your Excellency, it would be simpler to have left us with our own weapons and give out several automatics per vehicle…"

—"Yes… The English should not be believed,"— put in Yesaul Tchatchukh, as if answering his own thoughts. He had been silent until then.

—"Ilyass, so you believe it? Then why are you going?"

—"But what? An order of the Supreme Command concerns me less than you? This time and the second, I will go because I do not believe them… With what ease they fell into union with Stalin. With such perfidy, they will betray him, too. You are talking about an Englishman, not one of us. And he needs us now. You see, they are used to letting others rake their hot coals."—

Our discussion was interrupted by the approach of a Don officer, accompanied by an English one, who turned to a group that was standing on the side and speaking with those being sent off. He announced that it was time "to horse," that we were already a little delayed, and that it would not be good to arrive late.

Those walking along the highway hurried toward us to find out if there were some news. The Don officer, on seeing General Ye. seated in a vehicle, asked him to move to another vehicle, which had been designated for staff officers. General Ye. and Tchatchukh went off to the head of the column with both of the men.

And so I was again alone among strangers. After their departure, an old lady approached our vehicle.

… "Sons, perhaps some of you are thinking of remaining? Then come quickly into the barrack… And with her head, she pointed across the highway—There, our fellows will rip off these shoulder tabs and sew on new sergeant ones, and that will put an end to being led off!" And she hurried away.

—"Let's go. Let's take a look," a cornet sitting by the gate suggested.

—"Let's go!"—And we went into the barracks.

In the first room, where there were several bunk beds, there were nine officers.

—"How about you, have you decided to drop down in rank? Then go to that room."—And they pointed to a side door.

The cornet and I exchanged glances, but at that moment a girl came out of the door carrying several uniforms in her arms.

—"Well, choose for yourself, whichever you want. They are all the same now."—she said.

The uniforms were decorated with the shoulder tabs of senior sergeants. For some part of a second, I coveted the possession of one of these uniforms, but then I suddenly had a thought:

—"But how will these gentlemen feel about themselves when we return from the conference in the evening?..."—And I went out of the barracks.

Several officers were standing near the barracks, among them, my friend, Cornet K. M. (Terek).

—"Well what, Kostya, are you going?"

—"No. I was left here on guard duty."

The command, "to horses," passed through the column. The head of the column apparently began moving, signals could be heard for departure, and engines began to roar.

The cornet who had gone into the barracks with me ran out. This put an end to my vacillation. We quickly returned to the vehicle and took our places. After several minutes, it started off.

Kilometer after kilometer, the vehicle carried us. My head was ablaze. "This is a trick... What kind of conference can there be? ... I could understand if they called the higher command staff, or even regimental commanders—that would suffice fully; but the entire complement, to a man? ... How can the regiments be stripped so? And what if something happens? Ech! ... Why did I sit down in this vehicle? ... And what if I did not go? ... And it happens that they are truly taking us to a conference? ... Maybe it will decide questions on some new democratic structure I am ignorant of, as General Ye. said, where every officer, irrespective of his rank and position, has the right not only to express his views, but to also stick to his opinion. And what controversial questions might be decided by vote... And then, in the evening, when all have returned, what will we say to justify our staying behind? They will call us cowards. What could be more shameful for an officer? But to go like sheep, not even knowing where, is also not very flattering to an officer... And my brain woke up, as if instantly. They are taking us behind barbed wire! What kind of questions can there be at this conference? What kind of plans can they confide to us there, if they do not trust us enough to tell us where we are going, where the conference is to be? ..."

Then the thought ... "Jump out of the vehicle..."

Totally hooked by it, I got myself to the gate. But this would be true and stupid death! Well, but what if I succeeded? ... Will the soldier with the automatic shoot at me? No. He would not dare—the others would realize then what kind of conference they were being taken to.

But they could shoot from the cab of the vehicles following us... All the same, I made a decision. But there was no suitable place yet, and every minute, we were leaving kilometers behind us. Soon we will be in Nikolsdorf—the last place that I am familiar with. Here the road takes a turn to the left, and there will be no danger of hitting the tarmac—inertia will throw me to the side...

—Well, gentlemen, as you wish, but I go no farther, I do not trust them!

—Sotnik, you will smash yourself to bits!— I hear from behind me.

Rolling down the slope, I jumped to my feet. They waved their arms to me from one of the automobiles going away from me— obviously the one in which I had been.

Not having any injuries, I went into some low pine saplings. The columns moved on. Up ahead, where the road begins to wind through woods by the roadside, "our" column caught up with a column of tankettes, which wedged in singly, one per every five to six vehicles.

After the entire column had passed, I took off my uniform and hung it on a small pine, walked out onto the highway, and quickly made my way to the Stan.

What I lived through the rest of the days is hard for me to write. At times, I considered what I did justified; at others, I bitterly reproached myself for cowardice and lack of fortitude.

My deed, done entirely for my own escape was a poor argument for justification. Yes, and would anyone even want to hear my explanation? One fact was enough: I did not obey an order from the Field Ataman to go to the conference.

Remembering these immeasurably long hours makes me relive a pain that is inhuman, but no longer now for my own action, but the pain from expenditure of the honest and most loyal sons of the Homeland, among whom were not a few of my personal friends.

Sotnik of the Kuban Host
Alexander Shparengo

•

Record of the Words of a Former Officer of the Red Army, Kuban Cossack Yu. T. G.

The English took him with General P. N. Krasnov and other officers from Lienz on May 28, 1945. At Spittal, the staff officers, of whom he was one, were accommodated in a single barrack, in which General P. N. Krasnov was put in a separate room. Close by him was a bunch of Krasnovs—his distant relative, General Semyon Nikolaevich Krasnov, who served under him in his duties as Chief of Staff of the Central Administration of Cossack Hosts; Nikolai Nikolaevich Krasnov, of the General Staff, who had been only briefly in the Cossachi Stan in Italy; and the son of the latter, also Nikolai Nikolaevich, a young officer.

In the evening, the English commander informed Domanov that everyone would be given over to the Bolsheviks the next day.

This caused a tremendous sensation. Domanov lost his wits completely. The officers began to shed things that distinguished them as officers. They threw off coats, jackets, and threw away documents and other papers. There were quarrels and arguments. Several began to compose group requests for their release, based on them never having been Soviet citizens. This outraged those who had been under Stalin—When they needed to, they were with us, but now they separate themselves.

Of course, no one accepted any of the requests.

It was proposed that P. N. Krasnov meet with an English representative. They brought a chair out for it and placed it near the barbed wire fence. But no one came to speak to him, and an English soldier kicked over the chair.

Tarussky hung himself. Mikhailov tried, too, but was taken down from his noose.

The English ordered us to be ready to board the next day at four in the morning.

No one slept that night. G. thought about how to save himself. He tried to speak to several others about it, but most were afraid to even think about escape. But he resolved to escape.

The next morning, May 29, there was no reveille at four in the morning.

Toward six o'clock, everyone went out on the parade ground, where two priests who were with them began a prayer service.

Vehicles arrived at this time and English soldiers ordered the officers into them. The officers used passive resistance, linking their arms together. But they were broken apart by the use of clubs.

They grabbed the first officer and threw him into a truck. He jumped out. They beat him on the head with clubs and threw him into the truck again. He jumped out again. They beat him again, heavily, and threw him in the truck.

Apparently having no more strength, he stopped resisting, but just watched what took place with indescribable sadness in his eyes.

The incidence with this officer effected the general mood. Apathy befell them and they started to board without resistance.

Each vehicle took thirty men.

Several asked English soldiers for smokes.

Then an English soldier arrived with several cartons of cigarettes and offered them for a watch, regardless of the relative values.

Into his pouch flowed a stream of watches, among which were many valuable gold ones. He gave one cigarette for each. His large pouch quickly filled with watches.

Near eight o'clock in the morning, loading was competed and the vehicles went off.

Concerning General P. N. Krasnov, G. said that he did not come out for the prayers, but remained sitting in a chair by the window of his room, which looked out onto the yard.

When English soldiers noticed him, they ran to the window to pull him out through it. Cossacks lunged at them, chased them off, and, taking P. N. Krasnov carefully in their arms, took him out the window themselves to join the rest of the Cossacks.

G. goes on to tell how he escaped. He told Colonel B., who played a sad role in the last war, attempting to take a leadership role among the Kuban Cossacks, of his desire to avoid being turned over.

Colonel B. responded favorably to his suggestion. G. proposed hiding him in a dresser that lay upside-down on the barrack floor. He agreed, but after a while became very distressed. He said that he had shared the plan with a certain Colonel N., who figured it out and himself climbed into the dresser, from which it was impossible to pull him out.

G. suggested that B. hide under a pile of clothes, papers, and all sorts of other trash that had been thrown away by the officers in a corner of a room in the barrack. Then he began to look for a hiding place for himself. There was no attic in the barrack, but he spotted a place where the veneer hung down. Going to it, he tried to climb into the opening, but managed to do so only half way when he heard English soldiers entering the barrack. Making a last effort forward, he pushed himself through and, after a short crawl, found that he was beneath the roof, in something like a very small attic.

The soldiers walked through the barrack, making noise and laughing.

Making a small opening in the roof, G. watched the entire scene of those being taken away by force and thought about his plan for escape.

Wire surrounded the camp in three vertical rows. It was braided like a net, in large squares. He noticed one promising place across from his barrack. But he could not even think of making a break for it before the officers were taken out of the camp. Submachine gunners manned the towers. Beyond the wire was a thick circle of machine gunners. Several machine guns were aimed at the camp, ready to fire. A tank stood at the gate.

But after they took away the officers, the only English left were those on the towers. G. let himself down and told B. that they needed to make a break for it, but B. shushed him and said that he was going nowhere until nightfall.

Climbing back up, G. watched as two automobiles with officers in them came to the gate. They were additions to those taken from Lienz.

The English soldier in the nearest tower paid all of his attention to them, so G. decided to make use of it. Quickly running out of the barrack, he climbed under the wire and succeeded in getting through the first two rows, although very much scratched up, but on the third row, the openings turned out to be too small. Luckily for him, he managed to bend one of them apart and jumped out from the fence and into a German garden. There, he went to a building in which the people lived. Seeing that he was covered in blood, the Germans were first frightened, then let him wash up, put on new clothes, and go off into the woods. While he was in the garden, he saw N. follow his way out.

After several days, he met B., who told him how English soldiers discovered him burrowing under the trash. They had six automatic weapons pointed at him and told him to raise his arms. Then, pointing with his eyes, he showed one of them the gold watch on his wrist. That saved him. The soldiers lowered their weapons. Things went easier for him after that.

———————

G. also said that he saw Colonel Kuchuka Ulagay's great coat in the garden. He had also been at Spittal. How he succeeded in freeing himself, he did not know.

G. said that an English Major addressed Sultan Kelich Ghirey, saying that he was designating him as the leader of the Highlanders and making him responsible for their conduct.

To this, the Sultan proudly answered that when he had been free, he had been the dictator of the Highlanders. Now that he was a prisoner, he was the same as the others. They left him alone.

Then G. told how on the day of May 28, when the columns of trucks left the camp in Spittal, he saw a fine *kinjal* and sword in the hands of an English soldier at the gate. He suggested that they were General Shkuro's weapons.

According to his testimony, when the officers were taken from Spittal on May 29, Shkuro stayed behind. He was kept in a stone building, instead of a barrack.

Asked if he knew if anyone had escaped out of Spittal, G. answered that he knew of only one. That officer escaped *en route*.

As explained above, each truck took about thirty men. A submachine gunner lay on the roof of each cab, watching the vehicles traveling in front of him. A motorcyclist armed with a machine gun rode beside each one. Between every five vehicles, there was a tankette.

Getting away was very difficult. But God helps the bold.

The truck carrying that officer became temperamental and was taken aside, where it stopped. After being checked out, it started once more, but it was now closer to the tail. Then it failed several more times and, in the end, a final time. When it stopped once more, the vehicles still on the move were far ahead. Only a single motorcycle was left by it. After a while, the motorcyclist said something to the driver and left to catch up with the column. Out of this, the officer hatched a plan. The vehicle stood some ten or more paces before a small rise (ahead of which was a turn.) He reckoned that as soon as it started moving and crossed the bend, it would be hidden, and if he leaped just when it started to move, the soldier in the cabin would not be able to see him.

He shared his plan with several officers, but they protested firmly and did not want him to try from fear that, when a head count was made and it was one short, all would be in trouble.

But still, he carried out his plan with this result: as soon as the vehicle started moving, he tumbled out from its cargo space and hid unnoticed in the bushes.

V. N.

•

More on the Betrayal of the Cossack of the Cossachi Stan and the Highlanders

> Don Cossack I. N. S. lived through the days of the Cossack removal in a small camp next to the railroad tracks not far from Spittal.

By his own count, approximately three trains per day with Cossacks and their families passed through Spittal during the removals. There were forty cars in each, on the average.

He calculated that thirty to thirty-five thousand people were removed in those days.

Further, he tells that the doors of the cars where not locked, but the door latches were only twisted closed with wire.

Two armed English soldiers accompanied each train.

Most of the trains went through the Spittal station without stopping. Several did make stops and in such cases, according to S., he and his comrades succeeded in untwisting the wires on several doors and opening the latches. Several Cossacks took advantage of this to run away. He said that several cars were opened, but could not estimate even approximately how many.

He estimated that up to sixty people escaped from the trains.

To support his testimony, he noted the many different items being thrown out of the cars along the route the trains carrying the Cossacks and families being turned over followed: military insignias, shoulder tabs, caps, decorations, and various papers, money, photographs and the like.

•

On the Removal of Highlanders

This information is from two young Karachaevs from the Terek, belonging to the new emigration.

One of them served in the Red Army for a whole month and surrendered. The other did not serve at all, but left the Caucasus when the Germans retreated from there. They both wound up in Italy, and from there, in May, went into Austria, to the Drau River, where they shared the fate of the Cossacks and Highlanders.

When the Highlanders decided to leave Italy, German Captain Torrer [spelling could not be verified—*trans*.], liaison to the Highlander units, did not want to release them from Italy. But they knocked out the guards from a bridge and went through.

Coming to the Drau at Oberdrauburg, Highlander units headed into Lienz, where they settled. But when the English came, they moved to Oberdrauburg. There, they organized themselves in groups: Kabardins were mostly to the east, Ossetians were farther west, and Karachaevs even farther.

They greatly confuse the dates, but they relate events with full verisimilitude.

In their words, when it was proposed that the officers go "to a conference," it was obvious that a trap was being set. They concluded this from the tanks, motorcycles, and sub-machine gunners that were with the trucks.

Several officers—they gave three names—changed into civilian clothes, but were betrayed by their own hearts. An English officer approached one of them and began to ask whether he knew so-and-so, mentioning the name. He turned pale and said that it was he. They put him in a truck.

They also said that it seemed as if the English offered to let General Sultan Kelich Ghirey, an old emigrant, stay, but he answered that he would not leave his officers, but would go with them. The same offer was made to Colonel Kuchuk Ulagay. He made use of it and hid that day, although the English searched for him the next day.*

On the day after the officers were taken away, an English officer with a Highlander interpreter arrived, accompanied by a tank.

They gathered the people and announced that the officers had been turned over to the Soviets and that the people should prepare themselves for the same.

As soon as he said that, a terrible din arose, yells and screams. This so affected the officer and the interpreter that they both started to cry and left without finishing their announcement.

The next day, people began to run off. Several English soldiers themselves recommended doing so and even gave advice on the best directions.

It should be noted that English guards were not posted inside the camp, but some distance from it.

One of the Karachaevs left the camp with a group of more than a hundred people, among whom were children and oldsters. They grabbed what provisions they could take with them, several horses, and cows.

They spent the night in the cliffs above the camp. The next day they watched the picture of the removals from them.

They began with the Kabardins. Automobiles and tanks came, surrounded the camp, and began to force people into trucks.

The same took place there as in Lienz: women threw themselves beneath the wheels of vehicles, having first taken off their clothes. They were thrown naked into the trucks.

The same took place that day in the Ossetian and Karachaev columns.

More of the Karachaevs succeeded at getting away. It has to be suggested that they were the farthest and were not surrounded first.

By the estimate of these two young men, who gave plausible testimony about the Highlanders, sixty officers, in all, and six hundred others were taken away.

---

* According to the information of Yu. T. G., Kuchuk Ulagay was taken to Spittal, where he succeeded in freeing himself.

The next day, English soldiers and former Russian prisoners of war began searching for those hidden in the hills. Many were caught. Still, many succeeded in escaping and got to the area of Salzburg.

V. N.

•

Annihilation of Cossacks at Judenberg

> This testimony from the words of a local resident was communicated to Terek A. V. F., who lived for an extended time in the city of Judenburg.

My wife and I have been collecting evidence about the tragedy for a long time—says A. V. F.

Cossacks of von Pannwitz's Cossack Division, as were those from Lienz (Domanov's group), were brought to a former camp for Soviet prisoners of war close to the city of Klagenfurt. There, they were registered, then taken to Judenburg in small groups, with a tank going with every two automobiles.

The Mur River (a tributary of the Drau) washes the city on two sides.

A bridge had been built across the river, impressive in originality of construction and at a height of twenty-five to thirty meters above the water.

The English were in Judenburg, but the Soviets were on the other side.

Right past the bridge, to the left of the highway that goes through Bruck and Graz to Vienna, there was a huge steel mill. The Soviets dismantled it and took it to The Land of Soviets [совдепию —*trans.*]

Its gigantic steel and cement buildings, each of which, on its own, consisted of one huge room around two hundred and fifty meters in length, fifty to sixty meters in width, and fifteen meters in height, were being used like sheds, into which Cossacks were chased.

They were brought through the city and right to the mill without stopping.

When the vehicles went across the bridge, the Cossacks could see it by the side of the river, with a Soviet flag flapping above it. Several men jumped from the vehicles and threw themselves into the river. All were smashed to death. It is not possible to establish a number, as everyone names a different figure. Three, who to all appearances did not die right away, were pulled out by the English and buried on the bank of the river. But along the Judenburg—Weisskirchen highway, about half a kilometer from the bridge, there is a cross on a grave with the English inscription: "Here rest unknown Cossacks." Austrians attend to the grave with great care, and we have already held memorial services over it three times.

At the steel mill, there was once again registration and questioning. They were broken into groups.

Railroad tracks were laid from the railroad station to the mill, and railroad rolling stock put on it, into which Cossacks were loaded for return "to the homeland."

Still, to ascertain who was taken away and who remained there is totally impossible, but there is no doubt that many were left in that structure.

Day and night, executions were carried out beneath the sounds of running engines.

On the right of the highway, across from the mill were the workers' quarters. Several of them (former communists) managed to be in the factory and saw and heard much there.

Once, residents of the settlement, as those of the city, were surprised: the mill began to operate. Smoke came out of the mill's chimneys. All the while, the workers were at their homes and no one was calling them.

All eyes turned to those who were at the mill.

They sent someone to investigate. What the investigation showed was totally preposterous, and no one believed it—the Soviets were burning Cossacks...

Nonetheless, they soon did believe it. First the workers' village, then the entire city, was oppressed by the stench of burning human flesh.

The mill "operated" for five and one-half days.[*]

After this, the final echelon of Cossacks was taken away (this was July 15, 1945), and Russian girls who were working in the area were brought to the mill.

They were supposed to "clean the factory of the Cossacks' parasites." These were the words used by one of the Soviet officers.

V. N.

•

Information Obtained from Professor F. V. Verbitsky

> Professor Verbitsky was taken along with other officers, officials, and physicians, May 28, 1945, from Lienz "to the conference."

When we had gone some eighteen kilometers from Lienz, the entire column was stopped where tanks and English infantrymen were standing.

Two Englishmen armed with automatics stood at the back of each vehicle carrying officers. The vehicles continued under such convoy. The armored cars and English tanks remained and did not accompany the column.

When we reached Spittal, all of the vehicles went onto the grounds of a camp made up of barracks that were surrounded by barbed wire. They arranged themselves on the edge of a large square. The officers stepped out. After this, before anything else, they were called based on a list of staff with General P. N. Krasnov at its head. They were led off right away into the depths of the camp somewhere.

Then an English physician asked:—Is Doctor Dyakonov here? When he received a reply that he was, he called off fourteen physicians from a list, one of whom was Professor Verbitsky.

---

[*] In one of the San Francisco newspapers (regretfully, the name was not written down) in 1947, there was an article about the Cossack tragedy in Lienz in the spring of 1945, in which it was said that the English gave the Cossacks over to the Bolsheviks in Judenburg and that executions were carried out there, but no corpses were discovered after the Soviets left.

When all the physicians who had been called had stepped forward, the English doctor addressed F. V. Verbitsky, calling him professor, and asking him to go to one of the buildings of the camp in order to examine an ill Cossack general.

It turned out to be General Shkuro, who was brought there earlier and who was in a stone building with some seven officers, none of whom the professor recognized. Shkuro had called for a physician on the pretext of a heart attack.

The English soldiers who brought the professor led him to Shkuro's room, then went away for a short time, so that they had a chance to exchange several words.

Shkuro said that he was well. He only wanted to know who had been brought in.

For the sake of appearance, the professor asked him to undo his clothes.

General Shkuro asked several questions about those brought in, then he waved his arm and became silent. F. V. Verbitsky had the impression that he had not until then been completely certain of the prospective betrayal, but after he found out who had been brought in, he realized that it was inescapable.

Their meeting lasted about five minutes. Then the professor was taken away.

He spent the night, along with the other physicians, outside the wire, but under guard.

When they were taken from the barrack the next day, May 29, there was no movement within the wire-enclosed part of the camp.

All the physicians were returned to Lienz that day.

•

Mown Meadow

The journey winds like a marching song
Like a refrain suddenly bursting through…
Cossacks will not saddle, it will not come
To cinching leather saddle girths.
The heart of the Cossack has grown cold,

Does not beat. Tears command.
Someone whispers "Surrender,
Dishonorable, deserved peace"…
No blood in faces, no smiles…
At Cossack women and children,
Through ignorance or error
Tanks move in a tight row…
This is not what it seems, not a dream
But for real the Cossack flung himself
Under a rattling chain, to a way out,
To a sword abandoned by the Germans…
Swaying in the flesh of a neighbor,
In Solovka's silvery whisky,
Tumbled an old man, and along ruby footprints
Appears a *kinjal* in his hand.
In the year of forty-five, in Lienz
Where an enemy was made of a friend
Descended the Pokrova cloth of the
Mother of God on the mowed meadow.

"Roll Call" *No* 16.   **Pr. N. Kudashov**

•

From the Story of the Ural Host by Host Starshin U.

Host Starshin U. and Kuban officer V. were sent by railroad from Oberdrauburg to Lienz with a group of up to seventy Cossacks, but from there they were sent farther to the southwest, to the Italian border, to its last station, Sillian. While they were there, the burgomaster wanted to send them back to Lienz, but they objected and remained, settling in an abandoned "Oster" camp. There they joined a party of Poles who were working in Sillian at cleaning. Then, in part, the Cossacks returned to Lienz. Host Starshin U. tried to be counted as on the staff of the Field Ataman, but the Chief of Staff, General S., refused his request. Thanks to that, he escaped the bitter fate of the other officers. He did not witness the removal of officers and Cossacks from Lienz, but was told what had happened there by others. He personally spoke with two Ural Cossacks who were taken to Spittal, where they succeeded in escaping. They told Host Starshin U. what they had witnessed in Spittal. Based on his words, I have written the following:

In the first days of June, returning to Lienz from Spittal after being taken there May 28 along with other officers, were two Ural Cossacks, a father and son. The first was an old Russian officer, and both were new emigrants.

They told how when they were in Spittal, they were quickly divided into three groups: generals, staff officers, and ober-officers. Then, after being led off to barracks, the English officer in charge, a general they said, called three senior officers from those just brought to Spittal. They were General Domanov, General Tikhotsky, while the name of the third, they have forgotten.

The English informed them that in accordance with the Yalta agreement, all officers would be given over to the Soviets.

After this announcement, General Tikhovsky could no longer walk. He was carried away.

Once this became clear, a panic arose among the officers. They started to throw off their insignias, throwing away documents, photographs, money, etc.

The next morning, they were taken in trucks from the camp in Spittal to the Spittal Station, where they were locked into freight cars.

These two Ural Cossacks hid above rafters in an attic and sat there for three days, after which they came to Lienz on foot. The wife and daughter of the older (mother and sister of the younger) had been left there. On the eve of their arrival, both were maliciously [нальственно—*trans.*] taken away. Both Cossacks despaired. Seeing no other way out, they left voluntarily for the Land of the Soviets [Social Democratic Parties United, or SDPU—*translator.*]

V. N.

•

Essay of O. D. R.

> O. D. R. was an interpreter in Camp Peggetz during the tragic days in which the main act of the Cossack tragedy was played out on June 1, 1945. She was a direct witness to all that took place there and graciously agreed to provide material about what she saw and lived through in those days. She made her contribution more exact by answering questions posed to her.
>
> This essay is extremely valuable not only for us contemporaries, but for future historians investigating this dark chapter in the history of Cossackdom. It is valuable in the main because it has information on the behavior of those English officers who directly fulfilled the Yalta agreement.

I was transferred as interpreter to Camp Peggetz several days before weapons were taken away, and I write about what I myself witnessed in the camp.

There were twelve thousand five hundred residents.

May 28, in the morning,[*] British Major Davies came to the camp. As always, he was given a report in English on what the camp needed. He readily agreed to everything and even promised to comply with requests from several officers privately.

He left at eleven in the morning. I went to the Cadet Corps to give a first English language lesson.

Suddenly, at 11:30, the corps' director, Colonel T., came to ask me to terminate the lesson and, calling me into a neighboring

---

[*]   This was the day that officers were taken "to a conference."

room, announced that General Bedakov* wanted me to come quickly to his office.

I went there and found him to be pale and nervously pacing his room.

Seeing me, he cheered visibly. Nervously, he informed me that he had received an order by telephone from General Domanov to hurriedly gather all officers and military officials from all stanitsas and regiments, and that they should all prepare to go to a conference at one in the afternoon, which would take place in Villach. (For some reason, in all articles about Lienz, Spittal is written of. The order was to go to Villach. There had not been a word about Spittal. O. D. R.)

Liaisons were sent with this order to the regiments, the stanitsas, and the Military School.

Toward one in the afternoon, two officers arrived from the English staff and asked General Bedakov to provide a general number of how many officers there were, in order to know how many large automobiles to bring.

These officers, addressing me, spoke only about our officers. Did they mean also the military officials here?

Staying behind with me, General Bedakov asked me:

—What do you think, Olga Dmitrievna, what is this hurried conference—for the better or worse?

We thought and thought and, of course, could think of nothing—everything was so unexpected.

—Cross me, Olga Dmitrievna—Bedakov asked.

I fulfilled his request.

———

There were twenty-five large cargo vehicles provided to take away the officers. They were covered with tarpaulin and had benches along the walls. But when the English officer received the list and learned that we were still waiting for the officers from the regiments,

———

* General Bedakov, of the Kuban Tamanskoy Stanitsa, Ignat Maksimovich by name, belonged to the new emigration. General P. N. Krasnov had promoted him to general in Italy, not long before departing from it. On the Drau, he fulfilled the duties of Commander in Chief of Camp Peggetz for the Cossachi Stan.

he called for fifteen to eighteen additional vehicles. The number for each was to be twenty men, but up to thirty boarded, or maybe more.

When the officers left "for the conference," it was a hot day, and they all went without overcoats. All tried to dress well. Those who had them wore their Tsarist medals.

There were 1,600 men (not counting those leaving from Lienz. O. D. R.)

Of the two English officers at Peggetz, one, apparently the senior, gave out orders. He was the same lieutenant who oversaw the May 17 disarmament. I do not know his name.

He asked that one guard officer be designated for every three stanitsas to keep order until the officers returned from the conference. He wrote down their names.

As the officers were boarding, several of their wives were in tears and asked me, as interpreter, to ask the English officers if their husbands would return and when.

—But, of course!—the senior officer answered—By three o'clock, we will be at the conference. It will take one hour—one and a half, and, approximately at five—quarter after, the officers will return to the camp. Calm the wives. The officers really are going to a conference. They are crying unnecessarily!

I asked this lieutenant four times when the officers would return. Four times, he gave his word that they would return between five and a quarter after.

When our officers had gone, the wives and I discussed what sort of a conference it could be.

Time passed. Five o'clock went by. Six—no one had returned. We were gripped by worry and doubt.

Half past six, seven, seven-thirty—no one!

Finally, at eight o'clock, I was informed that the two English officers required an interpreter.

I went pale.

—Where are the officers?—I asked them.

—They will not return here.

—But, where are they?

—I don't know.

—You promised four times that they would return. You mean you deceived us?

Without looking me in the eyes, one of them answered:

—We are only British soldiers following the orders of our superior officers. Be so good as to call the three officers left on watch. We came for them.

Taking out a list with their names, he called them and took them away.

You can imagine the distress of the wives.

Following this, at half past one in the morning, an order was sent by Major Davies that all non-commissioned officers [вахмистры и урядники—*trans.*] be brought to his offices at half past nine in the morning, and also to prepare a list of them by stanitsa, regiment, and other units, with their names and ranks in English. He said that he would give an order that they should maintain discipline in place of the officers.

The lists were prepared. We sat and waited for the Major.

Ten, eleven, twelve o'clock that night, and he did not appear.

The non-commissioned officers decided to choose a leader and unanimously chose Under-*khorunj* [Cossack rank, equivalent to Cornet—*trans.*] Polunin.

Deciding that the Major would come in the morning, all went back to their barracks to sleep.

I was left with just the liaisons to the stanitsas. Our electric light went out. Our last candle burned down, and I decided to lie down. It was half past one.

Before I could fall asleep, at two o'clock that night, Major Davies came with interpreter Ya. and asked for the list.

When he learned that all had gone to bed, he said he would come at half past eight in the morning and sent an order to all units not to send wagons for provisions, but only one quartermaster per stanitsa with a list from each unit. The English would bring provisions in trucks.

At 3:30 in the morning of May 28th, we again gathered at the offices and waited for the Major.

At nine o'clock, instead of him, a lieutenant arrived with a Jewish soldier from Warsaw. He gave me an order written in Russian* and said:

—Read this.

Here is what was written on it:

1. Cossacks! Your officers deceived you and led you down a path of lies. They have been arrested and will not return.
2. You no longer need to fear and, free of their influence and pressure, you can tell about their lies and freely express your desires and beliefs.

—It has been decided that all Cossacks must return to their own homelands.

The remaining points of the order were about self-government, about order, which had to be maintained, and the need to obey the orders of the British Command without question.

A grave-like stillness fell as this order was being read.

Then, with constrained, but firm voices, the English officer was informed:

—What you said about our officers, that they deceived us, is a lie. We will not voluntarily go to the USSR. We all only ask one thing: return our friends to us, our officers, and then we will step as they tell us and go wherever they lead us. We trust them, we respect them, and we love them. Return our officers to us. We will maintain order, as they have taught us, so that when they return, we will be able to tell them honestly that we have fulfilled their legacies.

The English officer listened to all this in silence and said that he would pass it on to the Major. Then he left.

Within an hour, the Major arrived. It was ten o'clock on the morning of May 29th.

He said that the stanitsas and regiments would be sent to the Soviet Union on the 31st, that he would arrive at 7 AM, and would load them in order on trains that would be provided for the camp.

---

* This order was from the English staff and not signed by Major Davies. The signature could not be made out. The translation to Russian was obviously done by someone with a poor knowledge of the language.

First would be Don stanitsas (families) and, at the same time, Don regiments, then Kuban stanitsas and regiments, and after them, Terek.

He demanded a list of the stanitsas and in which barracks they were situated from the non-commissioned officers who had replaced the officers.

—This—he said—was so that families would not be divided.

He asked that people not resist. Those resisting would be loaded on the trains by force and families might be separated.

We provided the numerical composition, including the number of women, children, elderly, and invalids, of each stanitsa, but we refused to give a list of names.

All informed him that we would not leave voluntarily. All cried.

The Major was very upset. He went away, saying he would return in the afternoon.

During that interval, two trucks arrived to take away wounded officers and invalids.

Wives were permitted to send letters, overcoats, underwear, blankets, etc., to the officers.[*]

In a moment, letters, suitcases, packages with food, etc., were prepared and given to the English.

The unfortunate women cried as they sent their husbands things, but it did raise their hopes that their husbands were alive.

After the automobile with the wounded (those capable of walking) and the things left, the residents of Peggetz and those Cossacks from the regiments who had made their way to their families gathered in the 6th Barrack. People crowded in until they blocked the offices and the entire corridor of the barrack. They gathered to discuss the situation that had arisen. They decided to announce a hunger strike as a sign of protest and to hang black flags. Everything was organized quickly. Large placards were prepared with the inscription in English:

_____

[*] This was the next deception by the leaders of the English command. It was meant to calm the unfortunate women. Where those things wound up is not known, but in any case, they were not passed on to the officers who had been taken away.

"We prefer hunger and death here than return to the Soviet Union!"

When the English brought provisions, no one touched them. The English shrugged their shoulders, unloaded the food, and put it into a pile. The Cossacks put a guard on the food, so that certain provocateurs sent there did not drag it off.

Major Davies came at four o'clock. He was unpleasantly surprised on seeing the black flag and placards.

Everyone wanted to tell Davies that to return voluntarily to the USSR was impossible.

The Major answered that he could change nothing. The order came from his leadership, since, according to the Yalta Agreement, all Russians had to be returned to the Soviet Union.

On my question:—Do the Vlasovites have to go? the Major answered:

—Yes, even the Vlasovites.

—But old emigrants?

—Even old emigrants.

—Meaning myself?

—Yes, even you. In general, all Russians.

—Major, sir, turn around, look—men are crying…

—I can't look—he answered. His hands trembled. He smoked cigarette after cigarette and nervously folded the order just written.

Tears in every degree flowed from us. Even men sobbed.

I continued to try to convince Major Davies that our return to the Soviet Union was impossible, that the Bolsheviks would torture us, etc.

But it was all in vain. The answer was always the same:

—I am only a British soldier and must obey the orders of my superiors. This does not depend on me. I want to help and not separate families.

He drew up a plan of the camp and barracks, ordered that the women board the vehicles close to their barracks, and directed from which barrack the departures would begin.

I listened and thought:

—All the same, this order will not be obeyed, since everyone has already decided that, from four o'clock in the morning, we will hold prayers on the field and that the English would not touch those in prayer.

On the question of where the officers were—Major Davies insisted that he did not know.

—Where will they take the stanitsas?

He did not name a place, but he gave his word that they would be turned over to a different English unit.

—I do not believe you, Major—I said—for the officers also went "to a conference."

—I give you the word of a British officer that I, too, did not know until four o'clock that they would not return. And I lost the honor of a British officer by giving my word to my friend B. (Domanov's adjutant) that he would return. I myself believed it and against my will became a liar.

That day, the Major came to Peggetz two more times.

Day and night we had services going on in churches so that people could make confession and take communion.

In the interval between Davies' appearances, we discussed how best to organize for the possibility that force would be applied.

Long petitions were prepared to the English King and Queen, Archbishop of Canterbury, Churchill, and others from those with higher education, from Russian women, from wives, mothers, etc.

Translated into English, these petitions were handed to the English colonel* to be sent to those named. He promised to deliver them, but whether they ever were is not known.

Late in the evening, the Major came and informed us that, because of the Catholic holiday, "Blood and Body of Christ," departure was postponed until the 1st of June.

We all looked like those on Death Row, but some sort of hope of being saved still shone inside us.

The English brought produce daily and dumped it into a single pile. Our guards protected it.

Male and female Soviet agents moved quickly through camp, entreating people to return, for which several brazenly announced:

---

* The colonel was part of the English staff found in Lienz, and apparently was Major Davies' direct superior. About him and the English staff at Lienz, there will be more to be said.

—All the same, you will go to the homeland!

That same Jew—the soldier from Warsaw who came with the lieutenant to bring us the order to return to our homeland, propagandized into a megaphone from an automobile, calling for return. He spoke in Russian, but with a Jewish accent and halting speech.

No one liked him and all avoided him.

Something strange took place with us.

Was it autosuggestion? Was it a foundering hope? Was it some sort of well-thought-out enticement or a general hypnosis? But from everywhere was heard the advice:

—Hold on! Hold on and all will be well!

Various rumors spread through the camp. For instance, that two boys, one ten, the other twelve years old, were running somewhere and found our officers inside a barbed wire enclosure; that many wives wrote short notes to their husbands; that these boys forged an English pass and that one, at night, went secretly by automobile (there was one in camp) to the officers and returned with a note from one of them which said:

—Hold on these three days and all will be well!

Rumors also had English soldiers giving signs that we should hold on.

Rumors went around that Shkuro was free, that one lady saw him on the street in Lienz, and that he told her:

—Hold on! Everything will come out better than you think.

We all felt as if we were going to be electrocuted, but kept a firm decision not to give in.

We listened to the radio, which broadcast that Stalin had not accepted the American ambassador, that the ambassador had left Moscow, and that the allies had broken off diplomatic relations with Moscow.

Other, similar, information was broadcast.

From where and whom all of it originated is not known.

Now, when all of this is remembered, we begin to think that it might have been an intricately thought-out enticement to keep people from running away.

Since there were few healthy males in our camp, we asked to be reinforced from the regiments. It was decided that women, children, and the elderly would be in the center during prayers, while a chain of Cossacks from the regiments, linking arms with each other, would surround them.

May 30th, the day of the Catholic holiday, neither the Major nor the colonel came to the camp. A note was sent by the latter in the morning, asking that the mourning flags and placards be removed for the day of the holiday. We did not accede to the request.

Major Davies came the morning of the 31st. He was asked if there had been any response from London to our petitions.

He answered negatively.

Then we informed him of the radio broadcasts. He promised to check into them.

Mrs. L. asked:

—But what if it is true, Major?

—Then you will go nowhere—Davies answered—and I, with joy, will drink champagne with you here in the offices.

The information on the radio turned out to be all lies.

After lunch, the colonel came to camp and asked us to go voluntarily.

All refused.

Wives of the staff officers, led by General Domanov's (Field Ataman) and Solamakhin's (Chief of Staff), came from their Lienz hotel to our camp to be with the rest of us.

It was decided we would hide them in the middle of the crowd the day we were to load.

The Major came twice after midday, repeating his previous directions about departure.

—I will come at seven o'clock in the morning. You Madame —he addressed me— and Polunin will wait for me by the main gate.

I had decided not to meet the Major, but to stay in the crowd at prayer instead, so that he could not ask questions or give orders. But Polunin had to meet him, all the same. He did not know any English, so the Major would be unable to speak to him.

At seven o'clock, Davies came again.

—I wish to speak to the wives of Generals Domanov and Solamakhin—he said.

They were called.

When they came in, the Major stood and gave them his respects.

I translated the following unforgettable conversation with Domanova.

—Your Excellency—the Major began—you know that all the wives of senior staff officers must be taken first and first of all are to be you and Mrs. Solamakhin. I want you all to go with every comfort due your rank. For this, I ask you to be ready at 7:30 in the morning. In what barrack are your staying?

—In the 15th.

—A bus will be provided for the 15th Barrack. Prepare your things.

—I will not go voluntarily, so I will not pack my things— Domanova answered.

—I very much ask you to prepare for departure and not resist. For me, a British officer, it is unpleasant to use force against ladies, especially wives of officers. I would have wanted that you all, especially yourself, went in comfort. Otherwise, you will go by train with all the rest.

—I am a Cossack. There is no insult for me to be with the rest. At this time I sleep in a room with them. I thank you for the privilege, but I do not need that honor. I prefer to share the fate of the rest of the Cossack women. I will not go voluntarily.

She broke into tears that she tried to restrain.

—Could you give me a list of the wives of the senior officers?—the Major addressed her.

—No. I can only answer for myself.

—I repeat—the Major continued—at half past seven, there will be a bus provided at your barrack.

—I will not go voluntarily—was the answer that followed.

—You and General Solamakhin's wife will need to be taken first. Especially you.

—Good. If I am so necessary, and if by this I can save the others, then I will go voluntarily. I will sacrifice myself to save others. In such a case, I am ready to go now.

—No! That will save no one. All the same, everyone will have to go, but you first.

—In that case, I will share everyone's fate and will be with everyone. There is no reason for me to get ready to leave, because I will not go voluntarily.

—This is your last word?—asked the Major.

—Yes. This is my last word.

The Major rose.

—Think about it—he said.—In any case, the bus will be available at 7:30 in the morning at your barrack.

—I thank you, but I will not go voluntarily.

The Major gave Domanova his respects and left.

—You Madame—he addressed me—will wait for me at the gate at seven o'clock in the morning, and everything should be done according to the plan that I sketched for you—he said on leaving.

—I am listening!—I answered, but I knew that his directions would not be followed.

The evening of May 31st, someone turned off our water, so that we could not even wash up.

At one o'clock that night, a quartermaster, temporarily in command of the 1st Regiment, came to announce to us that he would send 1000 Cossacks at dawn to help us. At two o'clock, the commander of the 2nd Regiment came with the same news

Both asked me to cross them and hid.

At dawn, two thousand Cossacks and 100 *junkers* were in camp.

———————————

All of these days, from May 28 to June 1, were days of terrible inner suffering for us. I, personally, never had any time to myself and slept in my clothes and not more than two hours each day. All day and night, Barrack *No* 6 was stuffed with our unfortunate people. Many asked me to translate their personal petitions to Major Davies, pointing out relatives in the USA. Official group petitions were translated. People tried to stay together before the horrible day of betrayal. All fasted. Even had a notice not been given for a general hunger strike, we simply could not eat due to inner, heart-wrenching distress.

We considered what we could do, how to organize... We thought that they would not use force, that it would diminish them in the eyes of the Austrians...

For now, I will cut off my general account and switch to a separate question.

Under-khorunj Polunin had been in the trumpet orchestra of the staff of the Don stanitsas. He was twenty-five or twenty-six years old, of small height, brunette, nervous, and expansive.

Where he is now, I do not know, but, in any case, he managed to survive.

I met him two months after the tragic days of the betrayal, at the beginning of August at Camp Peggetz, when, having found my husband in Salzburg, I returned to Lienz for my modest baggage and paid a visit to Peggetz. Learning of my arrival, he ran to the barrack and we greeted each other like brother and sister, with kisses. Here, he led me through his difficult epopee, but how he saved himself, I do not remember.

I know that the commander of the 1ˢᵗ Regiment after the officers were removed also saved himself, which pleased me greatly. I do not remember his name, but he impressed me greatly with his performance on the eve of the hunger strike. He was a rare orator. He spoke of how necessary it was for everyone to take the announcement of the hunger strike seriously.

I also want to say a few words about General Shkuro and of Professor Verbitsky's remarks of having seen him on May 28 in a German uniform in the camp at Spittal.

I think the professor is mistaken. I met with the late General Shkuro twice before the Lienz tragedy. The first time was in Kotschach, before the English came. He was in a black *cherkesska* that time. The last time I saw him was in Peggetz, where he had come on the eve of his arrest, and that time he was in a black *cherkesska.* I doubt that, on returning to Lienz, he changed into a German uniform.

On that day, that is, the 26th of May, I stepped out of Barrack *No* 6, where General Bedakov's and Major Davies' offices were. I saw that the main street was full of Cossack men, women, and children. I thought that they might be some new arrivals, but to my question, I received the answer:

—No. It is Daddy [батько—*trans.*] Shkuro arriving.

Then I saw a small automobile within the crowd and, at the same moment, General Shkuro pushing toward me with arms already open wide.

—Greetings, kinswoman! Do not worry about your Mischa.[*] He is alive and well in Salzburg. I received a letter from him. He writes that they have formed a committee there against returning. Soon we will have ties with Salzburg. I will go there and take you as my interpreter.

We kissed again. He sat back down in the automobile. The crowd surrounded him. Everyone wanted to shake his hand. Arms were stretched out to him, offering cigarettes, tobacco, and cakes…

Cossacks followed him to the gate and beyond. It was as if they knew that they would never see him again.

I stood on the steps of the barrack and watched until the automobile was out of sight, while the people along his path, full of joy, all waved to him.

Later, O. A. Solamakhina told me that, in the evening, Shkuro had been invited to have dinner with Field Ataman General Domanov.

General Solamakhin, being Chief of Staff for the Field Ataman, had never been invited to such dinners, even though his room was across from Domanov's.

At three o'clock in the morning of May 27, Shkuro burst into his room, sat on the bed, and started to cry.

—He betrayed me, that scoundrel [м…ц, probably мерзавец. Russian sensibilities toward profanity are more refined than those of

---

[*]   Mischa—this is the husband of the author of the article, Colonel R., of necessity having left the Cossachi Stan not long before. After, he lived in Salzburg.

English speakers—*trans.*] Domanov—he cried out. Invited me, wined me, and betrayed me. The English are coming right now to arrest me and turn me over to the Soviets. Me, Shkuro, turned over to the Soviets... Me, Shkuro, Soviets...

He struck himself in the chest. Tears flowed from his eyes.

At six o'clock in the morning, he was taken away by two English officers.

Ideas were so mixed up at that time that the possibility of betrayal never came into our heads.

On the question of what unit carried out the forced removal of officers, Cossacks, and families from the region of Lienz, I can say in complete confidence that it was a Scottish unit of the English Army and not the Palestinian Brigade, as has been said by some who lived through the tragedy.

The Palestinian Brigade arrived later, about the middle of June.

The soldiers that used force spoke clear English, without foreign accents, and understood no Russian. I happened to have spoken with several of them earlier, when they came to provide Cossacks with shovels and such. All were surprised that we hated Stalin and argued with me, trying to convince me that he was a remarkable man and it was only thanks to him that they defeated the Nazis. They were overjoyed that the Labor Party, led by Clement Attlee, had won the English elections.

—Attlee is a remarkable man, and he is friends with Stalin, they said. They were surprised, too, by why we were not going to the Soviet Union. They did not believe me when I told them of the horrors taking place there.*

And to finish, here are several words about the English staff at Lienz, about the English officers, and about Major Davies. The English staff was located in Lienz, in the southern part of the city. They had a lame colonel there. What his name and position were, I

---

* That a Scottish unit was the one that used force is evident from the insignias on one of them from his certificate, provided by Major Davies. But the possibility cannot be excluded that, in their squads on June 1, were hidden NKVD agents, which would explain the rude remarks in Russian that were heard by many on the days force was used.

do not know. He was about forty to forty-five years old and made a good impression. He clearly suffered from all that took place.

Major Davies did not command the city, but was only an officer used in liaison to the Cossack staff. He was then twenty-six years old. In order to approve any serious requests, he had to go to the colonel. Davies had his own office with this staff, but he also had one in Peggetz, in Barrack *No* 6.

There were two majors on this staff. One was named Lisk and spoke a little Russian. The other was a redhead whose name I do not know. Besides them, there were many junior officers.

Anyway, Davies later explained that in the beginning, there was one major assigned to repatriation, whose name he did not know. This major was sympathetic to Russians and refused the post. They put him in the guardhouse. When he refused even after that, he was stripped of his rank and sent to the Japanese front.

Davies also first refused and was arrested for it, but after sitting in the guardhouse for fifteen hours, agreed, for, in his own words, he knew that, should he refuse, the redheaded Major, who was simply a beast, would be assigned and "things would have been even worse."

What insignia was on Major Davies' sleeves, or other officers' and soldiers', I do not remember, but I do know that Davies and all the other officers and soldiers in this unit were from Scotland. On parade, they wore Scottish kilts and the music they used was clearly Scottish. All were of the Anglican religion.

Their military chaplain was a kind man. He was greatly perturbed by the force that was unquestionably used by the Scots on the 1ˢᵗ of June 1945. On the next day, he gathered the soldiers who had taken part in the operation into church and said to them:

—Yesterday, you committed a great evil, even if not by your own free will. You used force on defenseless people; women, children, and the elderly. For this reason you must pray diligently to Jesus Christ, the Lord, so that He forgives your great sin.

Interpreter of Camp Peggetz R.

•

About General A. G. Shkuro

Telling of the arrival of General Shkuro to Camp Peggetz, May 26, 1945, the preceding essay states with complete confidence that he was dressed in a *cherkesska*. She saw him less than a day before his arrest, and it is difficult to allow that he had changed into a German uniform in this time, particularly since the German Army no longer existed—it had surrendered.

However, Professor Verbitsky, also with complete confidence, insists that, when he saw Shkuro on May 28 in Spittal, he was then wearing a German tunic, but whether it was that of a general, he could not say, since he could not distinguish insignias.

This is not an important question, but in view of the fact that it was raised, many Cossacks have taken an interest in it. The question has become a matter of principle.

There is no reason not to believe either witness. Without doubt, he was taken to Spittal in a *cherkesska*, and Professor Verbitsky saw him there in a tunic.

One insignificant circumstance might lead to the correct answer.

Kuban Yu. T. G., who was taken from Lienz with General P. N. Krasnov and the other officers of the Cossachi Stan, managed to escape being sent to the Soviets. He noted that, when the column of vehicles bringing officers to Spittal entered the gate to the camp, an English soldier came to meet it, carrying a sword and *kinjal*. Yu. T. G. suggests that these were Shkuro's weapons.

It is very probable that he is correct. Apparently, Shkuro was taken to Spittal in a *cherkesska*, but after, when the English took his weapons away, he took off the *cherkesska* and put on the tunic, which might have been of German style and make.

What clothes Shkuro was wearing has become a puzzle for many, as has the much more important puzzle: why did he, not having any direct relationship to the Cossachi Stan, appear in Lienz in those tragic days?

To the present, disregarding the opinion of several who served with and were subordinate to General Shkuro, it has not been possible to find any definite information about his presence in Lienz.

V. Naumenko

●

Tragic Days at Camp Peggetz

... When I came to the field on May 28, the officers organized themselves by Hosts: Don in front, then Kuban, Terek, and the rest.

I asked my father:

—Why so many? Are they all really going to a conference?

—Some conference!—he said.—They would not need so many for that. They will put us behind barbed wire in a concentration camp. The war is over, you see.

I tried to convince him to stay.

—No,—he answered,—it is better on legal grounds to be with one's own people. We will sit for a stretch. We will be sorted out and, God willing, will meet again.

Apparently, many thought the same way that Papa did. Colonels G. and M. said about the same thing. Many saw it as a logical conclusion to the war.

The column of officers set off. Don Cossacks boarded vehicles that stood on the road outside the camp first. Families saying farewell crowded around them.

When I wanted to put my arms around my father for a last time and cross him, an English soldier with an automatic appeared next to me.

He yelled very rudely to hurry. This struck me as being unpleasant, but I thought that prisoners of war are not treated any better.

The soldier and the chauffeur pulled down the rear curtain, and the vehicle moved into the general column.

I saw a soldier with an automatic next to the chauffeur of each vehicle.

The Tereks presented a beautiful and, I can now say, tragic picture.

Their ataman was small, elegant, and in a *cherkesska,* while strapping Cossacks were behind him, also in *cherkesskas.* They walked with complete precision. A handsome, tall old man in parade dress, his full bread flowing over a chest covered with medals, walked in the middle of the front row. He carried the tri-colored Russian flag. There were many more Tereks in *cherkesskas* than were Kubans, and all wore medals.

All this points to no one even having a thought of a betrayal. If someone now says that they foresaw a betrayal, they were very unusual—extremely sagacious and careful people.

… Major Davies came to Camp Peggetz repeatedly and used all his skills to convince people to go to their homeland. He even offered comforts. A bus, it seems…

I came into the 6th Barrack only on the last evening, that is, May 31st. He was still trying to convince people. The ladies were all alarmed, and all of his entreaties were in vain.

That evening depressed me. It was an image far worse than a cat playing with a mouse.

He sat at a table, posing a little, as if playing a role in a theater piece. Meanwhile, all around him, everyone was hysterical.

My heart was wrenched. It was frightening, sad, and somehow hopeless.

I left right away.

What happened the 1st of June you already know, and much has been written about it.

… At five o'clock, the English assured us that no one would be taken any more and that they were leaving the camp until tomorrow, but at seven o'clock that morning, vehicles would be provided for boarding and departure to the homeland. After waiting a bit, we started back to our own barrack. We lived in the 7th Barrack—next to the field. That night, Madame G. moved us in with her in the 6th Barrack, so that it would not be as frightening. Many rooms, and even barracks, were empty. Things had been plundered and thrown about.

That night, some people got a few of their things together and left for the hills. We suffered greatly during the bloody fight, especially Mama, and could go nowhere—we had no strength left and some sort of stupefaction had come upon us.

At seven o'clock on the morning of June 2nd, we were already prepared. Our things were outside, as instructed.

Our barrack was located at the end of the camp, and the entire street could be seen from it. We watched vehicles come to the barracks and people, no longer with any will of their own, in a kind of stupor, loading their things and seating themselves in the vehicles, which left immediately.

The camp became painfully empty. We waited our turn to load. At this time, a small automobile came to our barrack and Major Davies jumped out of it. He entered the barrack, with which he was familiar, and walked about the rooms as if looking for someone or checking to see if anyone was left.

Several ladies were crowded together in the corridor. I stood at the entrance.

Voices were heard:

—We need to ask him.—And, for some reason, they addressed me.

—Ask him in our names if he could leave us until tomorrow. Tomorrow, we will go ourselves, but until then, much can happen.

Davies was already nearing the exit.

I walked up to him and asked in Russian to leave us until tomorrow, pointing out our condition. It was awful: arms and legs with wounds, black and blues, swelling.

He looked at my leg, at the others, and answered in Russian:

—Good, go ahead and wait.

I think that if he could not speak Russian, then he could at least understand and say a few things.

He got back into his auto and drove off. At the same time, a truck came up to our barrack and began to load our things.

Natasha (my daughter) and I left the barrack, went to the truck, and started to explain that Davies said that we should wait. Natasha dragged our things back. A commotion arose: one group loaded, the other threw them back. An American interpreter drove up at this time and started to go around us. I rushed toward him and said that Major Davies gave us permission to stay.

He seemed not to believe me, said that he would check right away, and took off for somewhere in his jeep.

My heart stopped.

After about ten minutes, he returned to announce that loading had been changed and that, after dinner, we would all be able to register by presenting papers that we were old emigrants.

Regretfully, the camp was almost empty. Only four barracks remained unloaded: 6th, 7th, and the two across from them.

Toward evening, the camp began to fill anew, and more and more with every passing day.

L. S. G.

From the Travails of a Young Mother

... —How could it be?... I have already told so much about it!... I always get upset when I remember what we lived through,—a woman said, slightly out of breath with anxiety.

How could it be?—Here is how. When all the officers were taken to their deaths, our Papa among them, the camp was left without the intelligentsia. Almost all the barrack commanders had left with the officers. From that day, a young, clever Cossack named Kuzma announced himself to be the commandant, and all that time, he held the entire camp in his hands.[*]

Every type of rumor flew about. It spread everywhere that we all had to hold on together, since individuals would not count for much, but all together, it would be easy to maintain resistance. Only, God preserve us, do not touch the English, as that could cause serious consequences—was said throughout the camp.

Churches were full of worshippers day and night. Church services were continuous. The entire camp made confession and took communion. That is how it is, apparently, with prisoners before execution. After this, what began to spread was that, according to English law, churches were inviolable and worshippers could not be touched.

---

[*] Under-*khorunj* Kuzma Polunin was chosen by all the available non-commissioned officers to be the leader of the Cossachi Stan, May 28. Interpreter O. D. R. tells of this promotion.

Several times a day, we gathered together on the camp's field and there, by "consensus," prepared letters to the English King, Queen, Roman Pope, Madame Roosevelt. I remember some stirring expressions and entreaties from these letters: "Do not destroy totally innocent people," "Do not give them up to death and torture," "Take pity on the children," and others.

There were placards everywhere in the camp with the words: "Better death than going to the USSR." Many had notes pinned to their chests: "Kill me, but do not send me away." A hunger strike was declared: all cooking fires were extinguished; rations were not accepted from the English, and even children were not given food. Only the ill who were in infirmaries were fed, but the personnel refused rations.

People were anxious. Many wanted to run away, but most stayed in the camp in the conviction that there could be neither a massacre nor forced removal of defenseless people. Individuals from somewhere began to arrive, insisting that we needed to hold on only for three or four days...

... At six o'clock in the morning (1st of June), Mama and I spotted the religious procession through a window. At its front was a homemade birch cross. Priests and a mass of people walked behind it. We joined the procession then, but my brother went to join the chain.

The trucks came at eight o'clock. At the same time, the Liturgy was being read out on the field; most people were making confession and taking communion.

It was announced through interpreter R. that "we are being asked as a matter of honor to seat ourselves in the vehicles to go to our homeland." Over a graveyard silence, this order was repeated three times. At the same time, the firm advice: "Stay in place! Do not run off!" passed from mouth to mouth in the crowd.

Those in the first rows began to be beaten with rubber rods and two volleys were fired: one at our feet (there were wounded), the other—over our heads. When the volleys were being fired, mothers lifted their babies up to meet the rifle shots and I raised my baby. I wanted her to die right away, and then I could die in peace.

The rifle shots made the crowd squeeze together and sweep itself up; people were trampled; I myself stepped on someone's body, trying only not to step on his face. Soldiers grabbed individuals and threw them into trucks, which took off immediately, half full.

In the crowd, from all sides could be heard: "Chase off Satan! Christ has arisen. Lord have mercy!"

Those who were captured resisted desperately and were beaten. I saw an English soldier take a baby from its mother. He was intent on throwing it into a truck. The mother had firmly attached herself to one of the child's legs. They both pulled it: one to one side, the other in the opposite direction. Then I watched as the mother lost hold of the baby and the child struck the side of the vehicle. What happened later, I do not know.

The altar was knocked down, priests' vestments were torn... The crowd crushed us so that Mama, who was carrying the icon of the Kazan Mother of God, turned blue and started to lose her breath.

—Lord,—I prayed—how could I have had a child at such a time! Lord! What can I do? Saint Theodosius Tchernigovsky, spare my daughter! If I can save her even for only the course of this terrible Friday, I promise the rest of my life to follow a strict fast every Friday, so as never to forget this!

And then, a miracle occurred: the same crowd that had just been threatening to crush us now began to gradually squeeze us out, squeeze us out unbearably. And it squeezed us out. Not toward the circle of soldiers, but to the opposite side, toward a straight road that opened up before us to a bridge across the river and into the trees.

Yes, this was a miracle. And I devoutly fulfilled my vow: I eat nothing on Fridays aside from bread and cold water.

We headed for the bridge. And I did not even notice that I had lost my shoes and was running only in my socks.

A chain of *junkers* stood in front of the bridge, following some order or other to try to keep the crowd in place. They would not let us pass. I grabbed the chest of the *junker* who was stopping me. I tried to push him off the road, yelling:—Let me pass! I have a baby. Let me pass! English soldiers were just about to reach us... Only then did those blocking me seem to realize what was the matter and start to let people pass. Everyone rushed the bridge. One woman, right before my eyes, jumped with her baby and was swept away by the roiling Drau.

Once past the bridge, the main mass of escapees turned left, into the woods, and English soldiers took chase after them... Shots were fired and cries heard from the wounded and those being beaten, along with prayers for help.

Mother, my brother, and I, not knowing ourselves why, ran to the right, toward a village. Probably because we were so few, they did not chase after us. All that remains in my memory is that, when we ran past the village, Austrian farmers were peacefully working in their fields as if nothing had happened.

Running into the hills, we started to go up them, even though we were almost exhausted. We avoided roads. At times, some old Cossacks walked with us. Several of them lent us their footwear for a while. Then we lost them (actually, we fell behind), and we continued most of our trek by ourselves. We went almost always without footpaths. Our ascent was winding and difficult. My brother sometimes took the little girl in his arms and handed her up to me after I climbed a ledge. Then he climbed up himself. Mother could barely move along.

We got to the line where there was no longer any vegetation, just snow cover ahead of us... Snow began to fall. Bare mountains, swirling clouds, precipices everywhere, and ahead, snowy peaks. And below, people were moving and living. It was all so strange. We felt as if we were completely alone and were hunted animals. The farther we went, the more snow there was—above the knees in places, and we were bare footed... Strangely, no one even had the sniffles.

On our second or third day in the mountains, we came upon three corpses: a man in a military uniform, a woman, and a child. Apparently, seeing no way of being saved, they decided to end their lives.

We walked a fifth day. Ahead of us was nothing but snow. We ate the snow to ease our thirst in secret from each other. My little girl became weak. Her head hung down, and she appeared to be completely apathetic... Around us, everywhere, was the same bare rock. I thought that the child would not survive the trip, that she would die of hunger, as we all probably would... What to do? Who could we turn to? Who could help?

Again, I started to pray to Saint Theodosius Tchernigovsky: "Save us and help us! If I am not worthy, then send at least a crumb of bread for my child!"

I prayed, but at the same time thought:—What can I do? Is this not madness? Not even a dog will run through here, and I am asking for bread... And then I took heart—No! If I just believe, there will be bread!—And I prayed...

And then, completely unexpectedly, around a turn in a footpath, deep among the cliffs, a small tourist cabin appeared.

Apparently, a Cossack who had earlier walked with us was trying to break into the cabin by prying open a window. He made signs calling to us. We approached. Silently, he pointed within. I looked and was astounded: on a table right by the window were five loaves of bread, lying in a row. "Five evangelical loaves."

I grabbed one of them, pressed it to my breast, and kissed it ardently. At that moment, I truly felt that we would be safe.

A miracle! Another miracle! Aside from the bread, there turned out to be a small amount of semolina in the cabin, some flour, and other food. There was firewood. It was as if someone had prepared all of it in advance, especially for us.

We lit the stove, cooked kasha for the little girl, and ourselves ate. We took the bread with us, dividing it with the Cossack. This bread, softened in snow, nourished us for quite a while.

There were still unexpected new dangers ahead: how to cross over the ridge tops. Everywhere, there were cliffs and precipices, covered with snow. But here, too, the old Cossack helped us. He scouted for a long time to learn the area. Then he confidently led us in the direction he had chosen. It turned out to be the right direction, and within a few hours, we began to descend.

When I later looked at a map, it turned out that we had walked seventy versts [fifty miles—*trans.*] in those days and climbed over three mountain ridges.

Then we worked for a piece of bread at a "bauer," and here, too, there was a miracle: one time, two Englishmen came, in search of escaped Cossacks. The Cossack was "discovered" by them next to us, in a room in the attic where our chambers were, and began to cry unstoppably.

I grabbed my daughter by her hand and decided: I would not give myself up alive. I would simply jump out the window with her… I would kill myself and kill her… Only, I prayed:—Lord, do not let me come to such a sin. In walked a sergeant and asked for my papers. My hands trembled…

He looked at them, thought a bit, and then turned my brother's papers over for a long time. He was then only seventeen years old. Suddenly, the sergeant hissed: "All right," turned, and quickly left.

The Lord had saved us all for the third time.

F. V. V.

•

The Path to Treachery

What is wickedness? What is virtue?
Everything has been exchanged for gold!
Where will we now find earthly
Justice, mercy, and love?
  For what more is a heart needed?
  Without it, it is more peaceful, after all.
  And one can live peacefully with executioners
  And heartily agree to their butchery!
The world's shame does not much endure—
Let's extend its borders—
And in the presence even of God
Summoning when it occurs.
  Where is good? Where is evil?
  Everywhere, there is simply law
  And nothing can stand for long
  The response word: truth.
What then? Believe in tears, do not believe
And the price is written in blood!
There is in Europe a Valley of Death,

And leading to it is a path of treachery…
In that valley, forgotten by all:
Treachery is gotten used to quickly!
Oh, will there come such a time
When disgrace is called disgrace?
(From Cossack creativity of recent years)

•

June 1, 1945

The present essay is a continuation of the essay by the interpreter of Camp Peggetz, Mrs. R.

As in the first, the reader will find some repetition of previous information, but this could not be avoided without compromising the integrity of the account.

Both accounts are valuable mainly because they give several details about the behavior of those who directly fulfilled the Yalta agreement.

At 4:30 in the morning, all the inhabitants of the camp gathered on the field, where a platform had been built for religious services. Children, women, the old, invalids, and the wives of Generals Domanov and Solamakhin were placed in the center. I, too, stood in the crowd, supporting the ailing wife of Colonel M.

A chain of Cossacks and *junkers* stood with their arms linked all the way around us.

Te Deums were begun.

I think that rarely have people ever prayed as fervently as we did.

Thin, pale, with eyes sunken, thousands stood facing death, praying, with tears running down their cheeks.

—Look! A shooting star!—one of the Cossacks said. And truly, it appeared to all of us that a pale star was moving across the pale horizon.

—And it is moving straight. That is a good omen,—someone from the crowd said.

—God save Your people...—was sung and carried melodiously over the quiet field.

Suddenly, the roar of motors was heard. No one even turned to look. The sound came closer and closer and then... Major Davies came toward the crowd in a jeep. Under-khorunj Polunin, who had been ordered to meet him at the gate, was with him. Covered trucks arranged themselves next to the jeep. That meant it was seven o'clock.

Major Davies stood with arms crossed, apparently waiting for the worship services to end. How long he waited, I do not know. His motor began to hum—he drove away.

Soon, the roar of motors could be heard again. Tanks drove up (how many, I cannot say) and formed up next to the crowd. The crowd moved back.

A rifle volley was fired. They shot blanks, but it electrified the crowd, and it jerked back. Many of them, shouting, raised their arms.

The English apparently had counted on this and began to grab those standing nearest, drag them to trucks, and throw them inside. Those who had made up the chain were beaten with clubs and rifle butts. A second volley was fired... Tanks moved on the crowd. The crowd panicked. People retreated in horror, squashing their own women and children in the process.

Heart-rending screams and shouts were heard.

The British soldiers became bolder and began to beat people. They grabbed those who jumped back out of the trucks, beat them with clubs, and threw them back in... The crowd retreated with cries. Boards had been left in a pile in the rear; many, myself among them, fell over them. Half-crazed people ran over my legs. Everything was mixed up: prayers being sung, groans, wails, the yells of the unfortunates who were captured, children's cries, rude shouts from soldiers... Everyone was beaten, even the priests, who, raising crosses above their heads, continued their services... I prayed for the Lord to help me stand up. Rising to my feet, I ran along with the crowd through a break in the fence that surrounded the camp and into a different field. There, many people were on their knees while priests, their faces senseless, led them in continuing their prayers. Others rushed to the bridge leading across the river and, farther on, into the hills. All were guided by the same thought: "Soon, it will be my turn to be taken, thrown into a truck, and made to appear before the eyes of Red executioners." Horror took hold of everyone; like rabbits being chased, they ran here and there. I used handkerchiefs to bandage heads of two or three Cossacks that had been cracked open by rifle butts. The only refuge—the river… Throw oneself into the roiling stream and all would be over…

I ran to the river. Women, with cries, threw their own children into the stream and jumped after them into the water… This was so horrible, that I turned away for a moment—I could not look. Then yells were heard:

—Interpreter! Interpreter! Negotiations are taking place.

I crossed myself and returned.

Major Davies stood in front of the kneeling crowd. Seeing me, he said:

—Finally, I've found you. Why didn't you meet me at the gate?

—My place is with my Russian people.—I answered.

—Ask if anyone has seen Mrs. Domanov. I need to see her and Mrs. Solamakhin.

—The Major asks,—I addressed the crowd,—where is Mrs. Domanova?

A Cossack said that he had seen her being thrown into a truck.

—That's not true.—the Major answered.—I checked all the trucks, and she was not there.

Another Cossack said that he had seen her being beaten with clubs and then taken, it seemed, into a barrack.

—And where is Mrs. Solamakhina?

—We saw her run screaming to the river.

Major Davies turned to me.

—Be so kind as to accompany me through the barracks. I need to find Domanova. Perhaps she is in need of medical assistance.

We went by jeep to the first—the 6th Barrack. We went in. The Major went into the lavatory, while I was commissioned to check the barrack for Domanova.

—If you find her, come and tell me,—he commanded.

I went through the rooms, calling quietly—Maria Ivanovna!—and decided that I would hide her if I did find her.

But Domanova was not in the barrack. I went back to the Major. The door to the lavatory was open. He stood with a small glass in his hand and took a drink. A bottle of cognac stood next to him.

—I am searching for Domanova and Solamakhina not to turn them over, but I want to tell them something,—he said, addressing me.

—I do not believe you any more, Major,—was my answer.

We drove past several barracks without going inside. The Major merely asked people who were standing at them whether Domanova was there.

Everywhere, the answer was negative.

We returned to the crowd. The priest, Fr. A. B., stepped out from it, asking the Major to delay sending any more people for some three days, until an answer arrived from the King, Queen, Roman Pope, Archbishop of Canterbury, and others, to our petitions.

The Major listened, then said that he could do nothing. He called to a colonel.* The latter began to entreat people to go back to their homeland, but the reply to him was a firm: "We will not go voluntarily."

Several questions were put to the colonel:

—Tell us, where are our officers, and will we be reunited with them?

—I do not know where they are—the colonel answered.

—And where do you intend to take us?

—I only know that our unit will turn you over to another English unit.

---

* The colonel in question was the commander of the 8th Scottish Battalion, which conducted the transporting of people. His name was Malcolm, and his rank was Lt. Colonel. He is the one that the interpreter called "the lame Colonel" in her previous essay.

—And where will we be taken?

—To Judenburg.

—Good. We will go with you if you agree to let us go in marching order with our horse carts.

—No. That is not allowed.

—In that case, we will not go voluntarily. Give us a postponement until answers to our petitions arrive.

The colonel promised to call by telephone to get an answer. He left, but Davies stayed. The crowd, still on its knees, continued to pray. The sound of single gunshots reached us from the woods. These were from "volunteers" (or, as was said, Soviet soldiers dressed in English uniforms) catching people.

The Major stood, pale, downcast.

—Tell them not to resist,—he spoke up, talking to the crowd.

—Sir Major! Imagine a huge oven and a fire lit in it. You are ordering us to jump into it. Would you jump?

—I don't know.

—You know very well, Major, that you would not. Returning to the Soviets is worse than a fiery oven.

—But I, as a British officer, can no longer look upon unarmed people being beaten; women, children… I can no longer use force. I can't anymore. I can't…—Tears from his eyes traced small tracks—I can no longer. I can't…— And, waving his arm, he left in quick steps to find out the results of the colonel's conversation over the telephone.

Taking people away had been interrupted, because the trucks that had gone away loaded with victims had not returned from the train.

Polunin came up to me with two Cossack women.

—Mrs. R., come sit in the shade. You are about to fall down, —and they took me under a small curtain near the crowd, seating me there on a crate.

—Maybe something will be decided in our favor,—Polunin said.—Let's hope so.

English soldiers came up.

—Well,—one of them said to me,—now you will go by train.

—Why?—I asked.

—Aren't you Mrs. Domanov?

—No, I am your Major's interpreter.

—But tell me,—the soldier continued, looking at the crowd, —why, if they have so much faith, and there is a cross with them, are they so afraid? They should not be afraid, if they have faith.

—But we are also human,—I answered coldly.

In the end, the Major returned with the answer that old emigrants would not have to go, and that they needed to register with their documents with the English officers in the 6th Barrack. Registrations would be made according to the country in which they had lived as emigrants. He asked me to let them know about it.

The English soldiers put up a fence and made an entrance at which they put a guard, an English Captain, and myself, as interpreter.

Mobs of people began to come out of the crowd, holding documents in their hands, while others came without documents. Thanks to this, it was possible to save many new emigrants.

I told the Captain which person was from what country, and they went to register in the 6th Barrack.

At this time, motors could be heard once again, Trucks returned for new victims and arranged themselves near the crowd of worshippers.

Many women had suffered so, especially those in the condition or with nurslings, that when an English soldier came near them and helped them up from their knees, they were indifferent and walked to the trucks submissively, their faces puffy, supported by soldiers.

An English doctor arrived at the guard point, expressing his wish to help those suffering. He provided first aid gently, then he directed those who needed it to the dispensary or the infirmary.

Several women went into premature labor.

The doctor told me about his own indignation over the necessity of applying force against people.

—It is inhumane,—he said with tears in his eyes.

A Scottish officer came up to him. He had a swollen hand. He had obviously sprained it while wrestling with some unfortunate. I had personally seen this officer beating with a club people who resisted. Unfortunately, I have forgotten his name.

Those wounded by "volunteers" were brought from the woods on stretchers. One old Cossack was seriously wounded in the stomach.

Then a Cossack ran up to me and said:

—The wife of Colonel L. asks for you to come to her barrack. She is not well. She fell and had the crowd walk over her.

I ran to her. She lay in the barrack, moaning quietly. Many feet had trod her stomach. She wanted to see the Major. I went for him, and he came right away and was very concerned. Mrs. L. was taken to the hospital.

English soldiers were breaking open doors with their rifle butts and robbing rooms in the barracks. They slashed open the sides of suitcases or convenience and pulled things out: furs, shoes, silver, linens, etc.

Sobbing women ran across the field, searching for their children, while children, in tears, called to mothers who had been taken away. (Many parents were thrown into trucks, while their children were left behind, and vice versa.)

Later, the Red Cross sought out children and mothers in hope of reuniting them, but rarely with success.

At one o'clock, or two, perhaps three, and more likely the latter (my watch had stopped, which is why I do not know exactly), the Major sent me to a hotel.

—Your face is gaunt. [Interpreter Rotova had translated this to Russian as "You have no face"—*trans.*] You need to eat, then rest for three days,—he said.

When they took me in a large jeep to the hotel, I saw piles of things in it that were stolen by English soldiers, silver and gold things, shoes, boots, etc.

The next day, they loaded the poor *junkers*. It was said that several of them perished by jumping out of the trucks.

Then they loaded the regiments. But by that time, many had succeeded in escaping into the hills.

There were around seven hundred victims, trampled, beaten, killed, poisoned, hung, drowned in the river, or killing themselves in other ways, on the 1ˢᵗ of June in Camp Peggetz. Three of the *junkers* who had been sent to help us jumped from trucks at full speed and were smashed to death. A serious person, with higher education, now living in Australia, whom I believe without question, told me how he personally saw a Cossack tie himself to his horse and jump from a cliff into the stormy waters of the Drau. Supposedly, he had left a note on the cliff: "Here perished with his horse is Cossack So-an-so," with the date of his death.

All of this violence was the responsibility of the Scottish Battalion of the 8ᵗʰ English Army.

Approximately five thousand people were taken out of Camp Peggetz the 1ˢᵗ of June.

This tragic episode in the life of Russian people "in disseminating truth" will always remain a dark stain and mortal sin on the honor of the British leadership.

Ideas were so confused at that time and the English so softly "covered up," that it never entered anyone's head how tightly and basely they had worked out their plan for betrayal.

Even on the day of betrayal, everyone thought that unarmed people in prayer would never be touched. But, obviously, the "cultured" West in the 20ᵗʰ Century exceeded all expectations. The "humane" English raised their arms against defenseless women, children, the old, and invalids—without any sympathy for them…

On that day, the cries and tears of hunted people were heard over three kilometers away. Even the Austrians cried, hearing the desperate screams. Their horror can never be conveyed, never written by any pen. It needed to be seen and suffered…

May the souls of those who perished rest in peace, and may the Lord God help our unfortunate brothers and sisters who were given over to the Soviets.

Interpreter for Camp Peggetz R.

•

About Lienz

The author of the present piece held an administrative rank in the 1st Mounted Regiment while the Cossachi Stan was in Italy.

Before the move across the Alps, the sections that he led were disbanded, and he was left on the regimental staff without duties.

Apart from his personal experiences, this piece gives testimony on how the registration of regimental officials and their families was conducted. Also found in it is information on the fate of the Cossacks' friends—their horses.

May 27, at eleven o'clock, a messenger from the regimental staff came to my tent.

—You are urgently required by adjutant Yesaul Sh.—he pronounced.

—Tell him I am coming immediately.—But a thought flickered in me: so they have dug down even to me.

I went to the staff office. It was the first time I had presented myself to adjutant Sh. He did not know me before.

—Can you write in German?—he asked.

—Yes.

—Here is pen and paper. Allow me to see how you write.

He named two families. I wrote them down.

—Excellent.—he said.—Here are two clerks. One will validate the papers. The other will dictate names. You just write. By this evening, we need to give the staff of the Field Ataman a list with two copies on the receipt of equipment. You will write starting from under-khorunj and I will copy over the officer contingent.

It was already dark when I finished copying 1993 people.

The list was taken by Yesaul Sh. from the clerks, who had exchanged papers with me. He checked it against a list in Russian, rolled it into a tube with two copies, and sent it by special courier to the Field Ataman's office.

May 28, again at eleven o'clock, I was called to the offices and Sh. said:

—There are several officers' families with the 1st Regiment. Make a list of the wives and children.

Once more, a clerk dictated, I wrote, and, since there were few women and children with the regiment, I finished the list quickly.

That business was before lunch. The officers finished work, and I stayed with them to gab.

Soon, the regimental commander, Colonel G., drove up. He told the adjutant:

—Call all commanders of sotnyas and separate commands quickly to the regimental office.

After ten to fifteen minutes, the commanders stood next to the office. The Colonel stepped out and announced:

—Gentlemen officers! I have just returned from the Field Ataman. Inform all officers found in your commands to assemble quickly for a meeting of officers at lunch. English vehicles will be provided soon, and all officers will be driven to a conference with the English Command. Only a single duty officer will remain with a regiment. Do not bring anything with you, since we will return quickly.

I am neither an officer nor a combatant, so I went to my tent to have lunch. When I finished lunching, the officers had already left.

When the sun set, a car came, took away the duty officer and the ill Khorunj A.

The next day, there was an announcement that the families would be taken out of Camp Peggetz May 1st, followed by the 3rd Regiment, and after it, the 1st Mounted Regiment.

The Cossacks lodged a protest, announced a hunger strike, and hung black flags on all carts. Non-commissioned officers took off their shoulder tabs in order to act as ordinary soldiers so that they could protect women and children.

June 1st, the Cossacks assembled at field churches, raised regimental gonfalons, and went to Camp Peggetz, led by two priests.

After the slaughter, I returned to my tent at about three o'clock.

The hunger strike was ended—it had not helped.

There was a respite June 2nd, but on the 3rd, loading into vehicles resumed.

There were English posts on the bridges of the Drau during loading, but after loading, they were removed.

Cossacks began to leave. Women with their belongings in bundles and men mostly with foodstuffs climbed up the forests of the Alps toward the Italian border, along which they intended to go into Switzerland.

I stayed for a last day to ponder how to save myself from being turned over.

There were no direct guards, aside from those in the English tankettes that occasionally went through and who saw people with bundles going off into the woods, but never said anything to any of them. On a short summer night and day, one could not go far—one could only get to the alpine peaks.

From the indifference of the English toward those leaving, it might be surmised that they would not get far. The wooded regions could be taken and cleared—if they fired on an unarmed crowd, then why wouldn't the English be capable of shooting at those who had gone into the woods?

The 10th Sotnya (previously the 6th, commanded by Yesaul Z.) was located by the edge of the forest on the foothills of the Alps. I walked over to them. The Cossacks had broken up into small groups, each of which was working on a plan of action. They had broken into smaller groups because they were no longer maintaining an organized resistance, but only searching for ways to save their individual selves.

Six Cossacks from Yekaterinograd suggested that I join their group and go with them. I accepted the invitation. They decided to leave at night, but not into the hills. Given the location of the regiment in the valley, they would stay outside of the boundaries of encirclement during the loading process.

All night, people left for the hills. At two o'clock at night, we went down into the valley. A group of Cossacks stood next to a cart. Among them was a group of my "stanishniks," from the neighboring stanitsas of Rozhdestvenskoy and Philimonovskoy. We stopped. To the question of what they had decided to do, they answered that they decided to go, since no matter where they went, they would be in the hands of the English and would, in any case, be turned over. We said our farewells and left.

We lay in an orchard of the Austrian gardens on the banks of the Drau.

The sun rose, The regiment's place was surrounded by tankettes, provided with vehicles, and loading started. The Cossacks made no resistance.

We were outside the line of encirclement, so this time, we did not fear for ourselves, but nevertheless tried to keep out of the sight of patrols.

Here, our attention was drawn to an extraordinary spectacle. Several Cossacks, on saddled horses and paying no attention to the English soldiers, were herding horses.

Cossack horses, left without masters, had spread out over the valley in search of food. Several were not far from us. One of the Cossacks rode over to them.

The two S. brothers, who were in our group, called him over. He turned out to be a Cossack from the 1st Mounted Regiment from Ispravnoy Stanitsa. He said that the English offered willing Cossacks the chance to gather and pasture the horses for a two-week time. Sergeant P. was named the leader of their group. He had gathered his stanishniks, but they were short two men. P. was not far away. Riding over to us, he signed up the S. brothers for his group. They caught the first horses they could and rode off to chase all the horses into a single herd, They told us that they would keep us informed.

P.'s group consisted of eighteen men.

After about two hours, Aleksei S. rode up to us and said:

—Boys! We are going to drive the horses to the other side of the Drau. English guards are standing on the bridges. None of us has a pass. There is just one general pass with P. Catch some horses, mount them, and we'll see.

We quickly caught horses, found saddles, gathered about fifteen to twenty horses, and headed at a trot toward a bridge. The English gave way to us and we crossed over to the other bank of the Drau.

After some time, P. rode up. He told me that he had already signed me up for the group of horse herders.

By evening, we were 120 men. They separated us into two groups of sixty men each. P. sent the one I was in to Oberdrauburg. There, we gathered the horses of the other regiments and drove Circassian horses from Oberdrauburg.

After about three weeks, we were moved to Nikolsdorf. And after another two weeks—near Lienz, across from the Dölsach Station.

When we stayed near Lienz, our Cossacks first saw the Palestinian unit. Several of them spoke Russian.

I was designated as the one who got and distributed food for the group. For that reason, I stopped working directly with horses.

B. A. Ya. was the interpreter. He lived in Lienz and drove a car over to us with an English captain. Later, we went to England on the same transport with him, and even later, he moved to the USA.

Near Lienz, all Cossack horses were first registered, then branded—three stripes—and the numbers written down. After this, they were sent by rail (in freight cars). Where, I do not know. The English said they were sent to peasants in various places that had suffered in the war.

Several hundred horses turned out to have the mange. In one day, the English shot about two hundred such horses, along with several camels that had been in the Cossachi Stan, probably with Cossacks of the Astrakhan Host. After that, horses were no longer shot. A veterinary hospital was set up. Under-khorunj Z. was named the veterinarian. He was the former physician of the 5th Sotnya of the 1st Mounted Regiment.

Having finished dispatching all the healthy horses, the veterinary hospital and its personnel were left at Lienz, while our two groups were sent to Villach to tend to Hungarian horses. We took some of the horses that were across from Camp Kellerburg and combined them with the general herd of Hungarian horses outside of Lienz.

Over about a week, we sent them off from outside of Villach. I do not remember the number, because it did not hold any interest for us at that time. Each of us watched out not to end up in a freight car and find ourselves locked in it.

As we neared completion of the dispatching of the healthy horses, the mangy ones were loaded into open wagons and sent back to Lienz.

Our hospital turned out to be the "central" one.

One time, the English captain came to us with interpreter Ya., lined our entire group up, and posed the question of whether there were any among us who wished to return to the Soviet Union. Everyone kept silent. Then he asked:—No?

As if on command, we answered with one voice:—No!

He told us:

—You will no longer be sent back forcibly.

After some time, the interpreter informed us that the unit that oversaw us was leaving, and a new one would take over. Those soldiers who had sent people to the homeland by force had a sword on their insignias, but the new ones had something that resembled a sunflower.

Soon, the horses were cured and sent off. Our two groups were moved to the woods to get firewood for military units.

We worked until the month of November, then the interpreter came to announce:

—Good news. In days, you will receive documents from the civil guard and will be able to travel freely to work.

No more than three days passed. A commission arrived: a physician and some sergeant. There was no officer. They questioned each of us, filled in forms, and went away. We were not sent to work the next day, but were told that we were leaving for the Russian Camp Kellerburg that day. We knew of the existence of that camp some days before—that was where those who had formerly been within Soviet territory had been sent from the camp on the Drau and were free from barbed wire.

We settled into free barracks in the camp.

There was a meeting that night. Several men from the camp administration stood before us, calling on us to resist Stalinist messengers.

So that we would not be caught by surprise, the camp police posted guards against the chance of a night raid. In such a case, they would raise an alarm.

Several of us had worked in editorial offices, and one, Ye. S., wrote an appeal which was printed in the camp's offices and distributed.

Many Cossacks began to travel out of camp and corresponded with other camps: in Klagenfurt, in Villach, with Bulgarians, Rumanians, Serbs, etc.

I went in Klagenfurt in Lieutenant G.'s group. I had already corresponded with several men there of my acquaintance who were new emigrants and a stanishnik—an old emigrant.

Lieutenant G. showed great vigor in defending new emigrants from the Austrian police and did not allow Soviet commissions near us to examine who of us was new, and who an old emigrant. He told them that we were all old.

There were no longer any forced repatriations.

M. Alekseev

The Lienz Tragedy as Interpreted by an English Officer, One of the Parties Responsible for the Use of Force on Cossacks

This transcript was kindly given to us by the Honourable Secretary of the Managing Committee of the Russian Refugee Aide Society [English name could not be confirmed —*trans.*] in Great Britain, Count G. Bennigsen.

The Duchess of Atholl, who supposedly took offense to this English soldier, is the Chairwoman of the aforementioned organization.

She had previously been a Member of Parliament for fifteen years in the Conservative Party and holds the Order of the British Empire, Second Class; but at the time of the Spanish Civil War, her sympathy had been with the Reds. Later, on learning the reality of Bolshevism, she realized her confusion and went on the warpath against it.

1. Letter Printed in *The Times*, May 14, 1952, Under the Title, "Repatriated Russians."

M. G. Allow me, as one of the officers mainly responsible to the British Commander-in-Chief in Austria in 1945-46 for carrying out the policy of His Late Majesty's Government on the repatriation of POWs, to tell the Duchess of Atholl that she errs in taking offense that Soviet citizens were subject to obligatory repatriation.

In the British Zone of Austria, the only Russians forcibly repatriated against their will were those who, being citizens of the USSR on September 3, 1939,

A) Had taken up arms against Soviet nations ["their own country" in *The Times—trans.*] or the Allies or

B) Had a prima facie case of guilt for recognized war crimes established against them by ["in the opinion of" in *The Times—trans.*] Soviet authorities, and accepted by His Majesty's Government or

C) were deserters from the Soviet Armed Forces. I would like to point out that escaped or liberated prisoners of war and discharged hospital patients, who had not been recalled to the colours and were, subsequently deported by the Germans for labour, were not looked on as deserters.

I can assure the Duchess of Atholl, that Soviet citizens not included in categories A, B, or C, had the right to remain in the British Zone, if they wished.

Oswald Stein
99 Warwick Way, S. W. I.

[The version in Russian given by Naumenko above was checked against an English version in Peter J. Huxley-Blythe's *The East Came West* (Caldwell, Idaho: Claxton Printers, 1964). Neither gives the impression of being an original text. Huxley-Blythe's version is probably a translation from German—*trans.*]

2. Letter Sent to *The Times*. May 18, 1952

M. G. The letter of Mr. Oswald Stein in your May 14 edition demonstrates either his unfamiliarity with what took place in Austria in the Drau Valley or his desire to forget events in 1945-46 for which the leadership in this country can in no way take pride. Regretfully (for him), there are still survivors in existence who managed to save themselves from the evils of forced repatriation at Lienz, Peggetz, Klagenfurt, and Spittal, and who are capable of testifying that indiscriminate repatriation to Soviet authorities had not been limited to the categories given by Mr. Stein. In no way is it possible to include women and children in the category of Soviet citizens who took up arms against their country or the Allies, or were guilty of war crimes, or were deserters from the Red Army. No investigation (screening) was done, but on a designated day (June 1 in Peggetz), victims were surrounded by units consisting of tanks and the Palestinian Brigade,* who fulfilled their orders with extreme rudeness: refugees, preeminent women, and individuals incapable of bearing arms were forcibly driven into trucks and taken to the Soviet zone. When the terrified mass of humanity broke down a fence in an attempt to escape, they were pursued, beaten, and taken captive anew. Many committed suicide, and it was announced that more than seventy corpses were recovered from the Drau River.

G. Bennigsen

3-20 May 1952, the following postcard was received from the editor of "The Times":

"The editor of *The Times*, following established courtesy, gratefully acknowledges receipt of your communication."

The communication, itself, was NOT published.

•

---

* Force was used not by the ranks of the Palestinian Brigade, but by the Scottish Argyll-Sutherland Battalion of the Royal British Army.

The Last Days of the Cossachi Stan

This report was read by its author on May 31, 1953, at a gathering of Cossacks in Lakewood (USA) on the day of a memorial for the victims of Lienz.

It is quite natural that the author, who lived through the tragic betrayal with his wife and two small children, was not able to see all that took place on the large field of the camp, nor in some places near to him. However, he does give a clear picture of what took place before his eyes.

This report gives many details illuminating the inhumanity that took place on the Drau.

This frank, human document completely refutes the attempt by Mr. Oswald Stein to apply a legal basis to the illegal and inhumane acts of the English.

Much has already been written about the forced repatriation of Cossacks and their families that manifested itself at the end of World War Two on the Drau near Lienz, in Austria, carried out by the English from May 28 to June 5, 1945, especially about the betrayal of the officer staff. As an eyewitness to all these terrible events, I wish by sharing my impressions of what happened to the Cossachi Stan, from the betrayal of its officers to its final days, to set straight the record that has been given to the public by the publications of others.

The non-commissioned officers were not taken to the unfortunate conference and were left as the seniors in rank. One of them—Don Cossack, K. P., was presented to the English commandant, as it was then said, as the leader of the Stan. I first saw him in the following circumstance: on the day after the betrayal of the officers, that is, May 29, 1945, English tankettes drove through Camp Peggetz and other Cossack areas. Quartermaster P., dressed in a Cossack uniform, was in the third one of them. In no way do I bring this up as censure. One of the tankette commanders, a dark brunette who was capable of speaking clearly in Russian, was informing, with unconcealed spite, those who came near his tankette that everyone in the Stan had to be repatriated to the Soviet Union according to an agreement from the Yalta Conference. Therefore, he recommended that it be done voluntarily. Quartermaster P. was obviously vexed, as was the leader of the tankettes, a blonde Englishman, in appearance.

After the arrest of the officers, the priesthood became the moral leader, mainly (to June 1, 1945) the religious supervisor of the administration of the Cossack Diocese, Fr. V. G. (from the Don). Meanwhile, for organizational and disciplinary authority—the *junkers* of the Cossack Military School.

In order to bring to life measures directed at the prevention of the forced repatriation of Cossacks, group initiatives were organized through the good will of the intelligent youth of the Stan.

Those three powers, acting in concert, tried to do something to save the Cossachi Stan, left leaderless by the removal of its officers.

Their first act, under the direct leadership of Fr. V. G., was the completion of a petition that had been started by a group of individuals back before the betrayal of the officers. Among them was the betrayed Captain L. (from the Kuban), an old emigrant from Slovakia. This petition was rewritten in several copies. In what language it was prepared, I cannot now recall, even though I signed it, along with several thousand other Cossacks. Fr. V. G. submitted the signed copies to the English commandant of Lienz, Major Davies, for him to forward to: the English King, Archbishop of Canterbury, and Pope of Rome.

At the same time, as a sign of protest against repatriation, the entire populace of the Stan announced a hunger strike. In addition, everywhere in the Stan—on trees, telegraph poles, fence rails, buildings, and even on carts, black flags were hung. Notices in Russian were printed with typewriters and pasted in the name of the group initiating it. These warned that the English, in order to induce the residents of the Stan to repatriate, might turn to armed force and might even shoot to frighten people, but above the crowd, not at it.

The following situation, having the same aim, must be noted: under the direction of its priest, a large black flag was hung from the steeple of the Catholic Church in Dölsach as a sign of protest against forced repatriation of Cossacks. The church was within two or three kilometers of Camp Peggetz and the other areas of the Stan. It was removed the same day on orders from the English command.

In those days, the residents of the Stan resembled an aroused anthill. People went around lost in thought. Their faces were sad, because they knew very well what awaited them should they happen to fall into the hands of the Soviets. In various places, acquaintances and stanishniks gathered and discussed what to do. Many still tried to comfort themselves with the thought that the English would not undertake the heartless betrayal of turning over to the Communists tens of thousands who had showed through deeds their irreconcilability with Communism, and who could, in the near future, make true allies in the impending struggle with this world evil.

Rarely, in various parts of the Stan, groups of English appeared. Among them could be seen, dressed in the Cossack military uniform of the Siberian Host, with Russian epaulets, Ya.—an old emigrant. He served as interpreter, first with the staff of the Field Ataman, then with the English. Of necessity, they did not turn him over to the Soviets with the other officers. As I was told, Ya., lived at one time in Singapore as an émigré, where he learned English.

It was strange to see among the khaki uniforms of the English, the bright epaulets and cap band of a Cossack officer. Without words, with one sympathetic glance, he made it understood how heavy was his heart.

May 30, after lunch, Fr. V. G. informed the Stan through intermediaries that on May 31, after the liturgy, which would be held entirely in the church barrack of Camp Peggetz, he would explain all the measures being taken to accomplish the goal of averting forced repatriation.

At the time given, several thousand worshippers gathered in and around the camp church. During the liturgy, conducted by a gathering of the priesthood, many of those within the shrine gave confession (the sacrament of confession was given by five priests) and were administered the Sacred Final Rites, since they fully understood what awaited them. After a number of priests completed the administration of the rites, Fr. V. G. gave his sermon. This sermon was in answer to grumbling from several Cossack units about the former leadership of the Cossachi Stan, which in their opinion brought the populace of the Stan to such a terrible catastrophe.

Supporting the former leaders, Fr. V. G. called the criticism worthless, comparing it to a rosy apple filled with worms. Then he announced that he had done all that he could to prevent the forced repatriation of Cossacks, and that he considered himself free from having to fulfill the duties of Head of the Cossack Diocesan Administration after the reading of the petition.

After the end of the liturgy, the priesthood went in a religious procession onto the field inside the camp, since all of those who had gathered could not fit inside the church barrack.

Standing with the priests in the center, he loudly read the text of the petition, which had earlier been handed to Major Davies to be forwarded higher to those addressed. It was explained in the petition that, finding themselves in the Cossachi Stan, this irreconcilable foe of Communism—natives of the former Cossack Districts of Russia and their families, brought together accidentally. They had fought Communism from its inception, been in Soviet prisons and concentration camps, were treated as *kulaks* [property owners of all kinds, who were considered to be a criminal class by the Soviets, the term not unlike "usurer"—*trans.*], and had their right to vote taken from them. In the months prior to surrender they had been found in Poland, Czechoslovakia, Yugoslavia, and other countries, where they engaged units of the Red Army. Many were refugees, former White Army emigrants and their families. If the combat-ready units of the people of the Stan, with weapons in their hands, had to ally with the Germans to battle Communism during the period of the Second World War, it was because Cossacks hoped that, with the help of what they considered the lesser evil, they could carry on their fight with the greater evil of significance in the world—Communism.

The conclusion of the petition (about which, due to its expansiveness, it must be written separately) posed the question whether the populace of the Stan could be sent to do the hardest prison work, in any given part of the English territories, rather than be turned over to their most wicked enemies, without doubt for a tortured death.

After reading the petition, Fr. V. G. suggested that the day that repatriation was to begin, that is, the first of June, be greeted and passed in a Christian manner. Namely: with the priesthood, gonfalons, and icons, from seven in the morning of that day, gathered on the field of Camp Peggetz in worship services.

After this, those gathered began to disperse, while the priests returned to the church barrack. Only a single priest remained on the field. He began to sing a *Te Deum*. A small group stayed near him in prayer. Successive priests continued the service until the evening, before it became dark. When one set of worshippers left, they were replaced by another. At the same time, *junkers* went about the areas beyond the Drau, where Cossacks and their families were found among their covered wagons or in tents, in the woods, the side of the road, or in fields. They informed them of the coming worship services on June 1ˢᵗ, recommending that all gather at the designated time on the field of the camp, where it would be easier to give organized resistance against repatriation, should it be decided that force be used against a group of defenseless worshippers.

Night came. For many in the Stan, it was the last in their lives.

The fog that came off the Drau gradually veiled the river valley. The moon that appeared beyond it at the tops of the mountains at about three o'clock at night, could barely be made out. Before dawn, for the first time since the war ended, a long train, judging from the drawn-out sound that its wheels made, moved quietly along the railroad tracks on the Lienz side. We began to realize for whom it was dedicated.

Early that morning, even before the sun had arisen, priests in vestments appeared in various places in the Stan. One of the more senior Cossacks in age, either from a cart in which there were church belongings or from some place arranged for the purpose, brought out gonfalons and icons and stood beside them.

Tying horses to their carts or to nearby trees, entire families joined in. During the procession, several held icons in their arms that had been brought out of their homelands. They had managed to preserve them for decades, with great risk to themselves, while living in the impious USSR.

At the designated time, singing Easter songs, for it was just after Easter, the procession began to move along the road leading into Camp Peggetz. Along its route, Cossack men, women, and children, coming from the woods or their carts, joined the procession.

The nearer they approached the camp, the more of them there were. Entering the camp through the gates located in various places in the fence surrounding it, the religious procession stopped around the priesthood at the camp's field, where tables covered in white tablecloth for the altar and sacrificial table already stood on a platform for the liturgy. Those with icons or gonfalons stood on both sides of the priests. Two choirs (Kuban, led by Sh. and a diocesan choir, directed by A.) arranged themselves behind them. Around them were several thousand worshippers. All of them were surrounded in turn by *junkers* and young Cossacks, intent on protecting the elderly, women, and children.

It was a bright, sunny morning, boding a warm day. The songs of larks, rising high above the planted meadows, resounded through the air; the Alps that encircled the valley were colored with snowy peaks and, growing lower, there were green forests, in which picturesque Austrian settlements could be seen, along with their well tended yards. But all of this beauty had no charm.

Toward nine o'clock in the morning, when all the religious processions had converged, the Divine Liturgy was begun. This time, Archpriest Fr. V. N. (from the Kuban) led the priesthood—an old man of about sixty, having in the past finished two faculties of institutions of higher education. This reverent father was with the Cadet Corps as a teacher of religion and lecturer in Russian language.

At ten o'clock in the morning (at that time, the choir was singing "Our Father"), English automobiles, covered in yellow-green canvass, drove through the fence into the camp from the side of the railroad tracks. They came to a stop some twenty meters (on the Lienz side) from the worshippers. A platoon of soldiers came out of them. Half were armed with light infantry weapons—rifles with attached bayonets. Others had submachine guns, and there were even two machine guns. The rest of the soldiers had clubs, approximately a quarter meter long and as thick as a grown man's arm. On a command from their superior, the platoon formed up in two rows. With this, one of the machine guns was placed among the autos, with its barrel pointed at the worshippers, exactly like the second, which the machine gunners placed next to the array of soldiers. Their superior spoke to them for a full ten minutes. Obviously, he was giving them orders. At the same time, two airplanes appeared overhead and flew through the river valley and along the hills.

Religious services continued. Those who had fasted began to take communion.

On command from the senior officer, soldiers armed with rifles quickly aimed at the crowd and fired at the ground, below the legs of the worshippers. The bullets hit the ground and ricocheted toward it, hitting several in their legs.

After several volleys, when the crowd fell into disorder, the English came at it at an angle from two sides, with shouts and the most exquisite curses in English and Russian, and cleared a path for themselves with bayonets. They attempted to cut a part of the crowd out from the rest so that they could be taken more easily. At the same time, soldiers with clubs beat on defenseless people, mainly their heads. They lost consciousness and fell to the ground, their heads bloodied.

The worshippers, pressed by the ravishers, started to retreat toward the east, taking back from the hands of the soldiers anyone they could. During this, the altar and the sacrificial table were turned over. Archdeacon Fr. T., so as not to spill the Holy offerings, quickly drank them. Church vessels and prayer books were kept in the arms of the clergy.

Then, enraged soldiers, and there were more and more of these, began to beat people even more fiercely. Those who resisted or broke away were stabbed with bayonets or shot at.

One of the first to suffer a bayonet stabbing was killed. He was a Don Cossack who had stood in front. There arose such a roar then that even rifle shots could not be heard. One could only tell by the smoke that came from their barrels. Dead already lay on the ground, along with those wounded or knocked unconscious by blows from clubs. The valiant soldiers immediately picked them up and threw them into the back of trucks that were being driven right up to the crowd at that time.

Those who were deafened came to in the vehicles, jumped from them, and ran to the surrounded Cossacks. The soldiers once more beat them with clubs, and threw them into the vehicles. If they met resistance, they killed them.

At that time, apparently on orders from the English, an ambulance came to the Cossack hospital and stopped at the side away from the English. An experienced Sister of Mercy, dressed in the pre-Revolutionary uniform of the Red Cross, stood beside it, sobbing and wringing her hands.

After loading living and dead Cossack men and women, the motorcars, each with two armed Brits sitting in the back, rode off in the direction of Lienz, along the railroad tracks.

At that time, enraged soldiers began to beat and grab people with even greater persistence, trying to clear a way for themselves to the priesthood. The crowd, under the rain of blows from clubs, stepped back.

The priests, who were still holding icons and gonfalons, now turned out to be almost at the front, along with the singers.

Taking advantage of this, one of the monsters knocked the Gospel out of a priest's hands with a blow of his club.

At the same time, many singers and several of the clergy were grabbed and thrown into the motor vehicles. Some had soldiers tear their vestments off, right there on the field. Others were thrown into the motor vehicles while still in vestments. Before this, middle-aged I. M., of the Kuban, had been struck on the head with clubs and injured. He had been holding the image of the Holy Mother in his hands. The skin under his left ear had been split open. Along with some of his hair, it hung down from the ear. The neck, face, hands, and white shirt of this Cossack were covered in blood, as was the edge of the icon. A soldier tried to strike another from the Kuban on the head with his club—A. M., who carried the gonfalon of St. Nicholas, raised by the Yevkaterinskoy Stanitsa of the Kuban

District. But the club struck the braided edge of the gonfalon's cloth and tore it off, without allowing any harm to come to the Cossack.*

Fr. V. G., finding himself at the front of the Cossacks, retreated with them into a corner of the field that was enclosed by a tall, wooden fence. All the while, he was sanctifying with his cross the soldiers of His British Majesty who were trying to capture him.

When the latter had almost reached their mark, someone from the Cossacks yelled "Hoorah." Thousands in the crowd spontaneously picked up the call. The robust Russian cheer carried through the valley. The repatriators, assuming that the Cossacks were attacking them, became confused and, quickly running back to the motor vehicles, aimed their rifles and submachine guns at the crowd. One of the English, obviously an officer, yelled something at the machine gunners. Fearful that the English were about to open fire at the crowd, several of the Cossacks began to ask that the yelling stop.

A panic arose. Some tried to run off.

Noticing this was an under-khorunj from the 1st Mounted Regiment (Terek), some twenty-three to twenty-five years old, having an intelligent appearance and dressed in a blue work shirt, and K. Sh.—an old emigrant from Yugoslavia. They tried to yell over the crowd for people not to run off, since all who broke away from the general mass of Cossacks would be easily caught by the soldiers.

At the same time, under the press of the crowd, the fence separating camp territory from the fields was knocked over at one place. The crowd rushed out of the camp; but there, they came upon previously posted soldiers. Among them were machine gunners camouflaged by the tall rye grass.

Over the course of about ten minutes, everyone had run out of the camp and regrouped in the field to the east of it.

Father V. and the part of the priesthood that remained once more stood with gonfalons and icons before the worshippers, facing the railroad tracks.

---

* This gonfalon was raised the next day by the author of this piece, delivered to Munich, and turned over to the Host Ataman. Restored, it is presently found in the Kuban Host Museum—in the chapel of the Cossack Home in New York.

From the right side, about ten meters from them, all in a row, no fewer than ten tankettes had arrived from the direction of Dölsach, while all around was a chain of armed soldiers.

Father V. said, addressing the crowd:—Let us pray to God and His Immaculate Mother to save us.

His aged voice exclaimed: "Have mercy on us, Lord. Have mercy on us! Holy Mother of God, save us!"

The kneeling mass of worshippers, now significantly thinner, tortured by the horror they had lived through, the preceding hunger strike, thirst, and heat (the day was very hot), took up his exclamation.

After Father V., other priests made exclamations. And since it was just after the Easter period, all the Easter songs were sung in the general prayers: "Christ has Arisen," "The Angel Calls," "Yes, God has Arisen," along with the prayer to the Mother of God, "Hail Mary…"

In the distance, local residents watched all that was going on from the railroad tracks and surrounding villages.

For some unknown reason, the English left the worshippers alone, but burst into the barracks and grabbed people found there.

It became relatively quiet, so that gunfire from rifles and automatic weapons around the camp could clearly be heard. It was especially intense in the woods beyond the Drau.

About an hour after the Cossacks had broken out of the camp, the first trainload of captured inmates of the Stan left Lienz, headed toward Oberdrauburg.

It consisted of sixty freight cars, of which two were flat cars —one in the middle, the other at the end. Armed soldiers could be seen on each.

The doors to all the cars were closed. Here and there, people looked out from barred windows. Someone, apparently a woman, stuck her arm through the bars of one window and waved a white handkerchief in farewell to the still-kneeling crowd.

Soldiers then began bringing by those people they caught in the camp, who were hiding in the weeds or in the empty tents that were around the camp.

Three soldiers dragged out a Cossack who had earlier been wounded in the leg. He resisted, so they pinned him to the ground while a fourth beat him on the head with a club.

The following incident is engraved in my memory. A soldier was leading a young Cossack woman with a baby at her breast to a vehicle. The baby's arm had a slight injury—probably scratched. The "good-hearted" gentleman, stopped about ten meters from the crowd, wrapped a field bandage around the child's arm, and let him drink water from his flask. Then, ignoring the mother's pleas, he led her to the vehicle.

The behavior of the tank drivers was different. One of them (as I related earlier, a column of them had stopped some ten meters from the encircled crowd) said approximately the following in German:—Stay firmly in place. Do not agree to repatriation, and do not fear us. We, too, have human hearts. If we are commanded to drive our tanks at you, we will stop right in front of you.

A few minutes following the announcement, a young girl came out of the encircled crowd and walked over to one of the tankettes. She had a note in her hand, written earlier by her father at the request of the wife of Colonel T., who had been turned over with the officers. The text of the note was as follows: "It would be better to shoot my parents and me here, than to turn us over to the Communists from whom we escaped."

The tank driver took the note eagerly and read it. The girl's parents and those near them watched what was happening, knowing what was in the note. After reading it, the tank driver's face turned pale, and tears appeared in his eyes. He gave the note to his colleague to read, who had the same reaction. The first tank driver put the note in his jacket pocket as he watched the girl attentively to see if he could determine which were her parents.

After some time passed, at about four in the afternoon, a small military vehicle drove up to the encircled crowd and stopped between the camp and the Cossacks. Three men were in it: a fat military man [translated henceforth as officer—*trans*.], his interpreter, and a chauffeur. A loudspeaker had been set up on the car. Using it, the fat officer spoke in English, while the interpreter, standing beside him—in Russian;

—Maria Ivanovna Domanova! I have something very interesting and important to tell you. Come out!

The crowd answered:

—She is not here. (Domanova—wife of the Field Ataman.)

Ignoring them, the officer repeated what he had just said.

Then, addressing the crowd, he began in English:

—Cossacks! I am impressed with your bravery; but it is in vain, because, in agreement with the decision of the Yalta Conference, all who lived in the USSR as of September 1, 1939, must be repatriated.

The interpreter translated his words.

The crowd erupted with noise. In response to that, the fat officer announced:

—I cannot speak to everyone. Choose one person of your own to speak with me.

Someone recommended the priest, Fr. A. B.—a Cossack of Poputnoy Stanitsa, Kuban District, an old emigrant from Yugoslavia. The crowd approved the recommendation.

Father A. came out and told the officer approximately the following:

—We ask you to shoot us here, rather than return us to the USSR, to the Communists, with whom most of us have been engaged in armed conflict since 1917. Some of us were forced to emigrate from Russia in 1920, while others who were similarly minded, our near and dear, took on themselves all the horrors of life in the Soviet Union, serving time in prisons and places of exile. They only got a chance to emigrate later, using the arrival of the Germans. All of us, responding to the movement of the Soviet Army, hurried west, hoping that we would ultimately end up in territories held by the forces of the USA or England, whose leadership would provide us with asylum as political refugees. It is absolutely clear that the Communists consider us a dangerous foe, rain all manner of calumny on us, and make great efforts to capture us.

To this, the officer answered through the interpreter:

—The decision of the Yalta Conference must be carried out. All who left the borders of the Soviet Union before September 1,

1938, or lived until that time in other countries, as can be verified by documents in their possession, I ask to step out and stand to one side.

At least three families from Polish Belorus responded to this request.

The officer continued:

—All others, tomorrow, at eight o'clock in the morning, must be ready with their things to be sent to the USSR, but for now, you may disperse. No one will trouble you.

He waved a small red flag to the soldiers and tank drivers surrounding the Cossacks. The soldiers went to the side of the camp, while the tank drivers turned their vehicles around near the crowd and went in the direction of Dölsach. As they did, a husband and wife threw themselves under one of the tankettes, but the driver managed to stop in time.

It was close to five o'clock in the evening.

The officer rode off in his vehicle, while the Cossacks began to disperse, heading for their carts or into Camp Peggetz.

Only the last of the dead, not yet removed by the repatriators, were left on the site of the slaughter—the *junker*, Michael, born, as indicated by documents discovered on him, in Dniepropetrovsk, and the Kuban Cossack woman, Maria (who also had documents on her), along with a dead child.

As later became clear, the inmates of Camp Peggetz had to undergo the must careful investigation on the night of June 2nd and that day. At it, all foreign born and those with documents verifying that they were emigrants were allowed to stay in the camp. The rest (although there were instances in which the English destroyed documents of old emigrants on purpose) were grabbed by soldiers and taken to a large area near the railroad tracks, surrounded by barbed wire. Then they loaded them onto trains and sent them to Graz, where they were turned over to the Soviets.

Among those taken that night of June 2nd was Fr. V. N., whom the repatriators had sought especially. Apparently, by his self-disciplined example, he had interfered with the accomplishment of their plans.

Soldiers surrounded him and another priest, Fr. V. (Kuban), at the altar of the church barracks, overturning everything, including the altar, while doing so.

What happened to those few inmates of the Stan who on the day of the religious protest against repatriation stayed in the areas of what were then called stanitsas?

The measures taken for forced repatriation, as ordered by Major Davies, were carried out simultaneously in Camp Peggetz, Lienz, and beyond the Drau, in the area of the stanitsas. Tanks and tankettes with armed soldiers were on the roads and beside bridges, grabbing all those who did not have local documents. But, luckily, because there were woods that rose to the top of the Alpine ridges near the stanitsas, those who had remained by their carts, on hearing rifle fire from the camp and seeing soldiers approaching, went into the woody thickets. Through them, after crossing the road, where it was also guarded by tankettes, they made their way toward the ridges, with the intent of going higher. The repatriators who followed the escaping Cossacks fired into the thickets with rifles and sub-machine guns. This resulted in dead and wounded. A woman who hid in the thickets at the edge of a woodpile beyond the Drau across from the camp, was given away by the barking of a dog. A soldier followed the dog's barks and shot the woman.

That day and later, the victims of the Yalta agreement, preferring death to return to the "Soviet paradise," shot themselves, took poison, jumped from cliffs into the river, under tanks, and even threw themselves from the top-floor windows of tall buildings. One Cossack, at the time recovering in the Lienz hospital, threw himself through a window of the multi-floor building onto a bridge. Understandably, he was smashed to death.

There were places where entire families committed suicide. For example, engineer M., a Cossack of the Mishkino Khutor, Novocherkasskoy Stanitsa, Don District, used a revolver to shoot his year-old daughter, twelve-year-old son, and his wife, then himself.

Several women, whose husbands had been taken and given to the Soviets, tied their small children to themselves out of despair and jumped with them into the Drau. There, those Cossacks who tried to escape repatriation by swimming across the river also found death, from English bullets that reached them in the water. The flowing river carried away the bodies of those drowned and killed and deposited them farther down on the banks of the river, where the local residents buried them.

I saw one such grave near the bridge that was on the opposite side of the Drau, across from Dölsach. A cross made from branches tied together with rags was on it. During the course of 1945, someone periodically brought fresh flowers and water for a canning jar placed at the bottom of the cross. Toward autumn, the mound of the grave settled from the very rainy summer, and a small depression appeared on its place.

A sad picture was presented by the stanitsas on the evening of June 1. The Cossack men and women who remained left the forest thickets on returning from the slaughter, where they could have easily been caught, and went onto a field having several groups of carts, to which some of those who had successfully run off into the hills had begun to return. With feelings of dread, many of them untied their horses, in most cases brought all the way from their homes, and released them. It was the same way they treated the horses of those who were absent, known to have been captured or killed. The starving animals ran through the fields and hay meadows of the peasants, where they tried to graze. In order to protect their crops from destruction, the local residents had to guard them against the homeless horses. The better ones, they lured with oats to capture and take home. All that night, the neighs of horses were heard along with the mooing of cows and the noises of camels, upon which their masters, in most cases Kalmyks, had ridden from the distant Salsky and Stavropol Steppes.

The sobs of women and children could be heard from various places near the carts. They cried for those near to them they had lost that day, or they were crying over their own unfortunate lives.

Being ineffectual, the hunger strike was ended. Here and there, cooking fires were seen. Those few who had provisions left cooked food by them.

Night came. Under cover of darkness, many left for the hills. Each tried to save his life and the lives of those near to him in any way he could. But tanks and tankettes were next to the bridges across the Drau, patrolling along the road with the sentries.

Early on the morning of June 2nd, atop a small hillock on the field on the side opposite the carts, a venerable priest from a Don stanitsa, Father T. S., with the help of Cossacks, set up an altar for a field chapel. It was enclosed on three sides by small green saplings, cut and stuck into the ground. Attached to the saplings were two gonfalons and an icon. A table covered with a white cloth was placed inside the altar to substitute for a communion table, on which Fr. T. put all the things necessary to perform the Divine Liturgy, along with a painted image of Christ's Resurrection, erected by those from the Don several months before. At eight o'clock in the morning, Fr. T., in the service of Protodeacon T., began the oblation. People began to gather. Many gave notes for commemoration of their health and those near to them. Some prepared to take communion. All, with trepidation, awaited their executioners. At mid-day an automobile arrived with an English officer and an interpreter. People immediately gathered around them. Through his interpreter, the officer said that they would not be sent off that day, but the next. However it would not be to be turned over to the Soviets, but to a distribution camp, from which people would be repatriated only of their own free will. It had been decided that the area around Lienz be emptied of the foreigners that had accumulated. Furthermore, the English were interested in having a nominal number remain to deliver provisions.

What the Englishman said spread among the Cossacks immediately, but no one believed there was to be no further forced repatriation.

Before evening, the English did indeed bring provisions, giving out three days' worth, to those on lists prepared by Cossacks. For this, many, myself included, put on these lists not their own names, but contrived family names, as was recommended, in case we fell into the hands of the Soviets,

———————

Time went mercilessly quickly. It was another sleepless night. Again, many left for the hills.

The morning of June 3rd arrived. It was Sunday. Church bells could be heard ringing in the surrounding villages. People, after all that they had gone through, were weak and listless. Most, putting what was absolutely necessary into a sack or rucksack, wandered aimlessly from place to place.

Austrian women wandered among the carts. They traded pieces of pork fat or bread for the remaining cows of Cossacks.

In such a setting, I happened to see the following occur. Two children were left without parents: a brother and sister, three-four years old. Their mother had died several months before, while their father had been taken to the Soviet Zone on the first day of repatriation. A childless family that knew them looked after the two orphans. Wishing to save the children, they asked some Austrians to take them for their own. They agreed, but could not take them into one family. The orphans' names were given to them. When the latter came to take them, the unfortunate children, not wanting to be separated, cried and called to their father...

At about nine o'clock in the morning, tanks and tankettes surrounded the Cossacks and drove up close to them. At the same time, English military vehicles appeared along the road leading from the bridge over the Drau across from Dölsach. Driving up to the eastern end of a row of carts on the side of the road where the Terek-Stavropol Stanitsa was, they stopped. Armed English soldiers came out of several of them.

I was about a kilometer away with my family, in the tree-covered foothills on the side not guarded by soldiers. I watched attentively.

I had decided to hide in the woods only at the most critical moment, since we had several possibilities, even if tenuous, for passing ourselves off as old emigrants and escaping repatriation.

To our great horror, the inmates of the stanitsa showed no resistance whatever. They boarded the vehicles that came up the road one after another and headed for the railroad station. They returned empty for the others. Those who did not board a vehicle went off to the western side of the location of the carts, where the Kuban stanitsas of Tamanskoy and Slavyanskoy were found. Several of them left for the woods immediately after.

In this way, some three thousand people were loaded into vehicles.

The train was filled and left.

About five hundred people were left near the woods on the field. The English announced that they would be sent the next day.

An hour after the train left, a light Soviet automobile, a "G.A.Z.," drove by on the road where people remained. A Red Army man was behind its wheel, while an NKVD man, in full uniform, sat in the back seat. After driving quietly through the remaining Cossack carts, the car turned toward the bridge across the Drau.

All became perfectly clear.

My soul felt as heavy as a grave.

I decided to walk over to where religious services had been held a prior day.

A sad picture presented itself where the stanitsa had been. Walking among empty carts that stood in disarray, I saw harnesses, hitches, pillows, blankets, caps, hats, trousers with stripes, epaulets, dishes and various other things needed for domestic and field life thrown about.

I went farther across the field to the hillock where the altar for the field church had been set up. I saw an unmitigated insult: the table used for the altar was turned over. Its tablecloth lay beside it. Gonfalons had been thrown on the ground, as was the icon of Christ's Resurrection and, it seems, Mother of God (in its frame). In addition, commemorative notes were scattered everywhere. Crossing myself, I raised and returned the altar to its previous position, covering it with the tablecloth. Lifting the icon of the Resurrection of

Christ from the ground, I saw heel marks from military boots on its lower part, pressed deep with dirt. Wiping the dirt from the icon, I knelt and placed it on the altar. I did the same with the other icon. The gonfalon, I attached to the dried saplings on a spur that hung off one of them. Among the commemorative strips spread on the floor, I found my own. I collected them all and put them under the tablecloth.

Crossing myself once more, I set off to return straight to where my family was with those who remained. Halfway, I saw a boy of twelve to fourteen heading in my direction from the bank of the Drau on the side of the camp. At the same time, an older man came out of a group of remaining Cossacks and headed toward the boy. We all came together at the same time. As I later learned, the boy was the son of Fr. A. B., while the other—a stanishnik of this Reverend Father. The boy had a pass in his hand, given by the English. He had been entrusted with gathering the icons, gonfalons, vestments, and other necessities for worship that had been left behind on the field.

Explaining where I had just been and what I saw there, all three of us headed to the familiar-to-me woods. On the way, Fr. A.'s son told us that, after the Soviet citizens had been turned over, the old emigrants had organized themselves in Peggetz. His father was designated as their leader. He recommended that we make our way to the camp, where, perhaps, someone or other might vouch for us as old emigrants. Then we would be accepted immediately and enrolled into the lap of luxury. Getting there was not difficult, according to him, since there were no tanks or sentries on camp territory or bridges, or the road that went along the levee by the Drau.

Taking the gonfalons and icons mentioned above, Fr. A.'s son and their stanishnik headed toward the camp, while I, heartened by such important news, went to my family.

By the time I returned, the greater part of the Cossacks was already gone. Apparently taking note of the continuous presence of sentries, many left for the hills, while others managed to get to the camp.

Letting my family and acquaintances know what I had succeeded in learning, I decided to go immediately with them to the camp, pretending to be old emigrants. We had much to base this on, even if feebly. During the period of evacuation from the Kuban bridgehead, my family and I lived temporarily in Odessa, from November 1943. The entire Odessa District was then joined with Rumania, forming part of the Trans-Istrian Governorship. At that time, my wife and I had been given Rumanian *sogurantse*, that is, written police permission to live legally in that district. They were written in Rumanian. They were stamped with some sort of designation in Rumanian of "political police" printed around the outside of the circular mark, while in the center, it was decorated by a royal crown with a cross above it. Regretfully, there was that unfortunate word, Odessa, in the text of the permit, which could betray us. We had to put our trust in the help of God and in the ignorance of the ordinary repatriator.

Putting a rucksack on my back and the Rumanian documents in my hands, my wife, children, and I headed for a nearby tank. One of the tank crew was in the vehicle; the other, beside it. Approaching the latter, I showed him our documents and said in German that we were going to the camp. My plan was such: he would not be able to read the text of the document, but the stamp with the crown would grab his attention involuntarily. So it turned out: looking at the stamp where "political police" was indicated, he asked:

—Polish?

With joy, I answered in German:

—Yes! Polish."

The tank driver allowed us to follow his tank. He recommended that we not go through the woods in doing so, but along the bank of the Drau, were there were no sentries for some reason.

Praying with my soul to God, we quickly went in the direction given. Never in my life had I felt such joy as then, for without question, we had been destined before to an inescapable, tortured death.

Walking without hindrance along the embankment of the Drau, then across a bridge, we reached the courtyard of the camp. There turned out to be many people there already. Those meeting us gazed at us with amazement and sympathy.

We asked where we could see Fr. A. They told us.

We met him on the main street of the camp, as we walked toward the administration barracks. Introducing ourselves, we showed him our Rumanian documents and asked him to let us into the camp. He sent us to the 10ᵗʰ Barrack. We got there and shared our intentions with its commandant, F. F. T. The barrack secretary, P. F. M., registered us and sent us to Room 13, where its commandant, A. P. P., assigned us to bunk beds in adjoining corners. We got provisions.

That evening, Fr. A. and part of the remaining priesthood straightened out the barrack churches from the visits by English soldiers.

After three sleepless nights and terribly wracked nerves, we slept as if dead.

On the morning of June 4, all the inmates of the camp, my family and me included, went to register to the window of an office that opened that day. This time, I had in my hand letters from two old emigrants verifying that they knew my family and me from Yugoslavia.

At about ten o'clock in the morning, when it came our turn to register, we could hear train whistles from the direction of the Dölsach Station, taking away the rest of those who had stayed in the fields.

In closing, I consider it necessary to mention the fate of those Cossacks who went into the hills.

Ignoring the fact that during the days of repatriation, all movements along the valley and in the hills were controlled by English soldiers and airplanes, several groups of Cossacks succeeded in crossing the snow-covered passes to reach the American Zone of Austria—Salzburg, where one group moved into a camp, others found work.

Those who crossed the passes, also snow covered, into Italy, were in most instances captured by the English on the other side of the peaks as they came out of the gorges that led down into the valleys. They were then sent to a so-called Soviet Camp that was located some seven kilometers from Lienz and guarded by the English. Many Cossacks were successful in escaping from it. Those who did not or could not risk doing so were turned over to the Soviets. But those who had been brought to the camp after the critical period of repatriation stayed there until October 1945. They wound up in freedom after the camp was closed.

Those who stayed near Lienz in the hills that rose up to the peaks, served time in the thickets, a month or more, eating the meat of horses they had killed, or whatever they managed to earn or beg from the peasants.

Sadly, there were places where the latter turned them in to the English or the newly appointed Austrian police.

Toward autumn, learning that the main danger had passed while still hiding in the hills, they descended into Lienz and found work.

Only the nameless graves of the Cossacks who died there remained in the hills.

May 27, 1953.
Kubanets [from the Kuban—*trans.*]

•

The End of the Cossack Military School

To the present, there is the idea that most of the *junkers* of the Cossack Military School that was started at the Cossachi Stan succeeded in getting into the hills and avoiding being turned over to the Bolsheviks.

Careful investigation has established that it had not been so. At present, we have managed to establish that there were only twenty families of former *junkers* who successfully saved themselves. In the opinion of a former *junker*, a very serious and thoughtful person, ninety percent of the school was turned over based on the information given below on the fate of school.

> He begins his piece giving two events that
> influenced the mindset of the *junkers*.

Field Ataman Domanov came to our school some two days before, but perhaps on the eve, of the betrayal of the officers. It had to have been after the officers had given up their weapons, because the ataman's bodyguard, who always carried a submachine gun, was quite obviously unarmed this time.

General Domanov made a speech to the assembled Junker Division and its teaching and non-combat staff. He spoke for quite a while, but was not very articulate—he was obviously anxious.

As if it were yesterday, I remember his call to us to maintain strict discipline. He said that we Cossacks were being accused of banditry and put in the worst light. The ataman did not say who made such an unflattering assertion about us, but he doubtless had reason to be concerned.

Not long after Domanov's visit, a rumor went around that we would be transferred to civilian status. As if in its support, the sotnya's clerk, on higher orders, started to make a list of *junkers* in which, along with the usual questions, there was one about their civilian specialty.

As is now clear, this had been a ruse on the part of the English that gave them information they needed for repatriation. From the other side—a thin psychological step toward becoming victims, since the inclusion on the form of a question about civilian specialty, in connection with the rumor about transfer to civilian status, gave people hope that there would be no betrayal.

The above, in addition to an improvement in rations, the distribution of new uniforms, and the visit to the school by some senior English officer with a mustache, wearing a black beret, who smiled during the entire visit and expressed his pleasure with the appearance and bearing of the *junkers*, all gave us encouragement.

Rumors flew around that they wanted to use us somewhere in their colonies.

But after the officers were taken away and the English made the announcement about repatriation, our mood dropped sharply.

Junkers with relatives gradually left for the stanitsas. Almost all were taken away with them. A small portion went into the hills.

From these, the majority escaped. The rest, deciding to resist to the end, bravely stayed in Amlach, where the school was, and from there went to Peggetz for the mass prayers of June 1st, where many were captured and one or two killed.

The following is written from the words of Junker N. The author of this piece did not stay at the school, but went to his father's stanitsa. Then, together with his father, he left for the hills.

On returning from Camp Peggetz, it was announced that the next day, June 2nd, those in the school would be sent off. No one slept almost the entire night. They argued. Several decided to leave for the hills. They gradually began to disperse that night. N. too decided to leave in the morning with his friend, but the latter overslept and woke N. when it was already too late, that is, it was becoming light.

Those *junkers* remaining at the school, the non-combat staff, and the orchestra formed up on the plaza in front of a church. N. had by then hidden himself in the straw at the peasant hut where our platoon had been located. He watched the scene of the betrayal through a crack between the wallboards.

No more than a hundred had gathered. The scene of the betrayal was repeated here: tanks and vehicles drove into the village, but refusal followed the order to board the vehicles. Loading by force was resorted to. Even this did not break the spirit of the *junkers*— they held tight. Our Cadet A. disported himself with special courage. He was from the Bokovskoy Stanitsa of the Don, from which his aging parents had also come and shared his fate.

All of a sudden within this surrounded group, a cry was heard and someone fell. For an instant, the *junkers* gave way, while the one who had fallen jumped to his feet and ran toward one of the vehicles. This was V., a Cossack of the non-combat staff, a specialist in harmony who often favored us by playing his *bayan* [Russian accordion—*trans.*]

Cadet S., of the Don, ran to board after him. He had been the caterer and carried a sack of provisions with him. With the words:—I am going to my kolhoz!—he climbed into the vehicle.

Resistance broke off with these two actions, and the English loaded the rest without difficulty.

After this, English soldiers went about the huts and yards where our sotnya had stayed. One went into the hayloft where N. was hiding, but he did not look it over very carefully. Toward evening, its owner, an Austrian, came to the hayloft. He was frightened on seeing the *junker* climbing out of the hay, but then recovered and told him that the English had left the village.

In the evening, N. climbed out of the hut and bumped into an English patrol on the street, which did not notice him.

He spent that night in a lime pit.

Afterwards, he managed to find a place at Camp Peggetz and went to work for the English. Later, he left for Canada.

V. C.

•

About the Removal of the 1ˢᵗ and 2ⁿᵈ Don Regiments and the Don Battery of the Cossachi Stan from Lienz in Order to be Turned Over to the Bolsheviks.

A Cossack from the 2nd Don Regiment submitted the letter below. The text of the letter is given in full, with the exception of certain harsh expressions addressed at specific individuals.

I will not write about leaving Italy and crossing over the pass, which has been described by others. I will write about what took place on the Drau.

As is known, Cossack regiments were found along the valley of the river named, on the left bank of its flow, while stanitsas were on the right.

The Don Battery stayed in tents in a forested area some eight kilometers from Camp Peggetz. The 1ˢᵗ Regiment was another two kilometers farther. Even farther, some two kilometers from it—the 2ⁿᵈ Don Regiment, in Nikolsdorf. Each named regiment had a reserve sotnya of officers. During those painful times, I was in the reserve sotnya with the 2nd Regiment. My wife and daughter were in Camp Peggetz.

Colonel Rykovsky commanded the 2nd Don Regiment.

I asked for leave to visit my wife and daughter on May 2nd. I was given a pass that was good until May 28.

During this period, it was necessary for me to see Colonel K. On May 27, I went from Peggetz to Lienz, to the offices of Domanov's staff, to find out where the colonel was. There, I was told that no one knew.

Walking from the offices, I saw Colonel K., coming toward me.

—Greetings,—he said,—what's new?

I answered:—Nothing new for me, but, that is, May 28th, I am returning to duty.

—All well and good,—K. answered,—but before that, let's go to the staff dining room and eat. I will tell you how I got released from having to form a disciplinary battalion that Domanov commissioned me to do.

We sat down at the table to wait for our food. At this time, a priest I had seen before came into the dining room.

—Greetings, Sirs,—he addressed us.

—Permit me to sit down at your table to eat.

—For the sake of God.

The priest sat down and told us:

—I was with the Chief of Staff, General Solamakhin, who informed me there is an order from the English to take pistols away from officers.

This news so concerned us that we stopped eating and sat silently for almost five minutes. Then I asked Colonel K.:

—How do you feel about what it means to take away officers' pistols?

—Something suspicious,—he answered.

At this, I could only say:

—Pistols today, officers themselves tomorrow…

We finished eating and left the staff offices. On saying farewell, we decided that we needed to be on the alert.

About the Removal of the 1st and 2nd Don Regiments and the Don Battery of the Cossachi Stan from Lienz in Order to be Turned Over to the Bolsheviks.

On entering Camp Peggetz, I met Colonel Sh., who asked me:
—What is new at staff?
—There is news, but sad—the English have ordered that pistols be taken from officers.
—Let them take them,—Sh. said calmly,—they will give new ones in exchange.
—Well,—I thought,—everyone has his own beliefs.
I left Camp Peggetz for duty at Nikolsdorf at ten o'clock in the morning of May 28th. On the way, I went to the battery to see its commander, but a quartermaster met me, who said:
—Our commander and all our junior officers have gone to a conference.
—How did they go?—I asked.
—They rode their own horses over to the 1st Regiment,—the quartermaster answered—but farther, they will go by car with the other officers.
I explained what I was thinking to the Cossacks of the battery, that this was not a conference, but a heinous betrayal.
There was a silence that lasted some five minutes. The quartermaster was the first to recover. He posed the question to me:
—Tell me, what awaits us in the future?
I answered that I saw ruin ahead and considered the only way out to be to leave for the hills.
—You will not see your commander and officers again, but you can decide your own fate. I must leave. God bless you. Do not fall for any traps. Only in the hills will you be safe.
I went to where the 1st Regiment was. I saw—nine trucks standing there, guarded by approximately thirty English soldiers. Many of the officers were already near the vehicles. Others approached in groups. I heard someone from the command giving orders:
—Go faster! We'll be back sooner.
I was approximately a hundred meters from the vehicles when the idea popped into my head that I could be stopped and told to get into a vehicle. No one stopped me, though. I was worried,

because I was in a military uniform, but I had a pistol in my pocket. However, the cup passed.

I went into where the 2nd Regiment was. There, the quartermaster and sergeants met me. They told me that the officers had been called to the regimental office, where eight trucks awaited them.

—And our reserve sotnya is there. Go quickly. Maybe you can catch the conference,—they advised me.

—It is not a conference, but in reality a betrayal to death of the officers,—I answered, and it was as if I had scalded them with boiling water.

Our regiment was in a forested area of the Drau, while the regimental office was by the railroad line, where the loading of officers was taking place.

I went to the edge of the woods and stopped there. It was clear to me that those people had been sentenced to death.

Positioned some sixty meters from the place of loading, I saw and heard several officers ask if they should bring overcoats and the answer that they did not need to, since they would return soon.

The leader of the escort guard appeared to be a Jew. In excellent Russian, he turned to the regimental commander and said:

—Tell the officers to take their seats in the vehicles, and you with them.

When the commander heard this, he told the guard [конвоир —trans.] that he was unable to do so, due to illness.

The guard agreed to let him stay, but only if he named a substitute from among the quartermasters.

—As for you,—he added,—at six o'clock tomorrow morning, a vehicle will come for you to take you to a hospital for treatment.

After this, the command was given: "Be seated in the vehicles!"

I watched all that took place. Still etched clearly in my mind is how my acquaintance, Captain S. I. P., began to sing the song: "Beyond the Ural, beyond the river, walk the Cossacks..." as he climbed into a vehicle.

I started crying and thought:

—If you only knew where you are going. Then you would sing a different…—and I had the urge to jump from the bushes and warn them where they were being taken, but I realized that it would not help them. The thought of myself falling into a vehicle stopped me.

The engines of the eight vehicles with the officers from our regiment roared to life. At the highway, they were joined by a ninth vehicle, from the 1st Regiment. Then they went off in the direction of Spittal. Each vehicle had two submachine gunners. When they approached the village of Nikolsdorf, eight tankettes appeared.

After a few minutes, the column was hidden from sight and the sound of the engines was no longer heard.

I headed to where the reserve sotnya was, hoping that someone from among the officers was left. Sure enough, I saw my stanishnik, Khorunj L., the sotnya's ordinance master, seated there.

Some ten paces from him, I called to him and asked why he had been left behind. The answer that I received was that, as the commander of the sotnya was leaving for the conference, he ordered him to remain to keep order in the camp. To my question whether any other officer remained, he answered that there was only one regimental commander, who was ill and would be taken to a hospital tomorrow at six o'clock in the morning.

—See, had you arrived fifteen minutes earlier, then you too would have left for the conference—he added.

Hey, Cossack! Do not rush into battle; have pity on your life…—I said.—Had I wanted to go to the conference, I would have been here on time. I sat in the bushes for close to an hour and watched everything that took place.

Then I went to see the regimental commander to learn what the deal was, what was the conference?

—Ach, what a pity that you missed it!

—But I am very satisfied that I "missed" it and did not hurry to wind up at the conference,—I answered.—But what do you think? What do you make of this conference?

About this, Colonel Rykovsky answered:

—I think that the English general will give a report favorable to us and that will be the end of it.

—No, you are in error,—I said.—Why was your quartermaster changed? Why did they offer to give you a car to take you for treatment? Do you believe that Davies actually wants you to get treatment? No! He does not want to make you well, but to give you to the Soviets to be sent away. Well! Be of good health!

I went back to where my sotnya was. I asked Khorunj L. whether he had something to eat. We ate canned food and hard tack. I told the khorunj that I thought that the conference should be over. Suddenly and unexpectedly, seven officers came out of the bushes. They had intentionally stayed away from the conference.

The first one out of the bushes was Captain M. Addressing me, he said:

—And you, Mr. T., have also swerved from the conference?

—Yes! I was ready for it since yesterday, while you obviously only today understood that our end was being prepared there? Well, better late than never.

We were the lucky ones, the nine people gathered there, but our luck did not hold up.

Captain M. asked me what I thought should be done next, should our people not return from the conference.

—I am convinced they will not return,—I answered.—My plan is to go over to Camp Peggetz at night. It will become clear what needs to be done next.

No sooner did I say those thoughts than the sound of a motor was heard. It stopped near the regimental office. We stood on our guard. We heard talking. Colonel Rykovsky asked the leader of the escort guards why he had come. He answered that it turned out that not all the officers on the list had gone to the conference, and he had come for them, in order to take them.

Colonel Rykovsky answered that he would immediately order the quartermasters to collect all officers who remained and bring them to the office.

Hearing all this, we did not know what to do, where to hide.

I suggested running away, but it was late.

We barely got to the bushes when four quartermasters met us. The substitute regimental commander was in charge.

—Stop!—And the substitute started to reproach us for being deserters, and why were we not ashamed?

I answered:

—If we are deserters, then you are a villain and a traitor; but do not forget that today it might be us, but tomorrow it will be you who will be shot.

Three of the quartermasters agreed that we needed to hide, but the substitute commander said he was duty-bound to bring us to the commander. What came next was his business.

There was no escape. We went to the office. A large vehicle was standing by it. Close to it were two submachine gunners and the leader of the escort guards, who lied bare-facedly to Colonel Rykovsky that the conference had been delayed by the absence of several officers, and that if all had been present, it would have already ended.

I do not know how the other eight officers who had remained felt, but I was beside myself. The thought came quickly into my head that I had a loaded pistol in my pocket, and, so as not to give myself up into the hands of the Reds for questioning, I decided that as I was loaded into the vehicle, I would attack the guards. I wanted to do this not from any heroism, but only to have the guards kill me right there.

But there is a saying: "God is not without mercy, and a Cossack without luck."

Just before being seated in the vehicle, the regimental doctor, who had also stayed behind as ill, came up.

A new thought flashed through my head. I turned to the doctor and told him that, even with all of my desire to do so, I could not then get into a vehicle, since I had been suffering from dysentery for the last seven days. The doctor clearly understood what "ailed" me. He turned to the guard leader—with a request—to leave me behind as being ill. He agreed to it. Then I got bold and asked the doctor to also leave Khorunj L. behind for a similar reason. The guard agreed even to that, but with the provision that, May 28, at six o'clock in the morning, a car would arrive to take us for treatment.

In this way, of the nine facing death, two were left in freedom until the morning, while seven awaited the orders of the guard to board the vehicle.

The latter, in excellent Russian, asked those standing by the vehicle:

—And are you all healthy?

—Yes, we are well,—followed in answer.

—Well, get into the vehicle...—The engine started up, and soon it was out of sight.

When only the four of us were left: Colonel Rykovksy, Khorunj L, the doctor, and I. The doctor said to me:

—You are resourceful...To get out of that kind of situation...

—Yes, Doctor, Sir. I lived under the Soviets for twenty-five years, ten of them in prison, and fifteen under inquest. Because of that, I absolutely believe nothing from them.

After this, Colonel Rykovsky ordered us to be ready at six o'clock the next day to be taken to the hospital.

I answered him:

—You believe that they want to heal us? They want to deliver us.

—Well, what can we do?

—Khorunj L. and I will be at Camp Peggetz at six o'clock in the morning.

—What about me? Will I be the only one to go to the hospital?—asked Colonel Rykovsky.

On this, I advised him:

—Take off your uniform, put on an Austrian hat, and make your way to the crowd in the stanitsa. Then see what will be.

He took my advice, disguised himself, slipped in with the general masses, and then went into the hills. From there, he wound up in the White Corps of Colonel Rogozhin.

––––––––––––

When only Khorunj L. and I were left, the two of us decided to go to Peggetz early the next morning. My wife and seventeen-year-old daughter were there. He had a wife and married daughter there, whose husband, Yesaul P., had gone to the conference.

On May 29, early in the morning, the khorunj and I went to Lienz. So that we would not get caught together, we took different roads: he on the main road, while I went along the right bank of the Drau. He arrived without incident, while I came upon a patrol of eight English soldiers.

Well, I thought, now I'm done for.

They stopped me and asked:

"Who are you? Captain?

I answered that I was the coachman for the regimental doctor. I had an old bridle in my hands. It saved me.

They performed a complete search on me. Finding nothing, they asked where I was going.

I answered that my horse had gone off in the direction of Lienz, and I was searching for her.

—Well, go!

I got off cheap! Walking by the stanitsas, I spotted the three K. brothers. They were standing around deciding what was to be. They knew my family and me very well.

—What has you Don boys so in thought?—I asked from about fifteen paces.

—Ah, Mikhail Grigorievich! Can it be you? How did you get away?

—God only knows.

I told the brothers how I escaped, that I was being hunted, and that it would be dangerous to show myself in camp, as I might be turned in there. For that reason, I wanted to spend some time here.

The eldest brother suggested that I stay with them while he went into the camp to warn my wife about where I was.

I went with his brothers to the hut in which they lived. When I asked them why they were not living in a stanitsa, but on their own, they answered that General Shkuro's staff, on which they served, had been there. They said that a rumor was going around that Shkuro and his adjutant had been arrested.

As we were speaking, my wife and daughter arrived with the elder K. They had been very upset, because Khorunj L. had come into the camp and said that we had left at the same time, but I had not yet arrived. They thought I had been arrested.

My wife explained that there was an order to send us to the Soviet Union, that no one wanted to go, and that the priesthood had decided to go out on the square with gonfalons and hold religious services.

After accompanying my wife and daughter to the camp, I returned to the K. brothers.

The third day after the officers were taken away, the populace, led by the priests, went out on the square of Camp Peggetz. Exactly at eight o'clock, shots were fired, frantic shrieks from women. I quickly got ready, put on a black hat and glasses, and rushed to the camp. People were running toward me from the camp. I side stepped them and came upon a chain of English soldiers. Learning that I was going to my family in the camp, they let me through. At the bridge, I again came upon a guard post, with seven Englishmen, soldiers and officers. From their appearance, it was obvious that they were overwhelmed with what was happening on the square of the camp.

When an officer asked where I was going, I said to my family in camp. He sent a soldier with me to the barrack I had indicated.

As we walked, the soldier told me that the Cossacks had to hold out for three days. After that, no one would touch us. If we could not hold out, then we should go into the woods.

We arrived at the barrack. No one was there. Everything was overturned. An old woman answered from the neighboring barrack, saying that everyone had gone out on the square to pray to God.

I told the soldier that I wanted to find my family. He let me go and I went out on the square. A throng of thousands was there on their knees and praying to God. Approaching a woman I knew, I asked about my family. She said that she had seen my wife and daughter dragged to the vehicles, but did not know for certain whether or not they had been taken away. Moving farther through the crowd, I met one of my stanishniks, a woman who was crying with heart-rending sobs. She told me that mine were miraculously saved and were together. They had been grabbed, but they had held onto each other very tightly. They dragged them to a vehicle but dropped them there. Then they ran up to my stanishnik's family, deafened her husband with a blow to the head, and took him and their daughter to a vehicle. Now she was alone. She told me that my family was behind the priests, where I found them. My wife and daughter, in horror, said that they were about to take us to the Soviets. Right then, however, a small vehicle came up to the crowd, and from it was announced through a loudspeaker that the Cossacks were brave people, but that the next day, at nine o'clock, all had to be ready to board.

On hearing this, I told my family that it would be better to perish there and not go to the Soviets.

The auto left. The worshippers started to disperse to the barracks. I helped my wife and daughter up from their knees and told them that we should go to the camp to prepare to go into the hills.

In the barrack, I wrote up a slip for provisions in my name, got them, distributed them, and prepared for an expedition.

We left camp with Khorunj L. at three o'clock in the morning, having previously agreed to leave together. We kept strict silence, since there were English guards posted in the foothills. We stayed in the mountains for twenty days. I watched from there as people were taken from stanitsas and loaded onto trains.

After staying in the hills for that twenty-day period, my wife, daughter, and I came down from them and reached the White Corps.

In that way, with God's mercy, my family and I escaped the terrible betrayal to the Soviets.

Now I wish to write about how the Don regiments and battery were taken away. I did not personally witness it, but relate it through the words of another. My stanishnik, Quartermaster I., told me about the tragic betrayal of the 2nd Regiment.

When I came down off the mountains, I stayed for a while at a Bulgarian camp in Lienz. There was a large infirmary in the city. In it were many wounded Germans and Russians. I gathered berries and took them there to exchange for cigarettes.

One time when I came to the hospital, I saw a man standing with head and arms bandaged, but holding a cigarette. I asked if he wanted some berries. He nodded his head in agreement. I made a pouch from newspaper, poured out some berries, and offered it to him. In taking it, he asked:

—Don't you recognize me?

How could I have recognized him? His entire head was bandaged, but for his eyes and mouth.

He reminded me how, as stanitsa ataman, I had formed a regiment, and he gave my name.

I could not keep myself from exclaiming:

—Nikolai Ivanovich! Is it really you? What's up?

—Yes. So, I have been left among the living, as a permanent cripple. It would have been better if they had killed me, than to suffer as I do now.

He invited me to his tent and told me the fate of the Don regiments and battery.

On the third or fourth of June, a large train was provided at the camp of the 2nd Regiment. The regimental commander (the same one who, on May 28, did not want to let us go—the nine officers for which a truck had come to take to the "conference"), decreed that under no circumstances should any in the regiment agree to board. They would not be taken by force.

A large convoy of soldiers, armed to the teeth, came from the train, and the 2nd Regiment was ordered to board.

The regimental commander answered that the regiment would not board and would not go to the Soviets.

The convoy quickly opened up with machine-gun fire, resulting in over 100 dead and wounded. The quartermaster commanding the regiment was among those killed.

In all this that he told me, my stanishnik, N. I. T., was hit by five bullets: his lower jaw was split in two, and both arms broken—one by two bullets, the other by one.

After several rounds from the machine guns, the shooting stopped. Resistance was broken, and all the Cossacks were loaded into railroad cars.

A railroad train was provided at the same time for the 1st Regiment. Apparently, no resistance was given there.

About the Removal of the 1st and 2nd Don Regiments and the Don Battery of the Cossachi Stan from Lienz in Order to be Turned Over to the Bolsheviks.

The battery was taken by car to the 1st Regiment and loaded with them.

The English gathered the wounded and took them to the hospital in Lienz.

I thank the Lord God for saving my family and me!

We are now in America, but the old lady is still ill from all that she lived through.

My friend, Khorunj L., evacuated to Argentina with his family. Along the way, great sorrow befell him—he had to bury his wife, who so loved her grandson, Anatoly, at sea.

A Cossack of the Don Host **M. Titov**
February 1956
USA

**
*

From the Editor:

To complete the history of the tribulations of Khorunj L., it must be said that his daughter was squashed by the crowd during the Lienz massacre on the square of Camp Peggetz and gave premature birth to two boys. One died, but the other—Anatoly, happily greets the solicitude of his mother and grandfather that surrounds him.

•

The Drau Roars

Taken from the newspaper, "Russia," June 24, 1956

The Drau rolls its waters noisily,
Turbid, gray, like granite,
As in a storm—in bad weather
Day and night it makes noise…
"To fires or to meetings
You hurry in your course.

Either heavy suffering
Has upset your breast,
Or in unaccountable fear
You are running from enemies,
Or you have grown big with water—
Have your banks become too narrow?
Why so stormy and noisy?
Why not quiet down?"
Thus asked the willows of the Drau,
Disturbing their silence.
The Drau looked sadly
And said on the go:
"Earlier, I played, sang,
And did not know evil-misfortune.
I will tell you, my kin,
What I happened to see;
What horrors for the first time
God deemed worthy to see:
In forty-five (on a June day)
I ran through Lienz.
I saw people tortured there—
Frightened to death.
Roaring tanks, shouts, groans.
A solitary discharge.
Children cry, women cry
Screams of despair, prayers.
The English surrounded
The Cossacks of the peaceful Stan
Beat them, and loaded them
To betray to the clan.
Soldiers bereft of all humanity
Beat the elderly, beat children.
I am becoming a partridge
Flitting about its cage.
By the misdeed of the soulless, callous,
Innocent blood flowed.
Many victims, alive and dead,

At that time I took.
Such evil I will
Never be able to forget.
How can I not send out moans,
How not cry, not boil?
They nod their heads low
The willows, hearing the answer.
Bitter tears flow—
It is obvious that there is no justice in the world.

N. Tropin

•

The Priesthood of the Cossachi Stan and the Tragedy of the Cossacks

At the end of 1942, the Germans, unable to stay at Tsaritsyn on the Volga, needed to retreat on the entire front that stretched from Petrograd to the North Caucasus.

In June of that year, having gained a spectacular victory at Kharkov, the Germans secured the territories of the Don and Kuban Districts. With that, they gave Cossacks who had escaped to some place or other the opportunity to return with their family to their native areas.

Crawling out of "mouse holes," too, were priests, who had hid until then any way they could.

Religious services began in stanitsas.

But the German retreat compelled both Cossacks and their religious pastors to go West, into the unknown, with the hope that nothing anywhere could be worse than in the Soviet Union.

And off they went, driven by a blizzard, shod by crackling frost. The retreat from the districts began in January 1943.

They walked alone and with families. They were poorly organized at first, but then, as they went farther from their homelands, they began to group together. On reaching Belorus, the Cossachi Stan was organized near the city of Novogrudok under the command of the Field Ataman, Colonel S. V. Pavlov (a Cossack from the Don District, Yekaterinskoy Stanitsa).

Cossacks and their families were grouped into stanitsas according to their district. Formerly on their own, priests joined their stanitsas. Services began.

Here, Fr. Vassily Grigoriev (Don) moved into the foremost rank. He came into contact with Bishop Athanasius of Novogrudok (now in America), organized a diocese from the Cossack stanitsas, and was authorized by Bishop Athanasius to manage the Cossack Diocese.

The writer of these lines, Fr. Timofey Soin, did not reach Novogrudok in time, but joined the 6th Separate Sotnya, then under the command of Sotnik M. M. A., and found in the small city of Dvorets. This was when the Cossachi Stan had to retreat from Belorus to Poland.

On the way, the 6th Separate Sotnya joined the 8th Regiment. Then the 8th Regiment combined with the 9th to make up a brigade.

It was a long stay in Poland, three months (July-September), near the small city of Zdunska Wola. Here, there was a gathering of the entire priesthood, and Fr. Vassily Grigorievich assigned priests and named parishes. In a word, he organized the diocese. Fr. Vassily was a good organizer.

In September 1944, the Cossachi Stan was sent from Zdunska Wola to North Italy, in the area of Gemona.

Priests held services under open skies at all the stops on that difficult, long-suffering trip. Those who had sacred communion cloth —performed the liturgy, those who did not, served in masses and prayers.

We stayed in Gemona for several weeks in our carts. Here, near Gemona, a bomb fragment killed the priest, Fr. Dmitry Voynikov (Kuban Cossack).

From Gemona, the entire Cossachi Stan moved to the area of Alesso and Tolmezzo. The areas settled here were strictly allocated not only by districts, but also by circuits [округи—*trans*.] and stanitsas. All stanitsas were located within Italian settlements. A circuit priest was designated for each stanitsa. Services were conducted in Roman Catholic churches.

We lived this way until the end of April 1945. Then came the order to move the entire Stan to the East Tyrol (Austria).

This was a move with many difficulties: we had to cross a pass over Alpine peaks that zigzagged for eighteen kilometers.

There were some malicious ruses by Italians, They said that it should not be taken with heavily laden carts, and that anyone who did not cross the Rubicon by midnight would become a prisoner of war of the Italians. Many believed this and abandoned some of their worldly goods, which were meager even before. Near the settlement of Amara, the Italians blocked the hilly road completely and demanded the surrender of all weapons and transports. On the Italian side, a young Roman Catholic priest led the negotiations (demands). He was so insolent that he particularly angered the Cossacks.

Then, the *junkers* arrived. They had a cannon. A siege began.

The Cossacks quickly won a victory with their firepower. The "commanders" of the Italians were killed—that priest who led the negotiations and his father (also a priest). While the Italians ran away, nonetheless they did cruelly repay the Cossacks. Until then, there had been a Cossack hospital in Amara. There were up to twenty Cossack patients in one building. The Italians boarded the building up, then set it on fire. All the patients in the building burned to death. But the entire Stan, afterwards, traveled along that road without hindrance.

On the first day of Easter (May 6), almost the entire Cossachi Stan, having crossed over the ridge tops, was near Oberdrauburg. Then, day by day, they made small moves to Lienz. On reaching it, they settled according to stanitsas on the right bank of the Drau, with the Diocesan Office—on the left. Services—liturgy or mass—were performed throughout all parts on Sundays and holidays.

The evening before the disastrous 1st of June, Fr. Vassily informed the priesthood through messengers that the next day (June 1st), at six o'clock in the morning they (every priest) should go to Camp Peggetz in a religious procession with their stanitsas to hold a general worship service.

On the spacious square of the camp, capable of fitting ten thousand people, a platform was built from boards for an altar (one) and communion table (one) to be on it and to hold the priests.

To our surprise, Fr. Vassily Grigorievich did not lead the service, but rather Archpriest Vladimir N. Father Vassily had at that time gone into Lienz to "send" a telegram. When the Divine Liturgy approached its tragic moment, Father Vassily could be seen from the platform as he walked through Camp Peggetz from the city of Lienz, taking the back paths behind the barracks of the camp.

The following priests and deacons were with Fr. Vladimir as he performed the service:[*]

1. Archpriest Panteleymon T., 2. Priest Nikolai S., 3. Archpriest Aleksei A., 4. Priest Nikolai G., 5. Archpriest Mikhail D., 6. Priest Simon Sh., 7. Priest Victor T., 8. Archpriest Ioann D., 9. Priest Alexander (last name forgotten), 10. Priest Anatoly B., 11. Priest Vyacheslav (last name forgotten, he served in the Rostov circuit), [12 and 13 skipped in original—*trans.*] 14. Priest Vladimir Ch., 15. Priest Timofey Soin, 16. Archpriest Isidor B., 17. Priest Aleksei F., 18. Priest Grigory Ye., 19. Archdeacon Vassily T., 20. Deacon Nikolai K., and 21. Deacon (first and last name forgotten, served in the Starocherkasskoy Stanitsa of the Cossachi Stan).

Archpriests Nikolai M. and Victor S. were in the crowd of worshippers.

There were more priests in the Cossachi Stan, but they were not seen in the midst of the priesthood on the platform or in the crowd of worshippers. These priests: Pavel P. and Nikolai Ch.

When the Divine Liturgy reached the moment for those who wished to take communion, Fr. Vladimir N., leading the service, began to give communion ALONE, FROM ONE CUP. He only managed to give communion to a few score of people, as the multi-thousand crowd was captured by a ring of tanks, tankettes, and trucks. Soldiers armed with clubs and bayonets came out of the trucks. *Junkers* and young Cossacks took the entire crowd inside a living ring, linking their arms together, to prevent the attackers from breaking the crowd into small groups.

---

[*] Full names are listed for all priests in the article submitted by Archpriest Timofey Soin. But in view of the fact that many who lived through the tragedy do not wish to have their names proclaimed, while asking permission of all is impossible, prior to publication of this article, we decided to leave only each priest's first name and last initial.

Archdeacon Father Vassily quickly availed himself of the Holy offering and wrapped the cup in his frock [обернул чашу в плат—*trans.*] All the priests began to leave the platform, as the entire crowd was crushing one another in natural retreat from the attacker. Here, the platform cracked and the tables, the altar and communion tables for the service, were overturned.

Some people were squashed to death.

In this way, the worship service came to an end on its own. The entire crowd moved in retreat from the camp to the field between Barracks *Nos.* 5 and 6 on one side, and *Nos.* 7 and 8—the other.

After the fence was knocked down, the crowd went out on the field. Also on the field with the crowd were Cossacks who had held gonfalons and icons in their hands during the Divine Liturgy, along with priests in vestments with crosses (from the altar) in their hands. They sang a rotation of prayers from the beloved psalms: "Sweet Jesus, Save Us!", "Holy Mother of God, Save Us!", "Under Your Mercy We Resort, Mother of God!", "Open Your Merciful Doors to Us, Blessed Holy Mother!", "We Have No Other Help, We Have No Other Hope, Except You, Our Sovereign!"

When the prayers started to refer to the saints, Fr. Nikolai G. took the calendar in his hand and, starting with the 1st of September, read out every saint established by the church for each day. The rest of the priests, in concert with the crowd, sang: "Reverend Father Simeon (commemorated September 1st), Pray to God for Us!", "Holy Martyr Mamont, Pray to God For Us!" And so on for the whole year.

Once the tanks had the crowd on the square surrounded, they charged it. Like one, the whole crowd fell on its knees, resigned to await death on the field over suffering in the Soviet Union. But the tanks only came up to the crowd and turned sharply back again.

The priests continued singing prayers.

The prayers were interrupted repeatedly. An English officer arrived in a tankette and said through a megaphone: "Cossacks! We know that you are brave people, but in this instance, all manner of resistance is futile. You must be returned to your homeland."

There was one general answer to his call: "Better death here, than torture in the Soviet Union!"

At that moment, Fr. Anatoly B., in vestments, stepped out of the crowd and, speaking in French, explained to the officers that there were old emigrants from Yugoslavia in the crowd.

Either because of his boldness or his knowledge of French, the fact was that he was designated by the English Command on June 2nd to be the commandant of Camp Peggetz, destined for use by the old emigrants from Yugoslavia.

On the megaphone, the wife of General T. I. Domanov, Maria Ivanovna, was called out, with the promise "on the honor of an English officer" that nothing would happen to her, but that she was needed on a very important matter.

Exclamations could be heard from the crowd that Maria Ivanovna was not with them.

The crowd stayed on the field until five o'clock in the evening. Then, accompanied by tankettes, they were allowed to go back to the stanitsas.

Every priest, having first set out with his stanishniks at six o'clock in the morning for the general liturgy service in the camp, by five o'clock in the afternoon could barely weave along with his thinning group to his Stan.

During the time that the entire crowd stayed on the field, it was possible to go through the camp (Peggetz) without hindrance. Fr. Ioann D. took off his vestments and went in to get a drink of water. There, he was grabbed and thrown into a vehicle. Father Victor S., went into a truck voluntarily. Deacon Fr., who had served at the Cossachi Stan in Starocherkasskoy Stanitsa, was bayoneted by a soldier and taken into a vehicle. Deacon Fr. Nikolai K. was taken the first day in the camp.

Fr. Alexander (surname not known) was taken from the camp church the first day.

On the nights of June 1st to June 2nd, Archpriest Fr. Vladimir N. and Fr. Victor T. were in the camp church. They were taken to be loaded the morning of June 2nd.

May 28th, going "to take a ride" with their officers to the "conference" were Archpriest Fr. Alexander B. and Fr. Vassily M.

Fr. Pavel R. and Victor ("Little") disappeared without leaving any traces.

On returning the evening of June 1ˢᵗ, the fathers conducted prayers in their stanitsas early in the morning of the 2ⁿᵈ, while I gave communion to the Cossacks who remained and blessed them for their trips into the hills.

The evening of June 2ⁿᵈ, through a messenger, Fr. Vassily Grigorievich informed all of us, the fathers, that tomorrow, June 3ʳᵈ, early in the morning, we should come over to the left bank, where the Diocesan Office was, which we did, as there was to be a raid that morning.

All the fathers then gathered on the left bank near the Diocese office. But Fr. Anatoly B, the camp commandant, had already made arrangements with the administration of the camp to have us all considered as old emigrations from Yugoslavia.

So we all registered, each of us finding two guarantors to verify our having been in Yugoslavia.

They put us in Barrack *No.* 14. But several days later, the commandant's assistant, K. V. Shelikov, rudely moved us back to Barrack *No.* 34, on the edge of the camp (left bank of the Drau). But we were not embittered by the move, at least. The barrack turned out to be a large one. We ten priests settled in comfortably. There were even a few empty rooms that were taken by Slovenes.

There was a parish gathering in this barrack, which Fr. Vassily Grigorievich attended. He announced that he was resigning from his duties as head of the Cossack Diocese, and that he was moving to the Polish camp, since his son-in-law (Polish) was moving there.

For several well-founded reasons, we expressed our disbelief at this to Fr. Vassily.

He left, but we stayed.

It is fitting to mention here that Belorus priests, who had left Novogrudok with the Cossacks and at all times sought the shelter of the Cossachi Stan, stopped recognizing us or serving with us in the camp church. They formed their own separate group.

To our pleasure, they all soon moved to another camp.

The venerable and highly esteemed Archpriest Fr. Alexander Z. (Kuban, an old emigrant from Bulgaria) soon came to our Camp Peggetz.

We elected him our Elder, Fr. Nikolai M.—Father Superior, Fr. Mikhail D.—Secretary, while I—Confessor.

Fr. Anatoly, due to the intrigues of Mrs. Shelikhov was taken away to Camp Spittal in the course of administrative procedures. Fr. Alexander V. went with him voluntarily.

Soon we, all the fathers, sensed "trouble" in our new commandant after Fr. Anatoly was removed. (In his place, Mr. Shelikhov was named commandant.)

Several days after Fr. Anatoly was taken away, two five-ton trucks rolled up to our Barrack *No.* 34 with the demand that all priest board en route to their homeland. We argued that we were old emigrants, so that we were not subject to repatriation. How this miserable affair might have come to an end, I do not know, had not someone apparently well informed, a certain Lady (that is how she was called) with the military unit, run to our barracks. She used her authority to banish the vehicles, announcing that the priesthood was under her protection.

After this incident, which very nearly brought us to a dismal end, our life became quiet. But several of the reverend fathers, after living through the incident described and seeing that Mr. Shelikhov was handing over Cossacks, one after another, then in whole groups, moved to the American Zone, in the region of Salzburg, in Camp Parsh [English spelling could not be confirmed—*trans.*]. And so, in mid-1946, I was left all by myself in Camp Peggetz.

When life in camp began to settle down after the tragedy, a school for children of both sexes was opened in Camp Peggetz. There turned out to be several students who had finished the first levels of school, but found themselves in the first classes of the middle school. We had to open supplemental classes for them and put together a primer. Gymnasium instructors were found. In this way, two schools began to function in camp: beginning and middle.

Religious lessons at these schools were at first given by priests: Fr. Vladimir Ch. and myself. When Fr. Vladimir moved to Salzburg, I was alone.

When Camp Peggetz was liquidated in November 1946, the Yugoslavs who had settled in it were moved to Spittal; the Russians, across Spittal (we were held up in Spittal for three months)—to

Camp San Martin, near the city of Villach. Both schools were in operation in San Martin to 1949. There were two graduates, with certificates testifying to completion.

These testimonials were useful to the young people in South America. They were accepted without examination into institutions of higher education. In Argentina, meanwhile, examinations had to be taken, following even the six-year (first step) and gymnasium. Only then were they accepted into university.

On the first day of the tragedy (June 1st) and the days that followed, there were mortal victims. They were collected and moved to Camp Peggetz. A cemetery was created for them in a corner of the camp on the bank of the Drau River.

How many dead were buried there, I doubt that anyone can say. I know that Fr. Aleksei A. and Fr. Alexander V. performed several funerals.

Toward the 15th of September 1945, a monument was erected on one of the common graves during the time Mrs. Shelikhov was in charge: a concrete cross was put on a wide pedestal with the inscription: "To Those Who Perished, 1 VI 1945." But the fall rains soon caused the surface to crumble and erased the inscription.

Our Reverend Fr. Alexander V. designated priests to bless the monument: Fr. Theodore V., Fr. Vladimir Ch., and me.

I was required to say a word before the blessing of the monument.

Father Theodore V. came from von Pannwitz's corps after the tragedy.

October 17, 1945, the first group of priests left for Salzburg. A little later—the second. And so, all gradually went away. I was the only one left, as already described above, never abandoning my pastoral and religious instruction duties until the day of my departure for Argentina—November 9, 1948, from Camp San Martin, near the city of Villach.

Archpriest **Timofey Soin**

•

Three Documents About Archpriest Fr. Anatoly Batenko

These documents are reprinted from the Russian-American Orthodox Messenger, *No.* 6, June 1954.

1. Letter of Archbishop Stefan to Metropolitan Leonti

Your Most Eminent Eminence Leonti, Metropolitan of all America and Canada.

Now at your disposal is my Archpriest Fr. Anatoly Batenko. He is a serious person who never pushes himself forward.

I consider it my obligation to describe to you certain of his actions, which earned him a good name over all of Austria. Their memory will never fade from the hearts of those people saved by him from death.

On June 1, 1945, a betrayal of Cossacks to the Soviets by the English took place in Lienz. This is where Fr. Anatoly showed his heroism.

He organized a prayer service, formed a living ring out of the priests, and, when tanks approached, he shouted furiously:—Stop! We have citizens of Yugoslavia here.

It resulted in the command to stop and make all who were standing within the ring to register; in this way, they were spared and saved, and will never forget it as long as they live. I offer copies of documents safeguarded at the chancellery from that time.

Truly, an Orthodox priest does deeds with his right hand that his left hand does not know.

For this assistance, God helped him move out his entire household, even his infirm son, who began to improve in America.

I love this priest and deliver him to your love.

Please give your bishop's prayers.

Stefan, Archbishop of Vienna and Austria

P. S. In remembering the scene written about, I am unable to maintain my composure. There is no mention of this priest in print, or of such deeds by priests, and Fr. Anatoly, too, is silent on it.

Salzburg
March 10, 1954

—

2. Report of the Collected Priesthood in Lienz

The report of the assembly of the priesthood of the Orthodox Church of the United Emigrant Camps at Lienz, the year 1945, the 7th day of June.

In this difficult time of life, the priesthood assembled: archpriests, priests, and deacons, praising the Lord God for protecting them to this time, to recognize for his act of self denial—his heroic stepping forth in defense of the priesthood and Russian people—Priest Anatoly Grigorievich Batenko, and, in order to acknowledge his full worthiness, ask and intercede before the highest church authorities that he be rewarded with the following gifts: a gold pectoral cross and calotte, promotion to the rank of archpriest, and a mace.

Following are twenty-five signatures of priests and psalm readers.

Certified as a true copy:

Archbishop **Stefan**

—

3. Report of that Assembly of the Priesthood

The report of the assembly of the priesthood of the Orthodox Church of the United Emigrant Camps at Lienz (Austria), of the election by the church diocese in the year 1945, the 7th day of June.

Learning of the choice of the ecclesiastic superintendent of the Orthodox Churches at the United Emigrant Camps. Decision: to consider Priest Fr. Anatoly Grigorievich Batenko elected to ecclesiastic superintendent.

Signed by twenty-eight priests and psalm readers.

Certified as a true copy:

Archbishop **Stefan**

•

About Responsibility for the Lienz Atrocity

Below are submitted three articles which present themselves as if one series, since, with the exception of the second, carrying factual corrections of the first, they speak of the necessity to investigate the atrocity at Lienz.

Especially valuable is the article by the Dutch professor, L. G. Grondeis [English spelling could not be established—*trans*.], mainly not for an account of the tragedy, but because it is the first appearance in foreign presses asking for a careful investigation by an international commission of the atrocity, and the assignation of blame for it.

1. SPITTAL TRAGEDY

Excerpt from an article printed in the journal "Cossack Union," *Nos*. 16 and 17.

...For the seventh time, on June 1st of last year, the anniversary of the betrayal to the Soviet Army of many thousands of White combatants, who, together with the German Army, continued their old battle with a timeless foe, was solemnly noted by church and memorial services in Russian colonies spread over the entire world.

This is how this tragedy occurred, as far as can be established based on the many eyewitness accounts.

In May of 1945, a very large Cossack formation was in the northeast part of Italy in position against the Soviet Army, which was attacking the Balkans. Retreating to the north under that threat, they came into contact with the English Army in Lienz (a small city on the banks of the Drau River), where they were interred in a camp called the "Cossachi Stan."

Among the many reports at our disposal, we must give particular attention to the testimony provided by Professor of the Russian Medical Faculty Verbitsky, who was with the higher Russian staff, and, as a non-combatant, was liberated at the time by the English.[*] He reports having witnessed the Field Ataman, at the request of no other than Major Davies, persuade all his officers to prepare for a trip to a conference in Spittal with the English authorities, from which they were to return that same day. Because of this, he advised them not to bring overcoats, but to leave them in Lienz.

The Cossack officers that these means succeeded in removing without resistance numbered 2756 men, in which were 35 generals, 450 staff officers, 835 yesauls and under-yesauls, 1282 sotniks, khorunjes, and priests and military officials in officer's uniforms.[**]

The group was led by the Field Ataman, but its main personage was General Krasnov, the seventy-two-year-old Head of the Main Cossack Soviet, famous in the West for his novel, "From Double Eagle to Red Flag," which has been translated into many foreign languages.

The behavior of the English convoy guards opened deluded eyes. Of twenty-three officers who jumped from the train, eight succeeded in saving themselves. Guards shot the rest.[***] On reaching their destination, English soldiers discovered the corpses of two officers who had committed suicide on the train. Those who remained were conveyed to a camp surrounded with barbed wire.

That same evening, an English officer informed General Krasnov, then the other officers, that they were to be turned over to

---

[*] Professor Verbitsky was taken from Spittal on May 28 and freed from there the next day.

[**] It must be supposed that the number of officers taken away was obtained from the article of Vassyuta Serdyukov, found in *No.* 275/6, from July 1, 1948, of the journal "Sentinel," entitled "Tragedy of Cossack Forces." The data must not be considered absolutely correct, but close to the actual.

[***] There is a disconnect of some sort here. Eyewitness accounts specifically establish that the officers were transported not by train, from Lienz to Spittal, but by automobile.

the Red Army the next day.

Krasnov immediately sent a letter to English General (now, Lord) Alexander, who gave the order for the betrayal.* Apparently it was to remind him that in 1920, when the policies of Churchill, then First Lord of the Admiralty, were aimed at providing help to the White Army in Southern Russia, he—Krasnov, as the Host Ataman (1918), was one of the remaining leaders of the White Army. General Alexander did not answer Krasnov's letter, leaving him without resort.

The English let it be known throughout the camp that at four o'clock the next morning, May 29, loading into railroad cars would begin. Here is an eyewitness account:

"Everyone gathered at about six o'clock in the morning in the main square of the camp, where two priests in the group began a prayer service.

Trucks arriving in the camp quickly cut off the church service, and the order was given to load. The officers tried to resist at first by locking their arms together, but blows from clubs separated them. English soldiers grabbed the first one who fell and threw him into an automobile, but he managed to get out. Then they beat him on the head and once more pushed him into the vehicle. He jumped out of it again, but he was beaten until half dead and, in the end, injured, lacking any strength, he allowed himself to be thrown into the truck, from which he watched sadly as the drama continued. Such public abuse of an officer caused the others to cease resistance.

Up to fifty officers were loaded into each truck.

Several officers asked English soldiers for cigarettes. One soldier brought several packs and began to exchange the cigarettes for watches, which the officers would no longer need. One cigarette for one watch, regardless of its value, and his purse was soon full of watches."

General Krasnov was arrested as follows: "The old man did not come out for the church service, but participated in it as he sat by an open window. Seeing this, English* soldiers ran over to chase him off, but they were pushed aside by Cossacks, who took the general in

---

*   There is no support for General Krasnov having succeeded in sending a letter from Spittal to General Alexander. It is more likely that it never happened.

their arms and, lifting him through the window, put him back with the rest of the group.

At that time, it became clear that five officers had successfully escaped and that General Zhilkin, Colonels Mikhailov, Garushkin, and Kharmalov had committed suicide in their rooms.**

May 31, General Shkuro, who in 1918-20 heroically fought the Reds and whom the King of England, on the recommendation of the English military mission, had awarded the Highest Order of the Bath, was convoyed separately to Moscow in a light automobile, with his adjutant. One hundred twenty officers were shot on the road to Vienna by convoy guards.

Between Graz and Vienna, 1030 officers, after much questioning, disappeared without a trace and their fate is not known. From the concentration camp in Vienna, where they had been locked up, 983 officers were taken for interrogation and in all probability were shot as "white bandits."***

As confirmed by Russian newspapers, General Krasnov, his nephew, S. Krasnov, Shkuro, and Sultan Ghirey were publicly hanged in Moscow on June 17, 1947, after torture and interrogation.

Rumors worthy of belief have us consider most of the others, Whites and former officers, to have been executed, although several were sent to concentration camps in the Komsommol.

It must be brought to attention that only thirty-two percent of the officers who were turned over happened to be Soviet citizens when the war began and at that time joined national groupings that were enemies of the Soviet regime. The Germans, stepping into the role of liberators, convinced them to work jointly with them. The remaining sixty-eight percent had never been citizens of Soviet Russia and bore Nansen passports, which by statute guaranteed their independence from the government in Moscow in all European countries.

---

*   This account of what took place in Camp Spittal on May 29 coincides with the account of Yu. I. G., of the Kuban, who escaped from it.
** A misprint: it should not be Garushkin, but Captain Tarussky.
*** Data on officers perishing en route to Vienna are identical to the data of Vassyuta Serdyukov in the journal "Sentinel," *No.* 275/6, 1948. Ed.

In the course of all the trials of life to which they were destined, these people, while waiting for their homeland to be liberated, earned their daily bread through honest, if menial, labor. Most often, they were waiters, porters, elevator operators, and workers at mills and factories, while some were at times more professional, as journalists, professors, artists, and designers-inventors.

While they were refugees, most continued to live with the idea that, as soon as the situation allowed, they would resume the fight they broke off after failures in the Crimea and Siberia in 1920, which had been so energetically encouraged by the leaders of France and England at that time.

On agreeing to work with the German Army, General Krasnov stipulated that Cossack units should never be put in a position to fight against their allies from the First World War and that they wished for the creation of a free Russia.

After the Cossack officers were evacuated from Lienz, the English officers set out to forcibly send off the rest of the Cossacks and their families. When women and children closed ranks, categorically refusing to board the trucks, English soldiers beat them with clubs, then sent tanks against them. Eyewitnesses testify that a large number of women showed that they preferred being crushed under tank treads over being sent alive to Russia, and that several women, holding infants in their arms, jumped into the Drau, where they perished. From that moment, soldiers refused to obey their orders, and in that way, several women succeeded in avoiding butchery.

That these Whites suffered incredible cruelty when they were turned over to Soviet power should be obvious to anyone with the tiniest understanding of the implacable hostility with which both camps in the Russian Civil War conducted their struggle against each other.

One report said: "These people, who loved Russia, but hated the current government, came to meet their villainous foe, not with weapons in open battle, but unarmed, after being criminally betrayed. All the horrors of war pale in comparison with the torture that was used in their interrogations. The Soviet Command was well pleased with this unexpected prize, which promised them the opportunity not only for revenge, so long and futilely awaited, but of also receiving medals and promotions from the leadership in Moscow.

These reports, which I gave as briefly as possible in resume, merit being compared against each other and verified. It is not yet too late to do so. I have been given confirmation that Russian eyewitnesses, whom it would be easy to combine with a multitude of English ones, are ready to confirm their reports under oath and to submit to sworn questions, should an international commission decide to begin an investigation on the matter of "forcible betrayal of Cossacks from May 28 to June 1, 1945."

The inquiries into this inhumanity that were completed during and after the war were too one sided.

The inquiry I propose could be a worthy continuation of another one, of the mass slaughter at Katyn, which was conducted rather unsatisfactorily.

With what happened at Spittal, there is the great advantage that it would be very easy to name, accuse, and bring in those having a major guilt.

Professor Dr. **L. H. Grondeis**

—

2. On the Spittal Tragedy

Taken from the newspaper, "Russian Thought," *No.* 566, April 17, 1953.

The journal "Cossack Union," *No.* 11, printed an article by Professor L. Grondeis, translated from French, entitled "The Tragedy of Spittal." The journal printed:

"Among the many reports at our disposal, we must give particular attention to the testimony provided by Professor of the Russian Medical Faculty Verbitsky, who was with the higher Russian staff, and, as a non-combatant, was liberated at the time by the English.

"He reports having witnessed the Field Ataman, at the request of no other than Major Davies, persuade all his officers to prepare for a trip to a conference in Spittal," etc.

How could Professor Verbitsky be with the staff and at the same time be a non-combatant? Only one or the other can be.

But this is not important. More important is Professor Verbitsky's testimony. It seems that he was everywhere and knew everything.

In reality, Professor Verbitsky is merely repeating the rumors and misrepresentations, if not to say worse, which Lienz was full of in those days, especially in the refugee camp near Lienz in which Professor Verbitsky stayed.

What train in which two corpses were discovered and from which twenty-three officers jumped, eight of whom survived, is Professor Verbitsky talking about, when all the betrayed officers were taken from Lienz in English motor vehicles? And, as much as is known, no one ran away along the route between Lienz and Spittal. All arrived at Camp Spittal.

But in the end, even this is not important. Mistakes are always possible. In those days, so many incongruities and unsubstantiated rumors went about that it was impossible to establish anything. As concerns the day that preceded the handover, I can object with confidence and assert that neither Professor Verbitsky nor anyone else, other than Director Y. and interpreter Butlerov, were present at the conversation between Davies and the Field Ataman.

Davies made no request of the Field Ataman, but presented in written form, in English, the order from the English Command—to send all officers and officials to the city of Spittal for a conference.

Based on this order, the Field Ataman, in a subordinate position to the English Command, gave the order to gather the unit commanders in his office at eleven o'clock the day of May 28, 1945.

Persuading all the officers was physically impossible due to lack of time, since the military units where spread along a line from Lienz-Oberdrauburg that was twelve kilometers in length.

At one o'clock, they had to leave for Spittal.

At eleven o'clock, unit commanders were present at the offices of the Field Ataman. Professor Verbitsky was not there.

The Field Ataman, outwardly calm, but obviously worried, laid out the order from the English Command about sending all the officers to Spittal for a conference. After the order was read, a silence fell.

There was no opposition from the unit commanders. And the Field Ataman did not need to persuade.

Only a few questions were asked. Here are two of the most important:

Major General Tarasenko:—And what awaits us?

Field Ataman:—Little good. Probably barbed wire.

This phrase little resembles any kind of persuasion. The Field Ataman was hinting at the possibility of being imprisoned.

The commander of the 1st Mounted Regiment, Colonel Golubov: posed the second question—But what will be done to those officers who do not believe and begin to head off for the hills?

Field Ataman:—You are the commander of your regiment. Do you understand me?

This phrase from the Field Ataman let the regimental commanders know that they could do so if they thought it necessary.

This was the "persuasion" which operated on us in the course of an hour with the Field Ataman.

It was quite the opposite. The Field Ataman, having no chance to openly convey his true feelings, spoke through hints. And those who wished to understand, understood. Regretfully, there turned out to be very few of us.

It is relevant to note several instances that took place when the officers went off from Lienz.

There was no order, either English or from the Ataman, that priests were subject to being sent. Nevertheless, two of them went voluntarily, and one of them—Father Alexander, grabbing a boot brush to take along, said:—See, you will all get to the conference dusty, but I will be clean.

Colonel Khrennikov, who, two days before the betrayal, was put under arrest for three days by the Field Ataman for disobeying his orders and was not part of the general flow, the next day, after the officers had already left for Spittal, went there voluntarily. Nonetheless, his wife blames the Field Ataman. On just such unfair accusations were the reports of "eyewitnesses" built.

Host Starshin Zhuravlev, who was in the reserve officer's regiment, even pleaded with Sotnik S. to go, saying:—Fool. Do you know what kind of a conference there will be? They will be giving out duties in the British colonies.

Even Tarussky, the writer, went. He was asked by those around him:—And why you?—Tarussky answered:—Am I not an officer?

No! One needs to approach the question of the betrayal of Cossacks in Spittal seriously, not based on suppositions and rumors.

Steppenoy

—

3. Is There a Limit?

…And National Russia in the near future will request a moral accounting from the western world for being blinded by its own moral crisis of the soul to all of the atrocities of the Soviet monsters who sat at the same diplomatic table with the men of the official stupidity of this western world.

National Russia will likewise request the return of such war criminals as English Major Davies, who gave the word of honor of an English officer for the immunity of 30,000 Cossacks, who were then turned over at Lienz to the Bolsheviks.

This future National Russia will request a trial of the commander of the 8th English Army, who gave the order to shoot unarmed old men, women, and children in the Valley of the Drau in Austria…

If the Nuremberg trials washed with soap the nooses of German generals for the mass extermination of the peaceful and undefended populace of Europe, then why are they leaving unpunished the majors and generals—brave heroes of Lienz, Dachau, Kempton, and Judenburg?

"A single morality,"—then let it be single!

Peter Mar

●

Open Letter to the Editors of Newspapers and Journals Published in Western Europe and America

In connection with the continuation until the end of 1947 of Russian people being returned from Germany, Austria, and Italy, the editor of the journal "Russian Banner," N. N. Chukhnov, sent an open letter to editors of European and American newspapers.

Through the efforts of S. V. Zavalishin, then the director of a Russian press in Munich, and at present the publisher of this book, this letter from N. N. Chukhnov was published in a large circulation and was widely disseminated. It greatly raised the spirits of the emigration and helped it in its opposition. Almost all of the emigrant press organs and many of the foreign ones printed the letter.

The composition and publication at that time of the letter that follows required a great spirit of public responsibility.

The presence of many hundreds of thousands of people in the category of political emigrants, military refugees, and so-called DPs outside the borders of their native countries is a fact that on its own raises a majestic protest against that evil force that has seized a huge territory in Europe and Asia.

This protest is wider and deeper in its significance than that of Luther's Reformation protest against Papism, the fight of Balkan peasants against the cruelty of Islam, and, in the end, the ideals of American democracy against slavery.

It does not fit our purpose, within the limits of a newspaper article, to review the history of this contemporary "great exodus" and give its reasons. It has long been known to the educated public, for in our persons it has living witnesses to the horror that rules beyond the "Iron Curtain," where violations of human rights and God's Commandments have continued with great impunity over a decade now.

Here is why the new tyrants, with their obscene power eclipsing Caligula, Nero, and Persian despots, try so to physically destroy us.

For they know very well that as long as we emigrants exist, not one of their subterfuges has any hope. We are impartial witnesses. We are strict accusers.

According to the pronouncements of Molotov and Vyshinsky, the emigration represents a criminal element. It is asked: Why do they need this element so much? Wouldn't it be more logical to leave these people in the "rotting capitalist countries of Europe and America," rather than drag them to the "land of bright socialism?" Or maybe Mr. Molotov and Mr. Vyshinsky act out of altruism, striving to unburden Europe from us to ease an economic crisis?

No! Our existence represents the same danger to the occupants of the Kremlin as do their own soldiers who remained after the war in the garrisons of occupied Europe. These soldiers became enemies of the Soviet regime, for in Vienna, Berlin, and Budapest, they had the opportunity to compare their "socialistic homeland" with the "dismal capitalist system of the West." Not in vain do the Soviets carry out "cleansing" among the officers and soldiers of the Red Army who are returned in accordance with peace negotiations. Few of them are spared from returning to their homes without being accused of "bourgeois-capitalist tendencies" after such cleansing.

The gang of occupiers who now rule over almost a fifth of the globe are full of nothing other than feelings of fear.

It is a fear not for the march of history, not for future countries captured by them, not even for the ideas of Marx and their hope of world revolution, but only for their vile lives and personal welfare.

Oh, they have reason to fear: If their power wanes, even for a moment, their suffering people will tear them to pieces. That is why they need mass killings and famines, to hold in conformity through torture those bloody masses they have stupefied by want. This is why ten percent of the population of the West languishes in concentration camps, isolated from the rest of the world, while eighty-eight percent awaits its turn in them, and two percent rule. Fear, living fear, leads all the actions of the conspirators. They fear the atom bomb. They fear their own officers and soldiers. They fear *kolhozniks*. They fear their own workers. They fear emigrants. They fear every foreigner. They fear each other.

And here are we, a tiny part of an unfortunate people. Saved from the "good fortune of living under the sun of the Stalinist constitution" through the Providence of God, personal choice, and wartime circumstances, we merged into the background of world events.

There is a fight over our heads. Two camps of the current world wage it. One side's actions are led by fear for that truth which we brought to the world, base revenge, and hunger for blood; the other's, Christian morality and certain principles of Western democracy. Who will win?

For us, one thing is beyond doubt: no matter the circumstance, no matter how current society grimaces, truth will win.

It is not right to pursue those drowning in a river for overcoming the flow with great strength of will at the last minute and swimming to the safety of shore.

It is not right to criticize people who, having abandoned all their worldly goods, relatives, and friends, escaped to an alien world, not counting on any help, not counting on anything but fate...

It is not right to persecute people because they cannot accept the authority of those who killed those near and dear to them, took away the right to express their thoughts, took away the right to love their families, to raise their children, to have a home and the comfort of family...

It is not right to kill people because they believe in God and in higher values...

It is not right to torture people because they do not want to lie, denounce, betray...

It is not right to execute people for their unwillingness to participate in arguments against all humanity or participate in the epidemics of capital crimes that are blossoming in the rank light beyond the "Iron Curtain."

Have these people ever posed to themselves the question which shapes current policies: "Why are there millions of refugees from countries in which it is so good, so just, and honest?"

Have they ever posed the question: "Why does no other government experience anything similar?"

Have we ever heard of soldiers not wishing to return home from enemy imprisonment?

Have we ever known a political emigration, aside from Great Britain and the USA?

Have we ever seen thousands and thousands of Europeans and Americans refuse their own citizenship or curse the fate that gave them that citizenship?

On the strength of these conditions, on the strength of man's permanent right to life, we can not but object to those events that took place in our difficult lives as emigrants.

We insist that, once and for all, definitions be established— emigrant, refugee, military deserter, DP. All of us, regardless of the circumstances of our escape, represent a mass of people who knowingly and intentionally abandoned the territories of the Red Terror.

We protest against our heads being used in bargaining and, from time to time, having some number of people thrown into the bloody jaws of Moloch as ransom.

We ask that, on the basis of elemental rights protecting mankind, we be given the right to be refugees. We ask to be recognized as political emigrants without a country who have the right to live and work beyond the reach of our persecutors.

We ask that we be looked upon not just as consumers, but as a creative force. Do not forget that Igor Sikorsky, the main designer of the aircraft that defeated Germany—also a Russian political emigrant.

We want conduct toward us changed to conform to existing judicial norms, not random regulation.

In the end, we suggest that a million of us should not be looked upon as a million coal miners. Among us are scholars, writers, artists, physicians, architects, performers, and people of all levels of intellectual abilities, people for whom their homelands would normally raise monuments, and who could put their marks in the buildings of world culture and civilization.

Do not fear! Nowhere and under no circumstance has one Russian emigrant eaten another's bread without payment, but now... Now they make us eat bread without paying. Oh, how bitter the bread is.

Turning to the conditions of our personal lives, that of camp residents, we cannot help but smile when our supervisors, forced by instructions given to them, exhort us to return to our homelands.

Above all else, we have no homeland. We had one, but we left its borders, taking with us a small clod of soil and a hatred for the executioners of the Russian peoples. This way, all the attempts of our caretakers—without substance.

Then they hint that UNRRA is approaching the end of its existence. It no longer has any credit. We might lose our rations.

For people who have looked into the face of death thousands of times, for people whose lives—continuous battles for existence, battles for ideals, such loss is equivalent to the loss of a pocket handkerchief.

Know that no misfortune, no shortage, no amount of hunger will bring forth any foolish nostalgia in us.

We know that each of us—stepchildren of an overburdened world, but we are proud of our trials in the name of perpetual ideals of right and truth, even as they continue for us.

We know that our ideal of negating communist materialism, sooner or later, will conquer the entire world, independent of whether humanity understands us now or not, whether or not it wants to help us or refuses to.

N. Chukhnov

•

An Excerpt from the Article, "Western Betrayal of Anticommunist Forces," found in an Irish newspaper (in English)

The article begins as follows:

Many today speak of the "Russian menace," but neither Washington nor London points out that the most anticommunist country on earth is Russia.

This fact is demonstrated by consideration that when the German Army entered the USSR, it was greeted as a "liberator," and millions of soldiers surrendered to the Germans and asked permission to fight against the Red Kremlin...

...Anti-Red feelings in Greater Russia during the war were so great that Stalin, Churchill, and Roosevelt signed the Yalta agreement to give Soviet citizens over to Communist forces, regardless of the wishes of those to which it applied.

This agreement had the aim of destroying all active Russian anticommunists.

Keeping in mind what has followed from it, it is impossible to understand how Churchill could have agreed to it, since he had insisted that German turncoats working for the allies were heroes who had cast off a heinous terrorist regime that had been forced on them by secret police. Russian patriots fighting the same way against their government, which Churchill had many times pronounced to be the most heinous that the world had ever seen, were not only not called heroic, but traitors who had to be returned to the Soviets for punishment.

"Natinform"

•

On the Brink of Extinction

Human minds work nonstop in search of new ways. Centuries come at the change of centuries. New religious messages are hung, philosophical systems go out of fashion. Major reevaluation of values takes place.

From time to time, archives are shaken out and from the day that something is extricated from them, apparently from antiquity, it for some reason loses neither its substance nor its depth, even under ages of layers of dust. It has long been known, but what was forgotten transforms in the open and once more wins hearts and minds.

In our epoch, full of never-before progress and unbounded potential, the words of Goethe that "mankind continuously advances, but man stays the same," have particular resonance. From one side, no material civilization, no perfected technology, is in position to change the psychology of the cave dweller, with his instinct of self-preservation and tendencies of cruelty to, and destruction of, those like him. From the other—no external forces can put out the strivings for inner freedom and the comprehension of the perfect and permanent in a man granted authentically humane qualities. Between savages dipping their darts in lethal plant juices and chemists working to "perfect" a poison gas, there is no difference, in all honesty. Strictly speaking, some Hindu mystic, who day and night wraps his face in layers of gauze so that, if all goes well, he does not inhale a mosquito and become the involuntary cause of the death of a living creature, might be put in the same rank as the great Tolstoy, who in days not long ago preached an evangelic non-resistance to evil, no matter what. Here are the two extreme points to human nature: primitive animal ferocity and deep, tranquil humanity. One and the other—outside the conditions of time and space.

Can we be proud of the achievements of our age, surpassing as they do all contrivances of fiction? Can we say that they brought us happiness, benefited us?

All these achievements exist in the material plane. Man's spiritual aspect has not been enlightened! What is the point of technical work for the betterment and ease of life, if at the same time it threatens its complete destruction? What is the point of a head-spinning increase in tempo, if it only carries us down the slope?

We live under irreconcilable contradictions. How can we combine, for example, the broad dissemination of humanitarian ideals with the startling coarsening of manners, discarded often—must we acknowledge this!—toward the dark times of mid-century? How can we combine all the higher standards of living with all the declining levels of art? How can we combine higher civilization with contempt toward the basic rights of man? Obviously, that urge to reevaluate has led us into a blind alley. Not always is reevaluation justified: there are values that simply are not subject to it.

Ancient wisdom about good and evil has not yet lost its decisive meaning, not in our time and modern times, no matter how a modern person tried to divorce himself from them, no matter how he tried to destroy and level them as circumstances required!

The most frightening danger awaiting us is not from the arms of those who give primary meaning to matter in counterweight to spirit and openly carry out its destruction in principle. No, more frightening is he who underlines his belonging to the highest culture, Christian culture, even though he has taken from it only its external form, sacrificing its essence to his interests, its opposite. The history of the past years has regretfully given us many lessons on this concept.

Isolated instances of crimes against human morality are lamentable, but not catastrophic. Stretching shame over the scales of general, national, and governmental threatens us with indelible consequences.

Must we agree that for the acquisition of those or other genuine benefits, everything is allowed?

In a just state, common instances of duplicity, killing, violence, or treason are difficult to guard against. But if treason, treachery, betrayal, and the shedding of innocent blood serve the apparent benefits of the state in the whole, then they are simply reconciled with, as with facts, without calling them by name! People doomed to mass extinction sometimes provoke consideration of a higher purpose. Such consideration often allows even massacres.

We will not turn the pages on the chapters of colonization of non-European countries—a long, and in places, terrible chapter, and it already lies entirely in the past. But even our era, the era of illustrious achievements in everything, also celebrates great achievements in districts of betrayal, in the name of "higher" interests. Objecting to it is difficult.

The blood of humans—inexpensive goods. Russian blood has become especially cheap in recent times. There are many memories, with eyewitness proof for this. They have become history. They already cannot be brushed aside or extinguished or erased in any way. They will remain forever.

In the list of black deeds on the part of barterers in human blood, the last to appear for now, written in blazing letters, is the word

Lienz.

The tragedy of Lienz, not so far from us in time, has lost its reality. It burns and tears at the heart unbearably. The wound not only will not heal, but will not even be covered by a film of oblivion: everything can be understood, but not everything can be forgiven!

If one approaches with a measuring rod the mass killing of people in various places famous for it in the past two world wars, then the massacre of twenty, thirty, even forty thousand refugees makes no impression based on cold statistics. But the essential point is not in the statistical data—the essential point is in the very deed that clamors to the heavens!

Innocent, defenseless people perished. How they died—that is safeguarded in the unequivocal testimony of witnesses who lived through it. Memory is still fresh: less than ten years have passed. Loved ones have not been fully grieved over, the general sorrow has not been fully outlived.

It is insufferably painful that these people—our brothers and sisters—died before their time and without fault.

It is terrifying to realize that, in general, such things could even take place.

But hopeless despair is overcome by the thought that the world, that world which considers itself the bearer of the ideas of Christianity, HAS NOT CONDEMNED THE GUILTY!

The world walked silently past what should have been discussed. The world did not identify the evil as evil, did not turn aside from it with repulsion, indignation, and revolt. What a horror, what a black abyss!

If there is no condemnation, then it means that a passive acceptance exists, as if in justification of it by considerations of a "higher" order. Are we to be expected to await a future repetition of such instances of mass sacrifice on the altar of "general utility?"

What have we come to? And where are we going?

An Old Cossack Woman

•

To an Old Cossack Woman

Our good "Old Cossack Woman!" You grieve because the world walked away in silence from a terrible atrocity and did not repudiate it.

We all grieve over this. But glimmers can be noticed.

A number of journalists, American, British, and from other western countries, are stubbornly trying to get a clear picture of all the details of the inhumane turning over of our compatriots and to establish who was to blame. For example, we know that one Dutch journalist personally was at Lienz in order to clear up there, on site, several questions connected with the handover of Cossacks and their families.

The societies of the West and America are becoming more and more interested in the issue of the forced return of people to face reprisals from the Red beast.

The hour is not too far when the American Congress and the British Parliament will need to conduct a detailed investigation of all that took place in Lienz, Plattling, and other places in Austria and Germany, and to establish the identities of the guilty, as was done in the case of the killing of 10,000 Polish officers at Katyn.

V. Naumenko

•

Do Not Forget!

On a sad anniversary — June 1, 1945.

Do not forget Lienz, and tell posterity,
How Russian Bogatyrs, falling for the treachery
Of the high-handed lords of the British court,
With a single stroke of a filthy pen,
Were turned over to a tyrant's oprichniks.

Let Russians know, our native land,
Arising from the darkness of disgrace and misfortune,
When an old Brit, bearer of higher power,
Wishing to preserve the Kremlin's gratitude,
Suddenly sang a "Hosanna" to the executioner of Moscow.

Let the name of this vile old man in heart and soul
Become synonymous for the new generation
With moral worthlessness and the terrible crimes
With which the high lord was so open-handed.

The duty from the cradle of every mother of a child
To inoculate with hatred, if only for a talented land,
Where to raise stately traitors succeeded
In benefiting the lords and the devils with them.

Let him be cursed, who had better not been born,
Who, losing his honor, will at some time be judged
To find friends among eternal foes.
Enough lies, betrayals, and words,

And our goodness, famous for ages, —
Blood summons us to sound reasoning
Flowing in a river from British bayonets.

B. Patkovsky

•

289

Translator's Note

Although this compendium has been reprinted in Russian, to my knowledge, this is the first English translation. Too much time has passed for someone perhaps more capable to have done so, but for the descendants of the victims, a Russian-only version is insufficient. Thus, I felt compelled by duty to those survivors to take on this task, before the desire to translate the material passes away too.

It is a truism that some terms in one language are untranslatable in another. Because it is a compendium of reports, essentially intended as testimony—the authors are not professional writers, nor is Naumenko a trained editor any more than I am a trained translator—I have tried to keep the translation as close to the original Russian as possible in order to provide something of a facsimile copy. For example, I have left much of the punctuation as it is in the original, which, especially with dialog, will appear quaint or even jarringly wrong to the English reader, for which I apologize, as I do also for purposely passing on certain obvious errors without giving any indication of having done so. Much can be gleaned not just from what is written, but also from how. I have, however, whenever possible, to ease the reader's burden, broken up many long sentences made up of independent clauses being piled one upon another. The organization and the quaint delimiters of individual sections has also been kept as close to the original as possible given the restrictions of modern software. The Table of Contents, however, has been moved from its traditional place at the end of Russian-language books to the front.

Cossack ranks have been converted to their more conventional equivalents, but some special Cossack ranks, such as sotnik, have been retained, as have certain other words and terms. These have been transliterated and italicized, at least in their first use, in which I give a definition in brackets.

The reader by now should know that the officers were taken from Lienz in trucks. However, truck (or lorry) seemed not to have been in the vocabulary of most Cossacks, so that a variety of terms— auto, automobile, motor car, machine (translated as vehicle)—have been preserved in their English equivalent in the text. Train, too, seemed to have the same issue, as did its track, beds, and line. I retained the French Russification of "echelon" when I could not clearly determine that a train had been meant. Similar issues appear with "transport," "wagon," and "car." More problematic was the use of "wire" by the Cossacks. I translated it as "barbed wire," unless it was clear that the more general term was appropriate.

I have used my own judgment on capitalization of titles, which is somewhat arbitrary in the original. As for the poetry translations, I can offer only an apology.

Finally, and most significantly, there are several terms used by the authors that can be translated as "betrayal," but often have a less forceful meaning than that English word. Other than the word made use of in the title, I have translated them most often as some variant of "return" or "handover." They are the closest in English to describe the specific, simple physical action that took place. The morally judgmental term appropriately used in the title is, of course, defensible on the basis of the ramifications of that action.

William Dritschilo
Proctor, Vermont
November 11, 2011

Made in the USA
Coppell, TX
02 November 2022

85619114R00164